D0778876

Design for Democracy: Ballot + Election Design

Marcia Lausen

The University of Chicago Press
Chicago and London

Published in association with
AIGA | The professional association for design

Marcia Lausen, a founding member of Design for Democracy, is professor of graphic design at the University of Illinios at Chicago and principal at Studio/lab, a multidisciplinary design consulting firm.

The University of Chicago Press, Chicago 60637
The University of Chicago Press, Ltd., London

Printed in the United States of America

15 14 13 12 11 10 09 08 07 1 2 3 4 5

ISBN-13: 978-0-226-47046-7
ISBN-10: 0-226-47046-6

Library of Congress Cataloging-in-Publication Data
Lausen, Marcia.
Design for democracy : ballot and election design / Marcia Lausen.
p. cm.
Includes bibliographical references and index.
1. Ballot—United States. 2. Voting—United States. I. Title.
ISBN-13: 978-0-226-47046-7 (cloth : alk. paper)
ISBN-10: 0-226-47046-6 (cloth : alk. paper)

JK2214.L38 2007
324.60973—dc22

2007023282

This book is printed on a recycled paper, Knightkote Matte, that uses 30% post-consumer waste fiber, 50% total recycled fiber, and elemental chlorine-free pulps, and is both acid-free and chlorine-free.

Made possible by:

AIGA | the professional association for design
Richard Grefé, *Executive Director*

Chicago Board of Elections

Office of the Cook County Clerk
David Orr, *Cook County Clerk*
Scott Burnham, *Director of Communications*
Veronica Belsuzarri, *Designer*

Sappi Ideas that Matter

State of Oregon Elections Division
Bill Bradbury, *Secretary of State*
John Lindback, *Director of Elections*
Gretchen Schulfer, *HAVA Publications Specialist*

National Endowment for the Arts

University of Illinois at Chicago
College of Architecture and the Arts
Judith Russi Kirshner, *Dean*
School of Art and Design
Marcia Lausen, *Director, Professor*
Cheyenne Medina, *Designer, Teaching Assistant*
Stephen Melamed, *Clinical Associate Professor*
Elizabeth (Dori) Tunstall, PhD, *Associate Professor*

UIC Institute for the Humanities

contents

1 ballot design

2 design + the voting experience

3 design + election administration

4 election design system

An informed citizenry that actively participates in democratic processes will assure that government responds to the will of the people.

An informed and active citizenry is at the core of participatory democracy. In turn, citizens' participation in a democracy depends upon their trust in government. Trust, in general, will increase the motivation to participate; trust in the electoral process will increase the motivation to participate through voting rather than through less direct or more radically direct methods.

A government creates trust almost exclusively through communication—using words and images to convey meanings. Most of the communication between a government and its citizens consists of asking for and providing information. These interactions can be positive and engaging experiences, or they can be difficult, frustrating, disengaging ones. The difference is often a matter of communication design.

Design for Democracy began as an initiative of AIGA, the professional association for design, to apply design principles and solutions to government communication. It seeks to use the power of design to strengthen trust in government, increase the transparency of government activities, and facilitate citizen participation.

Nowhere in the realm of government communication is the impact of design greater than in the election process. As a result of the 2000 presidential election controversy, public officials began to better understand the need for design expertise in planning and conducting elections.

Thanks to AIGA's Chicago chapter, Design for Democracy launched two extraordinary partnerships with forward-thinking election officials in Cook County (which encompasses Chicago) and in the state of Oregon to take up the challenge of improving

foreword

election design. Under the project direction of Marcia Lausen, Stephen Melamed, and Dori Tunstall, teams of design and research professionals and design students met the challenge with energy and initiative.

Here, in association with the University of Chicago Press, we offer successful models and examples from these productive partnerships, with the full intention that others will draw freely and heavily from them. They were developed and tested within specific jurisdictions, but their lessons are straightforward and can be easily applied everywhere. Their impact may be more incremental than immediate, as voters gradually become more confident in and comfortable with the improvements. Yet we already have at least one objective measure of immediate improvement in voter participation as a result of the ballot redesign in the 2002 Chicago/Cook County judicial retention elections.

The Design for Democracy election design system is now being made available to election officials throughout the country, with support for dissemination provided by the National Endowment for the Arts, the National Institute of Standards and Technology, and the Election Assistance Commission.

AIGA is pleased to be able to make this contribution to a system of governance that has always been respected for its principles and its continuing desire to improve opportunities for civic engagement.

Richard Grefé

Executive Director
AIGA | the professional association for design

President
Design for Democracy

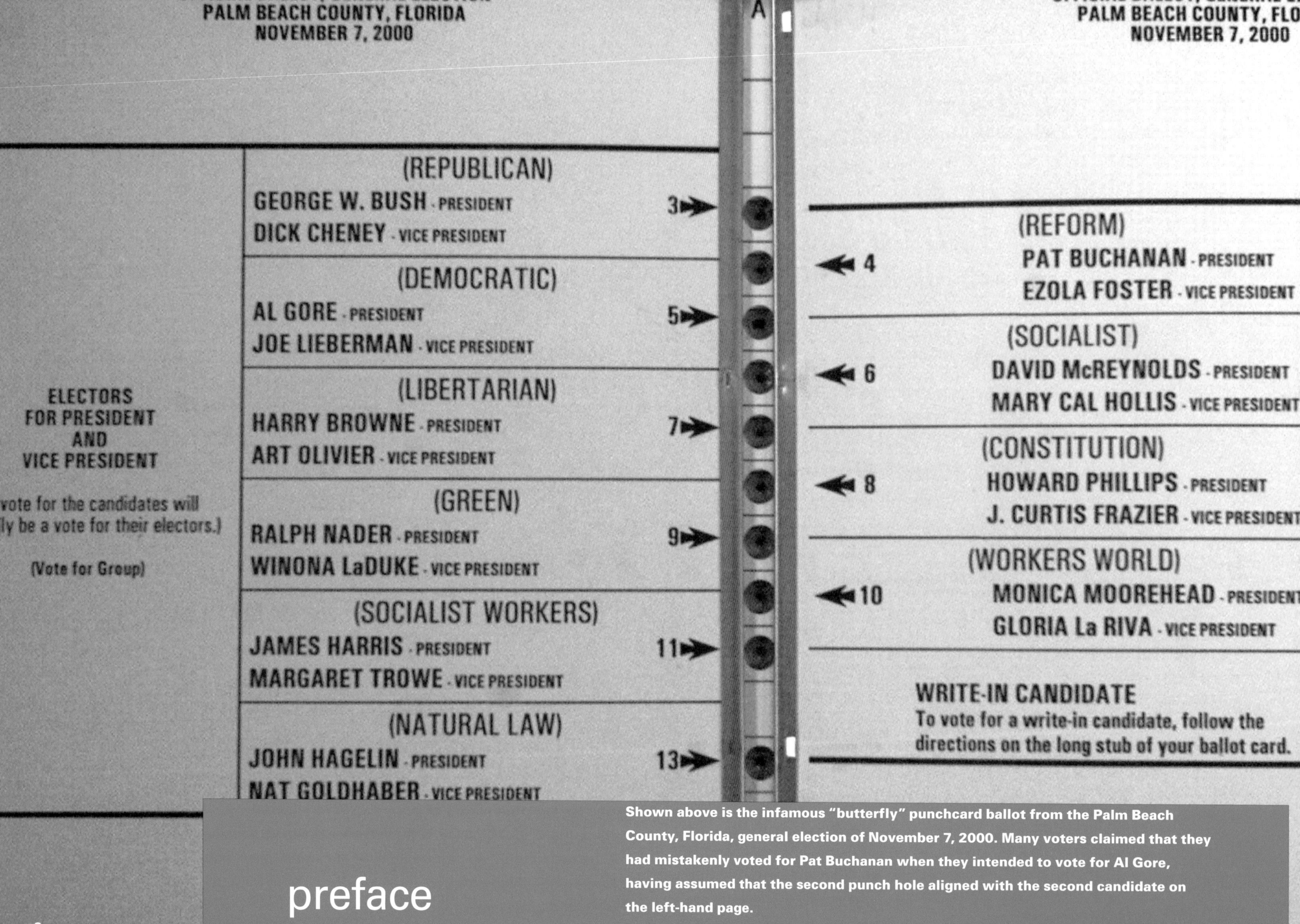

OFFICIAL BALLOT, GENERAL ELECTION
PALM BEACH COUNTY, FLORIDA
NOVEMBER 7, 2000
A
OFFICIAL BALLOT, GENERAL EL
PALM BEACH COUNTY, FLOR
NOVEMBER 7, 2000
ELECTORS
FOR PRESIDENT
AND
VICE PRESIDENT
vote for the candidates will
ally be a vote for their electors.)
(Vote for Group)
(REPUBLICAN)
GEORGE W. BUSH - PRESIDENT
DICK CHENEY - VICE PRESIDENT
3
(DEMOCRATIC)
AL GORE - PRESIDENT
JOE LIEBERMAN - VICE PRESIDENT
5
(LIBERTARIAN)
HARRY BROWNE - PRESIDENT
ART OLIVIER - VICE PRESIDENT
7
(GREEN)
RALPH NADER - PRESIDENT
WINONA LaDUKE - VICE PRESIDENT
9
(SOCIALIST WORKERS)
JAMES HARRIS - PRESIDENT
MARGARET TROWE - VICE PRESIDENT
11
(NATURAL LAW)
JOHN HAGELIN - PRESIDENT
NAT GOLDHABER - VICE PRESIDENT
13
(REFORM)
4
PAT BUCHANAN - PRESIDENT
EZOLA FOSTER - VICE PRESIDENT
(SOCIALIST)
6
DAVID McREYNOLDS - PRESIDENT
MARY CAL HOLLIS - VICE PRESIDENT
(CONSTITUTION)
8
HOWARD PHILLIPS - PRESIDENT
J. CURTIS FRAZIER - VICE PRESIDENT
(WORKERS WORLD)
10
MONICA MOOREHEAD - PRESIDENT
GLORIA La RIVA - VICE PRESIDENT
WRITE-IN CANDIDATE
To vote for a write-in candidate, follow the
directions on the long stub of your ballot card.

preface

Shown above is the infamous "butterfly" punchcard ballot from the Palm Beach County, Florida, general election of November 7, 2000. Many voters claimed that they had mistakenly voted for Pat Buchanan when they intended to vote for Al Gore, having assumed that the second punch hole aligned with the second candidate on the left-hand page.

Graphic design professionals rarely cross paths with election officials. Many election officials are unaware of the existence of our profession, let alone the value of our expertise. Designers often prefer to work in a world where clients come to us, understanding what we do and bringing well-organized projects with reasonable budgets and reasonable schedules—qualities that are not always present in the production of elections.

The complex workings of election administration are burdened with inherited, often antiquated, processes and systems of production that make change difficult, if not unwelcome. Budgets are small and time pressures severe. Most ballot design, if it can be called that, happens where election officials, lawyers, typesetters, and printers interact in a mad rush to "get it done on time."

In November of 2000, a confusing layout in the closely contested presidential election brought ballot design into the national consciousness. It also provided a rare opportunity for those of us in design leadership to step forward and demonstrate how design can improve election materials and processes.

In the days immediately following the November 2000 election, I volunteered on behalf of the Chicago chapter of AIGA, the professional association for design, to lead the development of a proposed redesign of Chicago's own butterfly ballot. The proposal was submitted to local election officials and to media outlets, and the response was enthusiastic.

Ballot design turned out to be merely the tip of the iceberg. Early in 2001, a group of design professionals, educators, and students began a dedicated collaborative effort to extend the ballot design initiative into the complete voting experience. Working with the University of Illinois at Chicago's School of Art and Design, and election officials in Cook County, Illinois, and the state of Oregon, the group developed prototypes designed to improve election administration materials, voting equipment, the polling place environment, absentee and provisional voting, and voter education and outreach.

This publication presents the election design system that resulted from our efforts. It provides visual examples and layout guidelines that can be adapted for use by all states and counties—to help make choices clear.

Marcia Lausen

Chicago, Illinois
May 2007

This book begins with the story of a confusing punchcard ballot — but it doesn't end there.

The ballot controversies that clouded the 2000 presidential election resulted in hasty and costly replacements of punchcard voting systems with newer technologies. Unfortunately, the implementation of these technologies has been uneven. States have invested millions of dollars to update voting systems, but the design of touch-screen and paper-based optical scan ballots is often as confusing and thoughtless as that of the punchcard ballots they replaced.

While focusing in part on ballot design, this book was created for a much broader purpose. It is intended to be a tool for designers, election officials, lawmakers, and the manufacturers and printers who serve the elections industry. It presents a comprehensive system of graphic standards that includes detailed guidelines for type, color, and image usage. It also provides numerous examples that show how this system can significantly improve nearly every aspect of the voting experience and of election administration. Most of these examples were developed in partnership with election officials in Cook County, Illinois, one of the country's largest and most complex election jurisdictions, and in the state of Oregon, which presents a unique design challenge as the entire state votes by mail.

The subject matter is organized into four sections. The first section focuses on the ballot. It presents five basic principles of ballot design and applies those principles to ballots used under differing local requirements and with different types of voting equipment. The second section shows how design can improve the total voting experience. From registration to information gathering to voting, information design principles are applied to produce improvements in forms, brochures, signs, posters, and even absentee voting materials and voters' guides. Behind-the-scenes aspects of election administration are examined in the third section, specifically those that pertain to pollworkers. Presented are instructional materials and

introduction

management tools that allow pollworkers to perform their roles more efficiently and more accurately. The final section provides specific guidelines and recommendations that are central to the Design for Democracy election design system: color palette, typography, and use of images such as logos, icons, illustrations, and photographs.

For designers preparing to embark on an project with an election agency, the Design for Democracy system provides a useful point of departure. It does not presume to cover every design issue that might be encountered in every jurisdiction. In the realm of elections it is impossible to anticipate all design-related problems that might arise. Rather, the goal here is to provide a detailed resource and a common point of reference for collaborative professional work. By collectively building from this base, designers throughout the nation become a network of creative professionals working toward a common goal.

For election officials and administrators, this work is intended to build awareness of the power of good design and the positive effect that it can have on both voters and election workers. The models, case studies, and guidelines presented on the following pages should encourage every state and local government to seek the services of design professionals. Experienced designers have the skills to expand, elaborate, build, and improve upon the system and the examples presented here.

Despite its seemingly straightforward visual simplicity, election design is not the least bit easy. It takes the combined effort of all parties working together to make improvements in the design of election materials and processes. From a design standpoint, work in elections is critically important and can be highly rewarding. More important, though, it can strengthen our democratic system by increasing the efficiency of the elections process and by inspiring confidence in the voting public.

in this section

information design

Functional, not decorative

ballot design case study

Proof that improved ballot design can increase voter participation

ballot design principles

The five most important things to know about designing a ballot

ballot design examples

Ballot design principles demonstrated on different voting systems

A ballot is a sheet of paper, booklet, or electronic interface that lists the candidates running for office in an election. The most crucial of the objects encountered in the voting experience, the ballot is the tangible record of the voter's choices. Unfortunately, design flaws can cause the ballot to become a source of controversy and contention. A confusing ballot suggests a disorganized election agency and results in voter frustration. Election officials want ballots that provide clear information to avoid misunderstanding and mistrust on the part of their constituency. Voters want ballots that are easy to understand to be confident that they have cast their votes as intended.

No one wants a ballot to be poorly designed. Bad ballot design often results from good intentions. Theresa LePore, the election official responsible for the infamous November 2000 Palm Beach County ballot, thought she was making the names of the candidates easier to read by increasing the size of the type, a change that led to a confusing butterfly layout. The problem in Florida in 2000 was the same problem that exists today: Ballots need to be well designed, and an election official is not a designer.

1 ballot design

information design

Information design is an area of professional expertise concerned with the visual display of data and instructions. Many of the materials used in elections are rich in information: registration applications, ballots, administrative forms and envelopes, polling place signs, and instructional diagrams. The presentation of election information demands accuracy and usability. While design for other subjects or industries might consider point of view, creativity, and expression, design for elections requires neutrality, legibility, and access.

In the design of a ballot, many types of information must be presented: labels that specify the date and jurisdiction of the election, descriptions of the offices and issues to be decided, names of candidates and their representative political parties, procedures for handling the ballot and casting votes, and instructions on what to do if the voter makes a mistake or has a question.

Information design professionals are ideally suited to address ballot design and related challenges. They are skilled and experienced in working with complex data; employing systems of alignment, hierarchy, and navigation; and developing layouts and typographies that maximize information access and comprehension. As systematic and innovative thinkers, they have the analytical skills to clarify information and the creative vision to see it in new ways. By adding information design expertise to election administration, ballots and supporting election materials will be made clearer and easier to use, elections will be more efficient, and voter confidence will increase.

One of the most pervasive examples of information design is the Nutrition Facts Label designed for the U.S. Food and Drug Administration.

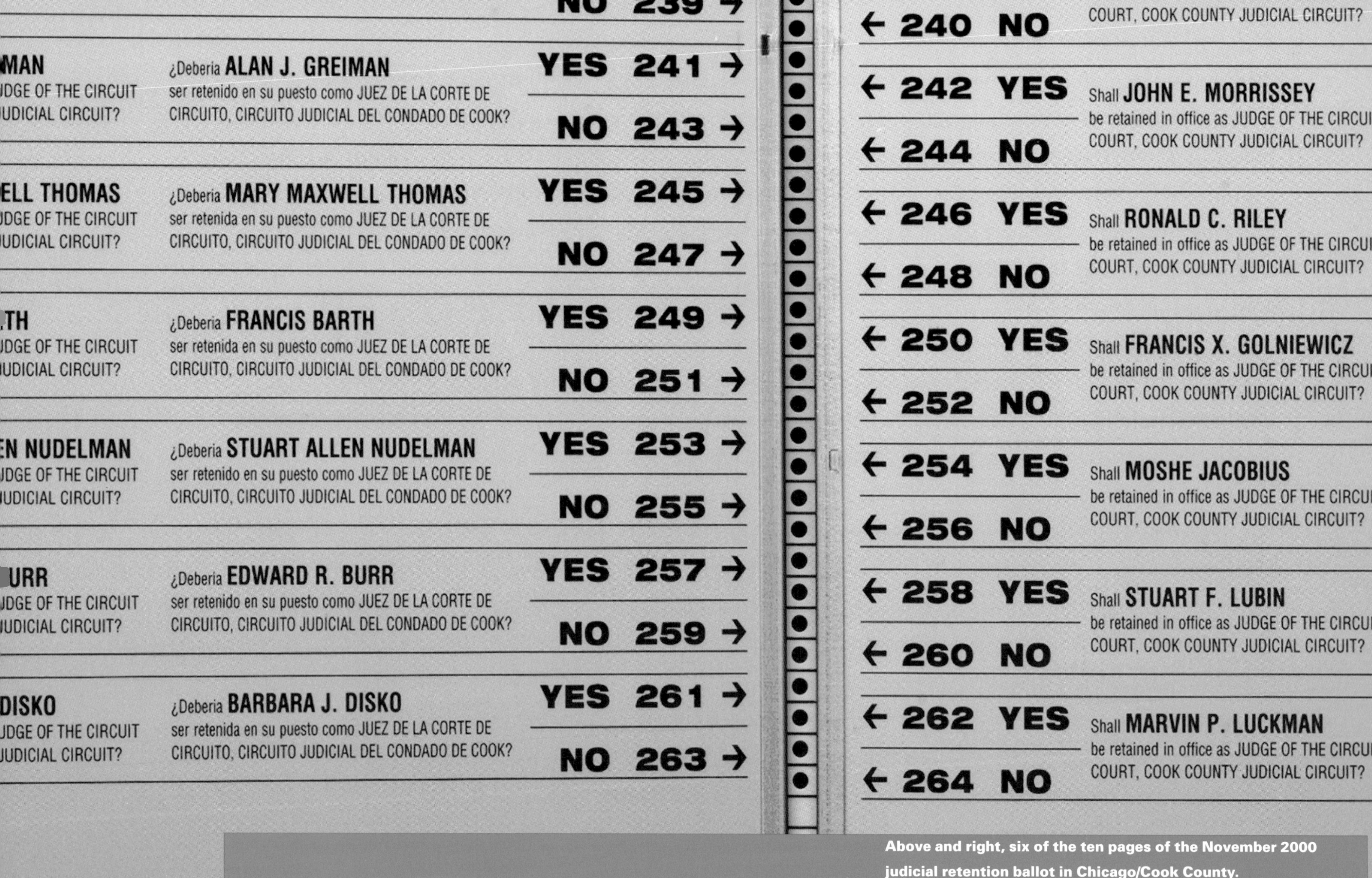

UDICIAL CIRCUIT? | CIRCUITO, CIRCUITO JUDICIAL DEL CONDADO DE COOK? | NO 239 →

MAN | JDGE OF THE CIRCUIT | UDICIAL CIRCUIT?
¿Debería ALAN J. GREIMAN ser retenido en su puesto como JUEZ DE LA CORTE DE CIRCUITO, CIRCUITO JUDICIAL DEL CONDADO DE COOK?
YES 241 →
NO 243 →

ELL THOMAS | JDGE OF THE CIRCUIT | UDICIAL CIRCUIT?
¿Debería MARY MAXWELL THOMAS ser retenida en su puesto como JUEZ DE LA CORTE DE CIRCUITO, CIRCUITO JUDICIAL DEL CONDADO DE COOK?
YES 245 →
NO 247 →

TH | JDGE OF THE CIRCUIT | UDICIAL CIRCUIT?
¿Debería FRANCIS BARTH ser retenida en su puesto como JUEZ DE LA CORTE DE CIRCUITO, CIRCUITO JUDICIAL DEL CONDADO DE COOK?
YES 249 →
NO 251 →

EN NUDELMAN | JDGE OF THE CIRCUIT | UDICIAL CIRCUIT?
¿Debería STUART ALLEN NUDELMAN ser retenido en su puesto como JUEZ DE LA CORTE DE CIRCUITO, CIRCUITO JUDICIAL DEL CONDADO DE COOK?
YES 253 →
NO 255 →

URR | JDGE OF THE CIRCUIT | UDICIAL CIRCUIT?
¿Debería EDWARD R. BURR ser retenido en su puesto como JUEZ DE LA CORTE DE CIRCUITO, CIRCUITO JUDICIAL DEL CONDADO DE COOK?
YES 257 →
NO 259 →

DISKO | JDGE OF THE CIRCUIT | JUDICIAL CIRCUIT?
¿Debería BARBARA J. DISKO ser retenida en su puesto como JUEZ DE LA CORTE DE CIRCUITO, CIRCUITO JUDICIAL DEL CONDADO DE COOK?
YES 261 →
NO 263 →

be retained in office as JUDGE OF THE CIRCUIT COURT, COOK COUNTY JUDICIAL CIRCUIT?
← 240 NO

Shall JOHN E. MORRISSEY be retained in office as JUDGE OF THE CIRCUIT COURT, COOK COUNTY JUDICIAL CIRCUIT?
← 242 YES
← 244 NO

Shall RONALD C. RILEY be retained in office as JUDGE OF THE CIRCUIT COURT, COOK COUNTY JUDICIAL CIRCUIT?
← 246 YES
← 248 NO

Shall FRANCIS X. GOLNIEWICZ be retained in office as JUDGE OF THE CIRCUIT COURT, COOK COUNTY JUDICIAL CIRCUIT?
← 250 YES
← 252 NO

Shall MOSHE JACOBIUS be retained in office as JUDGE OF THE CIRCUIT COURT, COOK COUNTY JUDICIAL CIRCUIT?
← 254 YES
← 256 NO

Shall STUART F. LUBIN be retained in office as JUDGE OF THE CIRCUIT COURT, COOK COUNTY JUDICIAL CIRCUIT?
← 258 YES
← 260 NO

Shall MARVIN P. LUCKMAN be retained in office as JUDGE OF THE CIRCUIT COURT, COOK COUNTY JUDICIAL CIRCUIT?
← 262 YES
← 264 NO

Above and right, six of the ten pages of the November 2000 judicial retention ballot in Chicago/Cook County.

ballot design case study

Many ballot design problems derive from the simple fact that U.S. elections are complicated. The tendency of our political system to put many candidates and issues before the electorate can create a burden for voters and election administrators. For example, in November 2003 there were 133 candidates in the California gubernatorial race.[1] While this seems extreme, it is not the first occurrence of a ballot of this length. In a 1969 primary election in Los Angeles, voters were asked to distribute seven votes among 133 candidates for Junior College Board of Trustees.[2] Similarly, judicial elections held in urban jurisdictions with large court systems can result in long, complex ballots.[3]

In November 2000 the Chicago/Cook County judicial retention ballot reached an all-time high in its level of complexity. With 73 candidates, this ballot section was compressed into a confusing butterfly layout that spanned ten pages of a dense punchcard ballot.[4] Four of the ten pages are shown below.

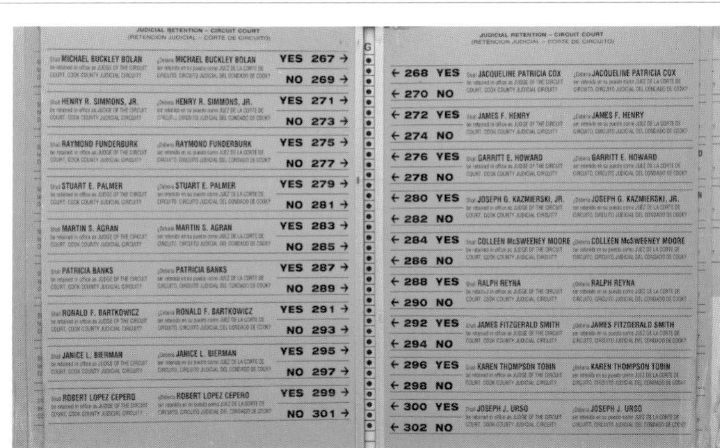

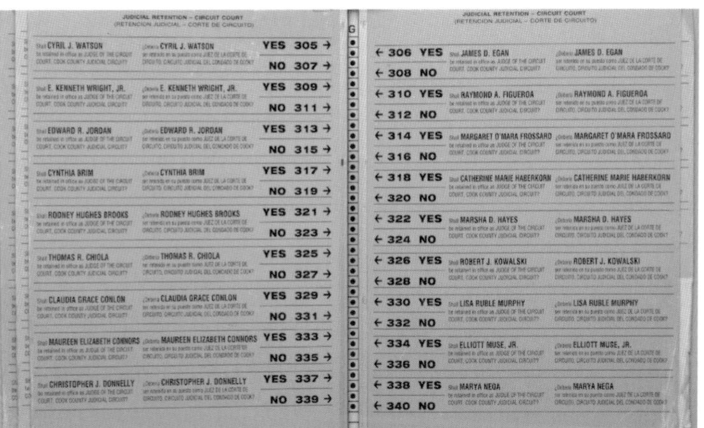

[1] For more information on the ballot design for the 2003 gubernatorial election in California, see Jessie Scanlon, "Wanted: A Legible Voting Ballot. Why It's Time to Redesign the Ballot Design Process" (www.slate.com/id/2089310).

[2] John E Mueller, "Choosing Among 133 Candidates," *Public Opinion Quarterly* 34, no. 3 (Fall 1970).

[3] Albert J. Klumpp, "Judicial Retention Elections in Cook County: Exercise of Democracy, or Exercise in Futility?" (Ph.D. diss., University of Illinois at Chicago, 2005).

[4] Ibid.

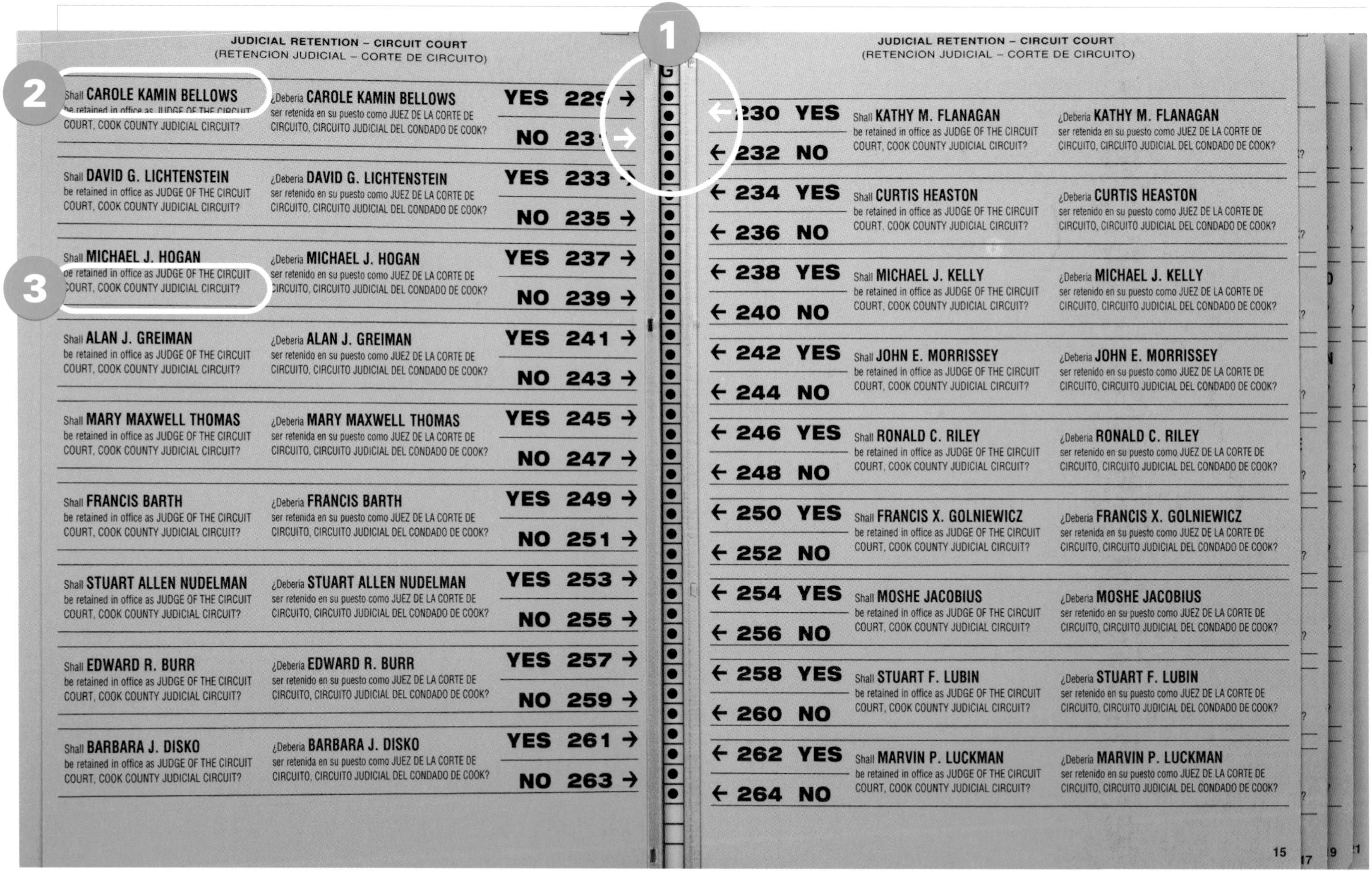

1

2

3

JUDICIAL RETENTION – CIRCUIT COURT
(RETENCION JUDICIAL – CORTE DE CIRCUITO)

Shall **CAROLE KAMIN BELLOWS** be retained in office as JUDGE OF THE CIRCUIT COURT, COOK COUNTY JUDICIAL CIRCUIT?	¿Debería **CAROLE KAMIN BELLOWS** ser retenida en su puesto como JUEZ DE LA CORTE DE CIRCUITO, CIRCUITO JUDICIAL DEL CONDADO DE COOK?	**YES 229 →** **NO 231 →**
Shall **DAVID G. LICHTENSTEIN** be retained in office as JUDGE OF THE CIRCUIT COURT, COOK COUNTY JUDICIAL CIRCUIT?	¿Debería **DAVID G. LICHTENSTEIN** ser retenido en su puesto como JUEZ DE LA CORTE DE CIRCUITO, CIRCUITO JUDICIAL DEL CONDADO DE COOK?	**YES 233 →** **NO 235 →**
Shall **MICHAEL J. HOGAN** be retained in office as JUDGE OF THE CIRCUIT COURT, COOK COUNTY JUDICIAL CIRCUIT?	¿Debería **MICHAEL J. HOGAN** ser retenido en su puesto como JUEZ DE LA CORTE DE CIRCUITO, CIRCUITO JUDICIAL DEL CONDADO DE COOK?	**YES 237 →** **NO 239 →**
Shall **ALAN J. GREIMAN** be retained in office as JUDGE OF THE CIRCUIT COURT, COOK COUNTY JUDICIAL CIRCUIT?	¿Debería **ALAN J. GREIMAN** ser retenido en su puesto como JUEZ DE LA CORTE DE CIRCUITO, CIRCUITO JUDICIAL DEL CONDADO DE COOK?	**YES 241 →** **NO 243 →**
Shall **MARY MAXWELL THOMAS** be retained in office as JUDGE OF THE CIRCUIT COURT, COOK COUNTY JUDICIAL CIRCUIT?	¿Debería **MARY MAXWELL THOMAS** ser retenida en su puesto como JUEZ DE LA CORTE DE CIRCUITO, CIRCUITO JUDICIAL DEL CONDADO DE COOK?	**YES 245 →** **NO 247 →**
Shall **FRANCIS BARTH** be retained in office as JUDGE OF THE CIRCUIT COURT, COOK COUNTY JUDICIAL CIRCUIT?	¿Debería **FRANCIS BARTH** ser retenida en su puesto como JUEZ DE LA CORTE DE CIRCUITO, CIRCUITO JUDICIAL DEL CONDADO DE COOK?	**YES 249 →** **NO 251 →**
Shall **STUART ALLEN NUDELMAN** be retained in office as JUDGE OF THE CIRCUIT COURT, COOK COUNTY JUDICIAL CIRCUIT?	¿Debería **STUART ALLEN NUDELMAN** ser retenido en su puesto como JUEZ DE LA CORTE DE CIRCUITO, CIRCUITO JUDICIAL DEL CONDADO DE COOK?	**YES 253 →** **NO 255 →**
Shall **EDWARD R. BURR** be retained in office as JUDGE OF THE CIRCUIT COURT, COOK COUNTY JUDICIAL CIRCUIT?	¿Debería **EDWARD R. BURR** ser retenido en su puesto como JUEZ DE LA CORTE DE CIRCUITO, CIRCUITO JUDICIAL DEL CONDADO DE COOK?	**YES 257 →** **NO 259 →**
Shall **BARBARA J. DISKO** be retained in office as JUDGE OF THE CIRCUIT COURT, COOK COUNTY JUDICIAL CIRCUIT?	¿Debería **BARBARA J. DISKO** ser retenida en su puesto como JUEZ DE LA CORTE DE CIRCUITO, CIRCUITO JUDICIAL DEL CONDADO DE COOK?	**YES 261 →** **NO 263 →**

JUDICIAL RETENTION – CIRCUIT COURT
(RETENCION JUDICIAL – CORTE DE CIRCUITO)

← 230 YES **← 232 NO**	Shall **KATHY M. FLANAGAN** be retained in office as JUDGE OF THE CIRCUIT COURT, COOK COUNTY JUDICIAL CIRCUIT?	¿Debería **KATHY M. FLANAGAN** ser retenida en su puesto como JUEZ DE LA CORTE DE CIRCUITO, CIRCUITO JUDICIAL DEL CONDADO DE COOK?
← 234 YES **← 236 NO**	Shall **CURTIS HEASTON** be retained in office as JUDGE OF THE CIRCUIT COURT, COOK COUNTY JUDICIAL CIRCUIT?	¿Debería **CURTIS HEASTON** ser retenido en su puesto como JUEZ DE LA CORTE DE CIRCUITO, CIRCUITO JUDICIAL DEL CONDADO DE COOK?
← 238 YES **← 240 NO**	Shall **MICHAEL J. KELLY** be retained in office as JUDGE OF THE CIRCUIT COURT, COOK COUNTY JUDICIAL CIRCUIT?	¿Debería **MICHAEL J. KELLY** ser retenido en su puesto como JUEZ DE LA CORTE DE CIRCUITO, CIRCUITO JUDICIAL DEL CONDADO DE COOK?
← 242 YES **← 244 NO**	Shall **JOHN E. MORRISSEY** be retained in office as JUDGE OF THE CIRCUIT COURT, COOK COUNTY JUDICIAL CIRCUIT?	¿Debería **JOHN E. MORRISSEY** ser retenido en su puesto como JUEZ DE LA CORTE DE CIRCUITO, CIRCUITO JUDICIAL DEL CONDADO DE COOK?
← 246 YES **← 248 NO**	Shall **RONALD C. RILEY** be retained in office as JUDGE OF THE CIRCUIT COURT, COOK COUNTY JUDICIAL CIRCUIT?	¿Debería **RONALD C. RILEY** ser retenido en su puesto como JUEZ DE LA CORTE DE CIRCUITO, CIRCUITO JUDICIAL DEL CONDADO DE COOK?
← 250 YES **← 252 NO**	Shall **FRANCIS X. GOLNIEWICZ** be retained in office as JUDGE OF THE CIRCUIT COURT, COOK COUNTY JUDICIAL CIRCUIT?	¿Debería **FRANCIS X. GOLNIEWICZ** ser retenida en su puesto como JUEZ DE LA CORTE DE CIRCUITO, CIRCUITO JUDICIAL DEL CONDADO DE COOK?
← 254 YES **← 256 NO**	Shall **MOSHE JACOBIUS** be retained in office as JUDGE OF THE CIRCUIT COURT, COOK COUNTY JUDICIAL CIRCUIT?	¿Debería **MOSHE JACOBIUS** ser retenido en su puesto como JUEZ DE LA CORTE DE CIRCUITO, CIRCUITO JUDICIAL DEL CONDADO DE COOK?
← 258 YES **← 260 NO**	Shall **STUART F. LUBIN** be retained in office as JUDGE OF THE CIRCUIT COURT, COOK COUNTY JUDICIAL CIRCUIT?	¿Debería **STUART F. LUBIN** ser retenido en su puesto como JUEZ DE LA CORTE DE CIRCUITO, CIRCUITO JUDICIAL DEL CONDADO DE COOK?
← 262 YES **← 264 NO**	Shall **MARVIN P. LUCKMAN** be retained in office as JUDGE OF THE CIRCUIT COURT, COOK COUNTY JUDICIAL CIRCUIT?	¿Debería **MARVIN P. LUCKMAN** ser retenido en su puesto como JUEZ DE LA CORTE DE CIRCUITO, CIRCUITO JUDICIAL DEL CONDADO DE COOK?

15

On the facing page is a two-page spread from the judicial retention section of the November 2000 Chicago/Cook County ballot. Here, in an extremely confusing array of information, the **yes** and **no** votes for the candidates on the left-hand page are actually interlaced with the **yes** and **no** votes for the candidates on the right-hand page. Moreover, the introduction of a reconfigured punchcard to accommodate more candidates resulted in punch holes that are squeezed much closer together than in previous elections.

In a retention election, the ballot identifies the judge and the relevant district and asks for each candidate *"Shall [the candidate] be retained in office as judge of the [relevant court]?"* Compounding the confusion on the ballot shown here is the inclusion of this text in a second language. The addition of Spanish was necessary to comply with federal election requirements, but in combination with the large number of candidates, it created space constraints that led to the adoption of the complex butterfly ballot layout.[5]

1

Punch holes are not sequential. Yes votes on left alternate with yes votes on the right, creating a complex weave of information from side to side.

Candidate names are difficult to read. Set in a condensed typeface in all capital letters, names are not typographically distinct.

3

A great deal of space is taken up with the question of retention. The problem is compounded by the addition of a second language.

[5] Klumpp, "Judicial Retention Elections in Cook County."

JUDICIAL RETENTION CIRCUIT COURT
RETENCION JUDICIAL CORTE DE CIRCUITO

vote yes or no
vote si o no

YES: Retain the candidate in office as Judge of the Circuit Court, Cook County Judicial Circuit.

YES: Retenga al candidato en su puesto como Juez De La Corte De Circuito, Circuito Judicial Del Condado De Cook.

NO: Don't retain the candidate in office as Judge of the Circuit Court, Cook County Judicial Circuit.

NO: No retenga al candidato en su puesto como Juez De La Corte De Circuito, Circuito Judicial Del Condado De Cook.

Carole Kamin Bellows	YES 229 →	NO 230 →
David G. Lichtenstein	YES 233 →	NO 234 →
Michael J. Hogan	YES 237 →	NO 238 →
Alan J. Greiman	YES 241 →	NO 242 →
Mary Maxwell Thomas	YES 245 →	NO 246 →
Francis Barth	YES 249 →	NO 250 →
Stuart Allen Nudelman	YES 253 →	NO 254 →
Edward R. Burr	YES 257 →	NO 258 →
Barbara J. Disko	YES 261 →	NO 262 →

Official Ballot
Balota Oficial

G

JUDICIAL RETENTION CIRCUIT COURT
RETENCION JUDICIAL CORTE DE CIRCUITO

← 231 YES	← 232 NO	Kathy M. Flanagan
← 235 YES	← 236 NO	Curtis Heaston
← 239 YES	← 240 NO	Michael J. Kelly
← 243 YES	← 244 NO	John E. Morrissey
← 247 YES	← 248 NO	Ronald C. Riley
← 251 YES	← 252 NO	Francis X. Golniewicz
← 255 YES	← 256 NO	Moshe Jacobius
← 259 YES	← 260 NO	Stuart F. Lubin
← 263 YES	← 264 NO	Marvin P. Luckman

vote yes or no
voto si o no

If you spoil your ballot, ask the judge for a new one.
Si usted daña su balota, pídale una balota nueva al Juez.

Turn page to continue voting.
Voltee la página para continuar votando.

15

Replacing the Chicago/Cook County ballot's capital letters with more legible lowercase letters required legislative revision of the Illinois Election Code. Revision was also required to limit the statement of the retention question to once per page in English and in Spanish. These revisions were enacted in September 2001.

The proposed redesign of the Chicago/Cook County judicial retention ballot (facing page) solves many of the original ballot's legibility problems. By changing only the design—not the printing specifications (black ink only) or the voting system (punchcard)—the redesign greatly clarifies the information.

Here, the repetitive language is removed, voter instructions are placed in a designated area, and the interlacing of **yes** and **no** votes for different candidates is eliminated. Candidate names are presented in a larger, bolder, more legible typeface (Univers 65). The **yes** and **no** votes for each candidate are tightly grouped, and graphic devices and shading connect the names with their corresponding punch holes. These features are also employed on prior ballot pages, shown below, on which the butterfly layout is used to group candidates by contest. The purposeful use of both the left- and right-hand pages prepares voters for left-right voting before arriving at the dense judicial retention pages.

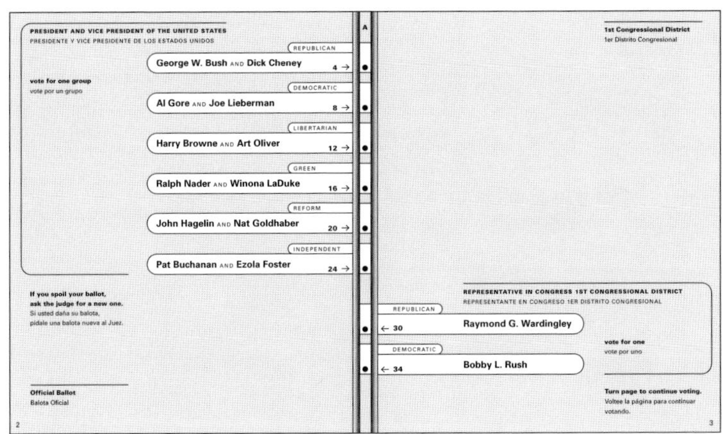

The proposed redesign as applied to presidential and congressional contests.

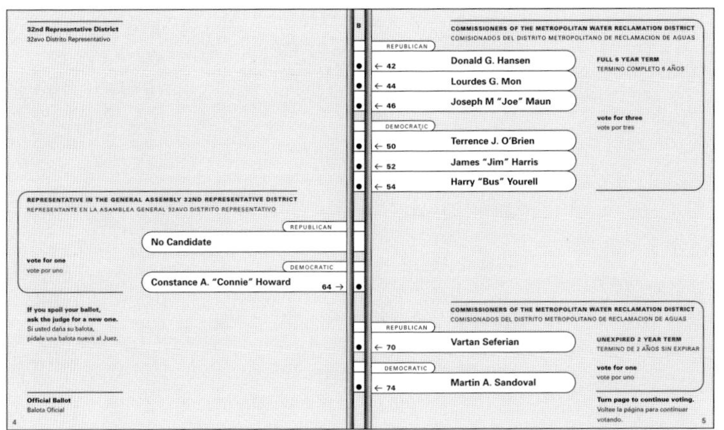

The proposed redesign as applied to state and local contests.

JUDICIAL RETENTION CIRCUIT COURT
RETENCION JUDICIAL CORTE DE CIRCUITO

Shall each of the persons listed be retained in office as Judge of the Circuit Court, Cook County Judicial Circuit?

¿Deberia cada uno de las personas enumeradas ser retenido en oficio como Juez de la Corte de Circuito, Circuito Judicial del Condado de Cook?

	Vote Yes Or No VOTE SI O NO	G
Judy I. Mitchell-Davis	YES (SI) 267 → NO (NO) 268 →	● ●
Mary Ellen Coghlan	YES (SI) 269 → NO (NO) 270 →	● ●
Sebastian Thomas Patti	YES (SI) 271 → NO (NO) 272 →	● ●
Michele Francene Lowrance	YES (SI) 273 → NO (NO) 274 →	● ●
Kathleen Marie McGury	YES (SI) 275 → NO (NO) 276 →	● ●
James P. O'Malley	YES (SI) 277 → NO (NO) 278 →	● ●
Shelley Lynn Sutker-Dermer	YES (SI) 279 → NO (NO) 280 →	● ●
Gay-Lloyd Lott	YES (SI) 281 → NO (NO) 282 →	● ●
Lynn Marie Egan	YES (SI) 283 → NO (NO) 284 →	● ●
Gerald C. Bender	YES (SI) 285 → NO (NO) 286 →	● ●
Andrew Berman	YES (SI) 287 → NO (NO) 288 →	● ●
Patricia Martin Bishop	YES (SI) 289 → NO (NO) 290 →	● ●
Diane Gordon Cannon	YES (SI) 291 → NO (NO) 292 →	● ●
Evelyn B. Clay	YES (SI) 293 → NO (NO) 294 →	● ●
Sharon Johnson Coleman	YES (SI) 295 → NO (NO) 296 →	● ●
Clayton J. Crane	YES (SI) 297 → NO (NO) 298 →	● ●
Wilbur E. Crooks	YES (SI) 299 → NO (NO) 300 →	● ●
Daniel P. Darcy	YES (SI) 301 → NO (NO) 302 →	● ●
Donald M. Devlin	YES (SI) 303 → NO (NO) 304 →	● ●

If you spoil your ballot, ask the judge for a new one.
Si usted daña su boleta, pidale una boleta nueva al Juez.

Many of the proposed recommendations were implemented in the November 2002 Chicago/Cook County judicial retention ballot.
Candidate names are larger and more legible, and the question of retention is not repeated excessively.
The improved design substantially increased voter participation in this section of the ballot as compared to the 2000 election.

On the facing page is the actual ballot used in the November 2002 Chicago/Cook County retention election. This ballot layout utilized many of the recommendations of the proposal. The names of the candidates are set in large bold upper- and lowercase letters, emphasizing them as the most important information on the page; the question of retention is asked only once per page in each language; and the graphic devices are used to group the **yes** and **no** options for each candidate. Opting to avoid the butterfly layout entirely, the names are placed on a single side of the punch holes. In this arrangement the action of voting is consistent from left to right throughout the ballot, but as a trade-off, the information in this section is uncomfortably dense. Statistical analysis of the numbers of retention votes cast in recent Cook County elections documents the success of the improved design, even while retaining the denser punchcard.[6]

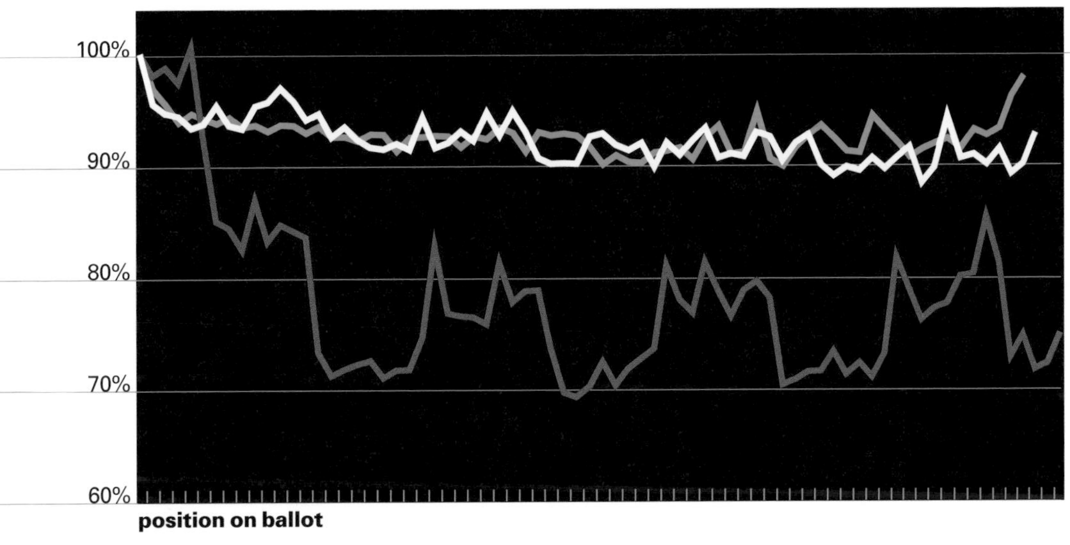

blue line:
average votes cast 1982–1998, no butterfly, 312-hole punchcard

red line:
votes cast in 2000, butterfly layout (pages 14–15), denser 456-hole punchcard

white line:
average votes cast 2002–2004, improved design (facing page), 456-hole punchcard

[6] Klumpp, "Judicial Retention Elections in Cook County."

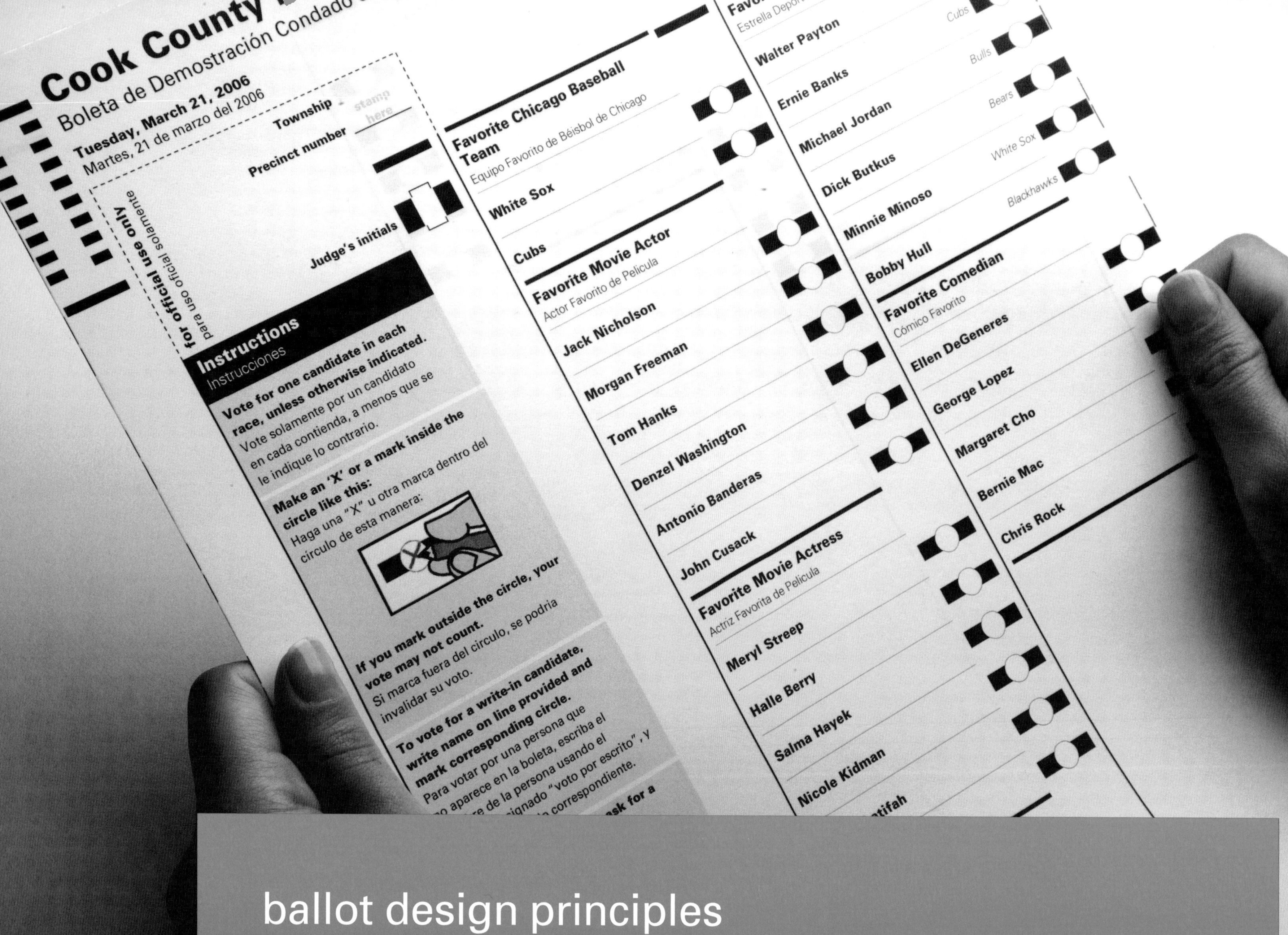

ballot design principles

While the preceding case study focuses on a highly dense punchcard ballot, similar design principles apply to all ballot types. Design improvements can be made regardless of ballot complexity or voting system technology: punchcard, optical scan, direct recording electronic, paper, or lever.

Additional improvements can be achieved with design refinements that result from usability testing. For example, it was discovered through observational research that instructions placed in the first column of a multiple-column optical scan ballot (shown on the facing page), rather than placed across the top of all columns, increased the likelihood that voters would read the instructions.

Illustrated on the following pages are five basic principles of ballot design. By developing and testing ballot layouts that adhere to these principles, clarity and legibility can be significantly improved.

The five principles of ballot design for all ballot types:

→ Use lowercase letters for greater legibility
→ Understand and assign information hierarchy
→ Keep type font, size, weight, and width variations to a minimum
→ Do not center-align type
→ Use shading and graphic devices to support hierarchy and aid legibility

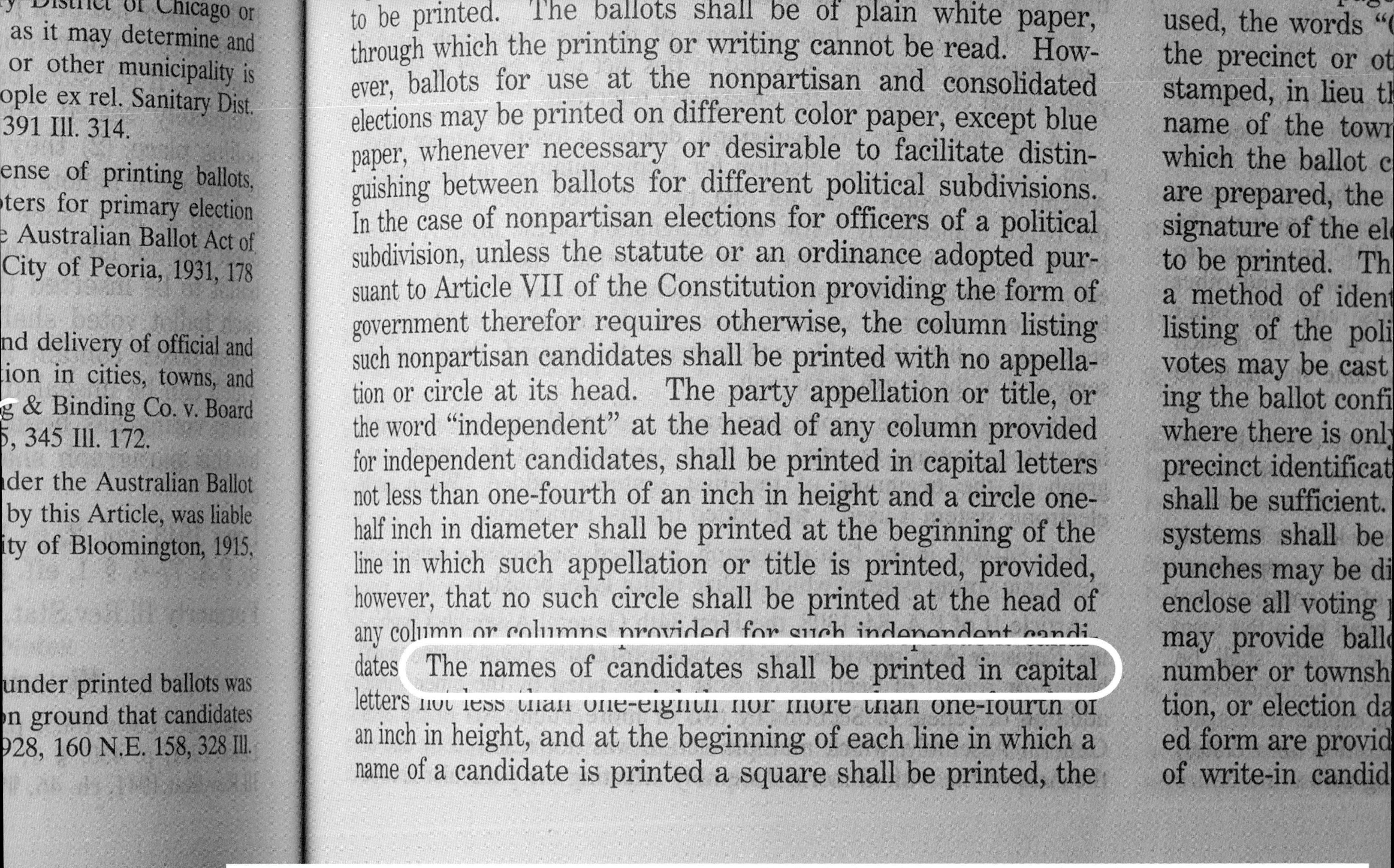

to be printed. The ballots shall be of plain white paper, through which the printing or writing cannot be read. However, ballots for use at the nonpartisan and consolidated elections may be printed on different color paper, except blue paper, whenever necessary or desirable to facilitate distinguishing between ballots for different political subdivisions. In the case of nonpartisan elections for officers of a political subdivision, unless the statute or an ordinance adopted pursuant to Article VII of the Constitution providing the form of government therefor requires otherwise, the column listing such nonpartisan candidates shall be printed with no appellation or circle at its head. The party appellation or title, or the word "independent" at the head of any column provided for independent candidates, shall be printed in capital letters not less than one-fourth of an inch in height and a circle one-half inch in diameter shall be printed at the beginning of the line in which such appellation or title is printed, provided, however, that no such circle shall be printed at the head of any column or columns provided for such independent candidates. The names of candidates shall be printed in capital letters not less than one-eighth nor more than one-fourth of an inch in height, and at the beginning of each line in which a name of a candidate is printed a square shall be printed, the

lowercase letters

Election law typically dictates typographic specifications in dense legalese. As of November 2000, the use of all capital letters for candidate names on Illinois ballots was mandated by state election code. In September of 2001, Illinois House Bill No. 1914 was signed into law, allowing the use of lowercase letters.

One of the most common errors in ballot design is the overuse of capital letters. This is especially problematic with candidate names, which need to be the clearest, most accessible information on the ballot. Unlike the simple rectangles formed by groups of all capital letters, groups of lowercase letters form distinctive silhouettes. Ascenders (strokes that extend above the standard height of lowercase letters) and descenders (strokes that extend below the baseline) provide visual clues and help readers to more quickly and accurately identify words.

The decision to use all capital letters for candidate names is often made with the intent of signifying importance. However, there are better ways to achieve this. In the redesign of the Chicago/Cook County ballot, larger and bolder type was used to place greater emphasis on candidate names.

KATHY M. FLANAGAN

Words set in capital letters all have a similar silhouette.

Words set with lowercase letters have a unique shape, providing visual cues for identification.

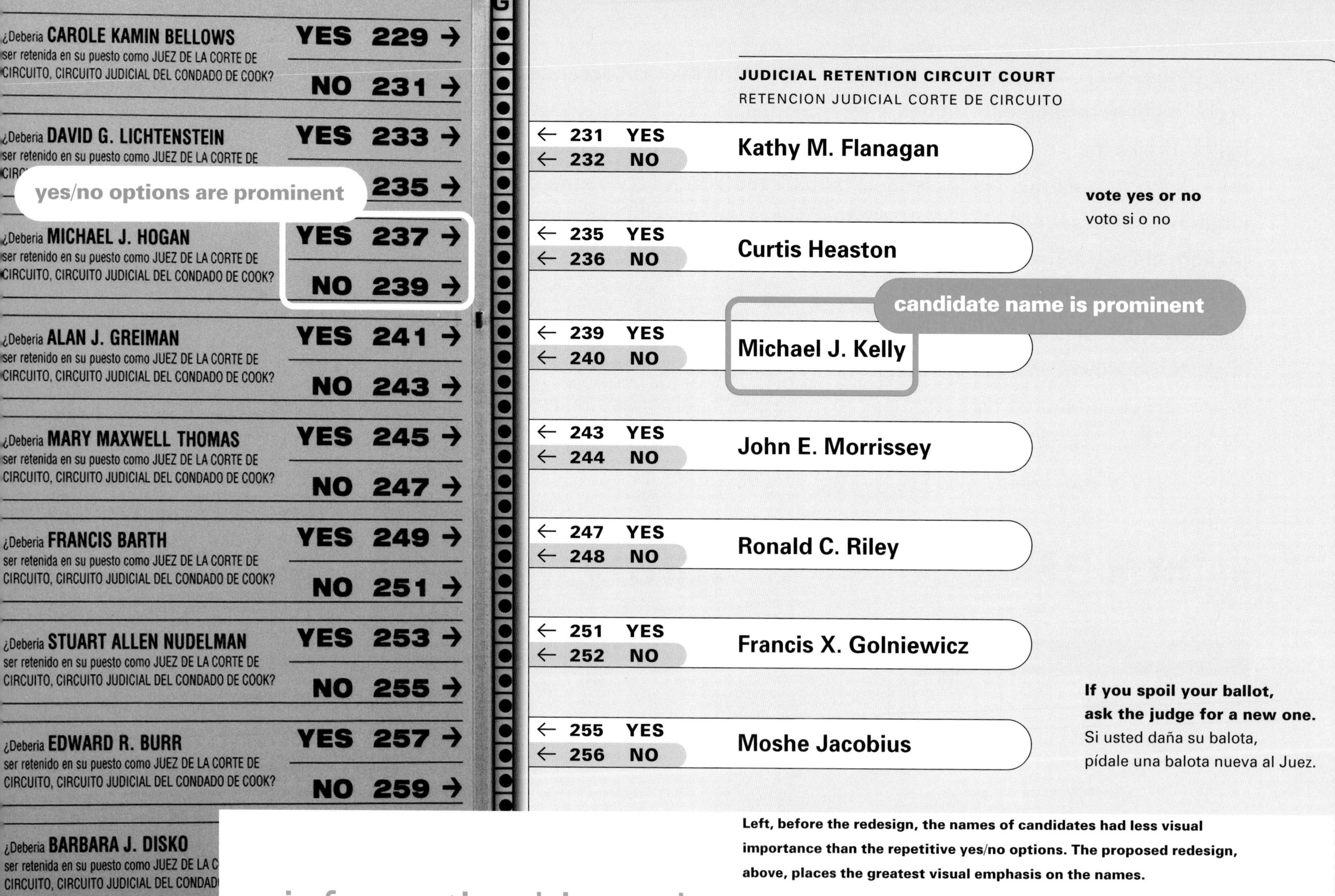

ON JUDICIAL – CORTE DE CIRCUITO)
¿Deberia CAROLE KAMIN BELLOWS ser retenida en su puesto como JUEZ DE LA CORTE DE CIRCUITO, CIRCUITO JUDICIAL DEL CONDADO DE COOK?
YES 229 →
NO 231 →
¿Deberia DAVID G. LICHTENSTEIN ser retenido en su puesto como JUEZ DE LA CORTE DE
YES 233 →
235 →
yes/no options are prominent
¿Deberia MICHAEL J. HOGAN ser retenido en su puesto como JUEZ DE LA CORTE DE CIRCUITO, CIRCUITO JUDICIAL DEL CONDADO DE COOK?
YES 237 →
NO 239 →
¿Deberia ALAN J. GREIMAN ser retenido en su puesto como JUEZ DE LA CORTE DE CIRCUITO, CIRCUITO JUDICIAL DEL CONDADO DE COOK?
YES 241 →
NO 243 →
¿Deberia MARY MAXWELL THOMAS ser retenida en su puesto como JUEZ DE LA CORTE DE CIRCUITO, CIRCUITO JUDICIAL DEL CONDADO DE COOK?
YES 245 →
NO 247 →
¿Deberia FRANCIS BARTH ser retenida en su puesto como JUEZ DE LA CORTE DE CIRCUITO, CIRCUITO JUDICIAL DEL CONDADO DE COOK?
YES 249 →
NO 251 →
¿Deberia STUART ALLEN NUDELMAN ser retenido en su puesto como JUEZ DE LA CORTE DE CIRCUITO, CIRCUITO JUDICIAL DEL CONDADO DE COOK?
YES 253 →
NO 255 →
¿Deberia EDWARD R. BURR ser retenido en su puesto como JUEZ DE LA CORTE DE CIRCUITO, CIRCUITO JUDICIAL DEL CONDADO DE COOK?
YES 257 →
NO 259 →
¿Deberia BARBARA J. DISKO ser retenida en su puesto como JUEZ DE LA C
CIRCUITO, CIRCUITO JUDICIAL DEL CONDAD
G
JUDICIAL RETENTION CIRCUIT COURT
RETENCION JUDICIAL CORTE DE CIRCUITO
← 231 YES ← 232 NO Kathy M. Flanagan
← 235 YES ← 236 NO Curtis Heaston
← 239 YES ← 240 NO Michael J. Kelly
candidate name is prominent
← 243 YES ← 244 NO John E. Morrissey
← 247 YES ← 248 NO Ronald C. Riley
← 251 YES ← 252 NO Francis X. Golniewicz
← 255 YES ← 256 NO Moshe Jacobius
vote yes or no
voto si o no
If you spoil your ballot, ask the judge for a new one.
Si usted daña su balota, pídale una balota nueva al Juez.

Left, before the redesign, the names of candidates had less visual importance than the repetitive yes/no options. The proposed redesign, above, places the greatest visual emphasis on the names.

information hierarchy

When presenting information, the use of different weights and sizes of type should establish a clear and manageable hierarchy. Type variations must be carefully considered. Too much variation and the hierarchy is lost. Emphasis on the wrong information and the hierarchy is incorrect.

Before the redesign (facing page, left), the most prominent information on the ballot was the grouping of **yes/no** options with the corresponding arrows and punch numbers. Unquestionably this information is important, but is it more important than the names of the candidates? The **yes/no** options are repetitive information, easily accessed and understood by the voter. The unique names of the candidates should be the most prominent information on the ballot.

The proposed redesign (facing page, right) clearly establishes the candidate names as the first priority.

Recommended typographic hierarchy for all ballot types:

1. Candidate names
2. Ballot-marking device (arrows and punch numbers, optical scan ovals or arrows, etc.)
3. Candidate party or professional affiliation (if applicable)
4. Instructions, headings, and all required and/or repetitive information

JUDICIAL RETENTION – CIRCUIT COURT
(RETENCION JUDICIAL — CORTE DE CIRCUIT)

3

1

YES 230
NO 232

2

5

Shall KATHY M. FLANAGAN
be retained in office as JUDGE OF THE CIRCUIT COURT, COOK COUNTY JUDICIAL CIRCUIT?

4

Before the redesign, the Chicago/Cook County retention ballot had too many variations in type size, weight, and width.

minimal variation

The original Chicago/Cook County retention ballot had five variations in the size, weight, and width of type. At left, in order of descending visual importance: 1] very bold, very large, all caps for **yes/no** and punch numbers; 2] medium weight, large, all caps, condensed for candidate names; 3] medium weight, extended, all caps for ballot page heading, with lighter-weight version of the same style for the second language; 4] light weight, all caps for title of the office within the retention question; 5] light weight, lowercase for the remainder of the question. This is a confusing and unnecessary amount of variation. In ballot design a change of typographic style should always indicate a change in meaning.

As shown below, the redesign limited typographic variation to two sizes and two weights. At the first level of importance is the name of the candidate and the punch number. At the second level are headings and instructions. A lighter weight of the secondary type size is used for the second language.

Kathy M. Flanagan

YES 229 →
NO 230 →

Vote yes or no.
Voto si o no.

If you spoil your ballot,
ask the judge for a new one.
Si usted daña su balota,
pídale una balota nueva al Juez.

The information displayed in a ballot layout can be grouped into a two-tier visual hierarchy using only two sizes and two weights of type.

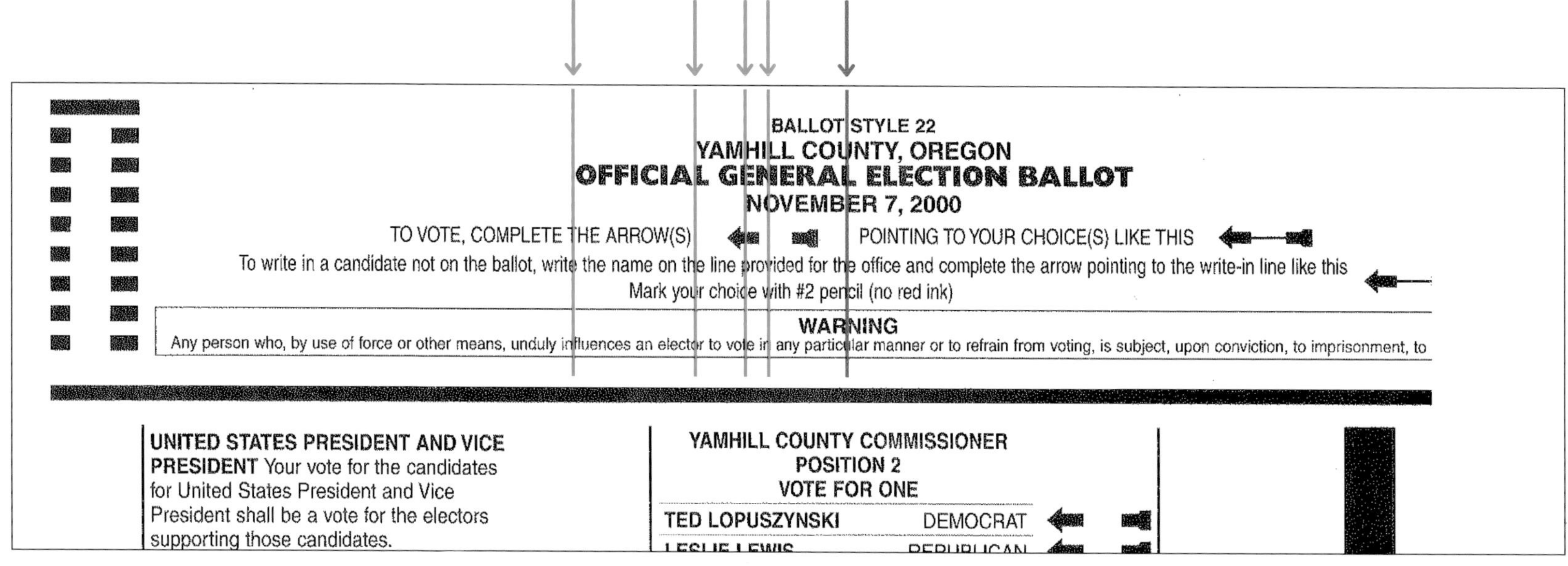

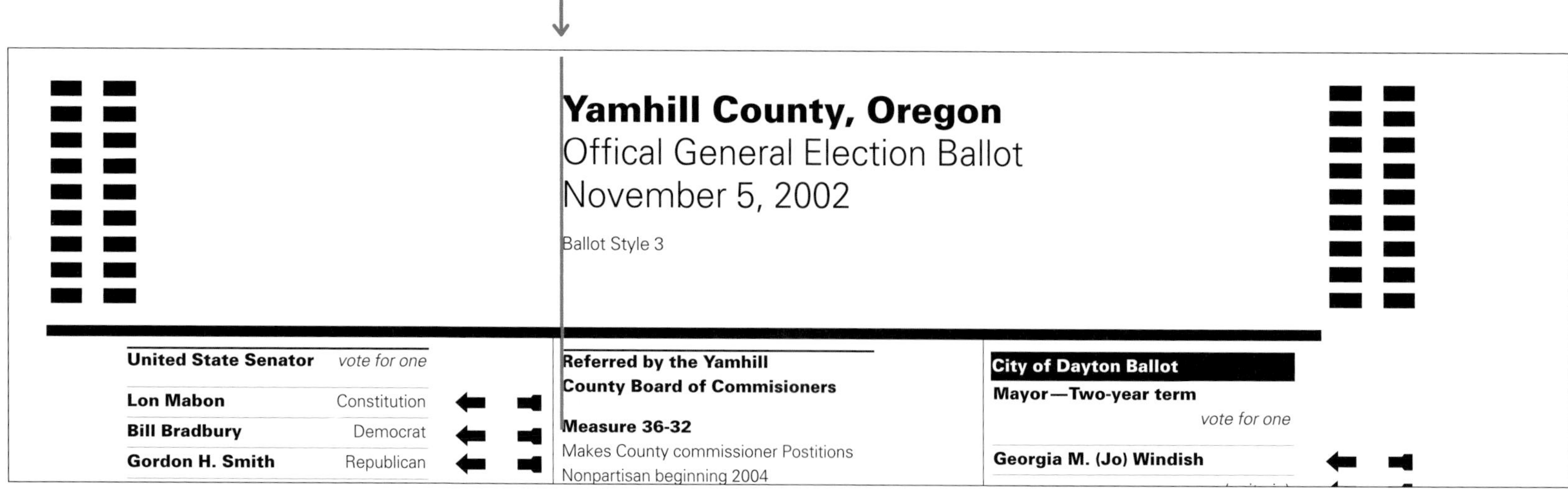

Center-aligned type requires our eye to search for the beginning of each subsequent line. It is a decorative form of typographic alignment, but not a functional form.

asymmetrical alignment

We read from left to right. From the end of one line to the beginning of the next, our eye seeks the place to begin again. Flush left (asymmetrical) alignment is simple, practical, and highly legible. Centered (symmetrical) alignment is complex, decorative, and more demanding to read. In center-aligned typography the placement of the beginning of each line is inconsistent and unpredictable. There is very little practical use for centered typography, and no need whatsoever for centered type in election design.

The principle of asymmetrical alignment is demonstrated below in the redesign of the Yamhill County, Oregon, ballot heading, which also uses lowercase letters to increase legibility. In the improved version there are only two type sizes. The information determined to be most important, the name of the county, is set in bold. Secondary information, the election type and date, is set in a lighter weight of the same size. The ballot style, of least importance to the voter, is set in a significantly smaller size.

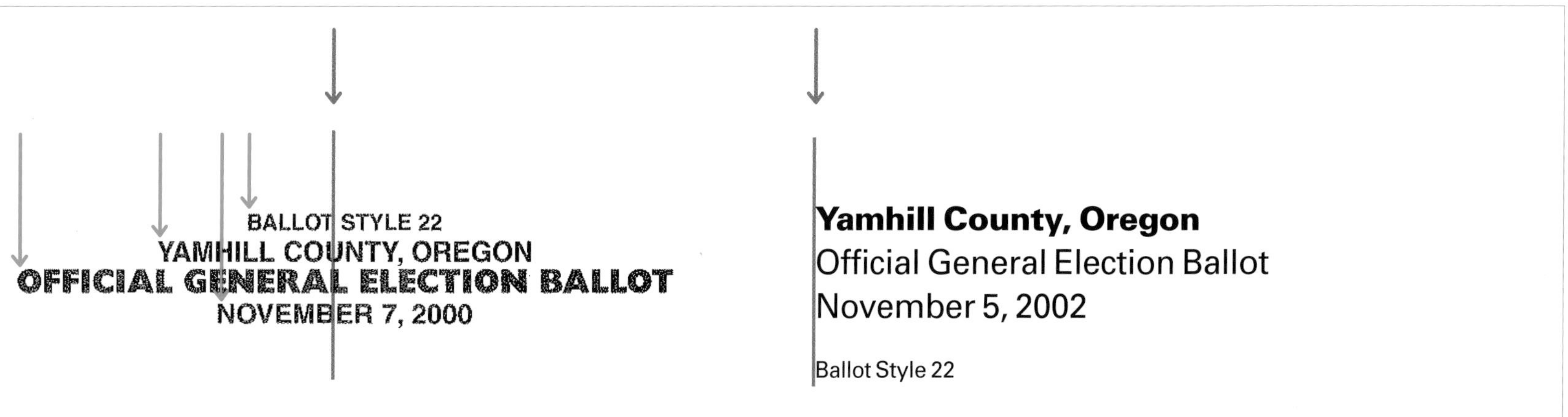

Centered alignment, all capital letters, and indistinct variations in type size make this ballot heading complex, decorative, and difficult to read.

Flush left alignment, lowercase letters, and limited type sizes make this ballot heading accessible and legible.

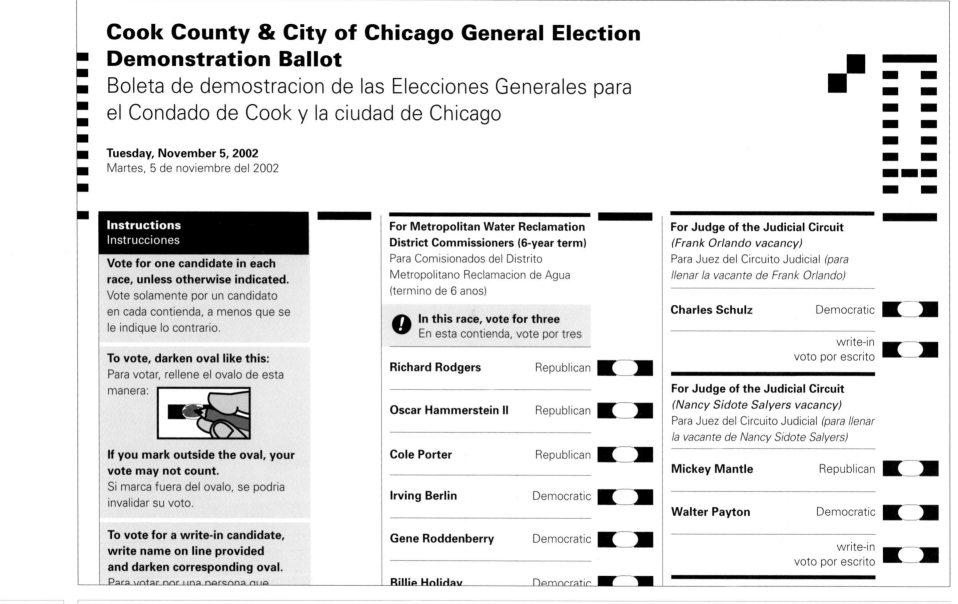

Cook County & City of Chicago General Election Demonstration Ballot

Boleta de demostracion de las Elecciones Generales para el Condado de Cook y la ciudad de Chicago

Tuesday, November 5, 2002
Martes, 5 de noviembre del 2002

Instructions
Instrucciones

Vote for one candidate in each race, unless otherwise indicated.
Vote solamente por un candidato en cada contienda, a menos que se le indique lo contrario.

To vote, darken oval like this:
Para votar, rellene el ovalo de esta manera:

If you mark outside the oval, your vote may not count.
Si marca fuera del ovalo, se podria invalidar su voto.

To vote for a write-in candidate, write name on line provided and darken corresponding oval.
Para votar por una persona que

For Metropolitan Water Reclamation District Commissioners (6-year term)
Para Comisionados del Distrito Metropolitano Reclamacion de Agua (termino de 6 anos)

In this race, vote for three
En esta contienda, vote por tres

Richard Rodgers	Republican
Oscar Hammerstein II	Republican
Cole Porter	Republican
Irving Berlin	Democratic
Gene Roddenberry	Democratic
Billie Holiday	Democratic

For Judge of the Judicial Circuit
(Frank Orlando vacancy)
Para Juez del Circuito Judicial *(para llenar la vacante de Frank Orlando)*

Charles Schulz	Democratic
	write-in voto por escrito

For Judge of the Judicial Circuit
(Nancy Sidote Salyers vacancy)
Para Juez del Circuito Judicial *(para llenar la vacante de Nancy Sidote Salyers)*

Mickey Mantle	Republican
Walter Payton	Democratic
	write-in voto por escrito

contrast + graphics

Contrast can aid legibility and support hierarchy. Black type on a white background or white type on a black background provides the highest possible and most legible visual contrast. The names of candidates should always be displayed in black type on a white background. Alternate forms of contrast can be used to distinguish headings and instructions. On the facing page, a heading appears in reverse form—white letters on black—and on-ballot instructions appear on a light gray background.

Additionally, in the proposed Chicago/Cook County ballot redesign, a graphic device surrounds the candidate names and party affiliations. Shown below, this device visually groups the candidates and their parties and directs the voter's attention toward each corresponding arrow and punch number. When using graphic devices (lines separating candidates and sections, warning icons, ballot-marking devices, etc.) it is important that they be simple and functional—never decorative.

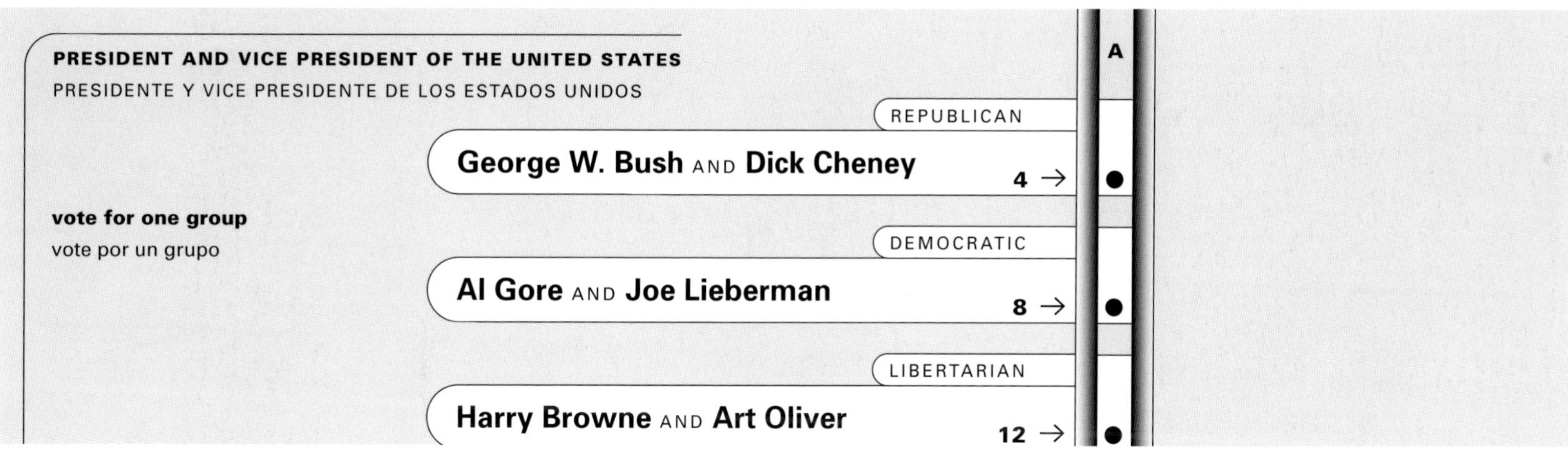

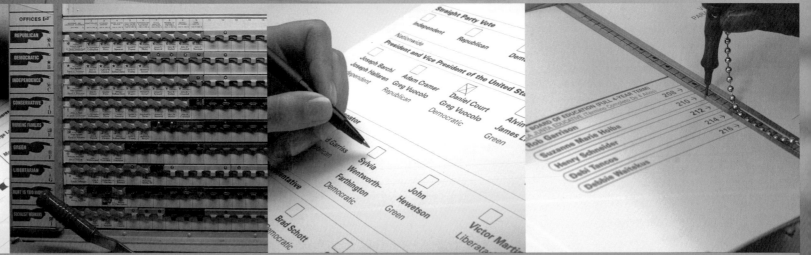

The five basic voting systems in use in the United States are, from left to right directly above, optical scan, lever, paper, punchcard, and top, direct recording electronic.

ballot design examples

There are five basic types of voting systems currently in use in the United States: optical scan, direct recording electronic (DRE), punchcard, paper, and lever.[7] While punchcard, paper, and lever systems are still in use in some areas, most states and counties have by now adopted optical scan or DRE technologies. The federal government has assisted in this transition through the Help America Vote Act (HAVA) of 2002. Enacted in response to the controversies surrounding the 2000 presidential election, HAVA provides federal payments to states to update voting systems. HAVA also established the U.S. Election Assistance Commission (EAC), which is responsible for disbursing HAVA funds and for various informational and administrative tasks pertaining to federal elections.[8]

Design for Democracy has worked with the National Institute of Standards and Technology, election offices in Chicago and Cook County (Illinois) and the state of Oregon, and voters' rights groups and election consultants to develop actual and prototypical ballot designs in both print and electronic media. The group will establish universal models and best-practices guidelines for optical scan and DRE ballot design for the EAC in 2007.

The following pages present current examples of Design for Democracy work for optical scan and DRE ballots. These examples apply the same design principles described on previous pages: the use of legible lowercase letters; a clearly established information hierarchy; minimal variation in type size, weight, and width; asymmetrical alignment; and strategic use of contrast and graphics. Design for Democracy encourages the adaptation of these examples for use by other election jurisdictions.

[7] Election Data Services, Inc. (www.electiondataservices.com) tracks the use of voting equipment usage in the United States.

[8] Visit the U.S. Election Assistance Commission website (www.eac.gov) for more information on the Help America Vote Act.

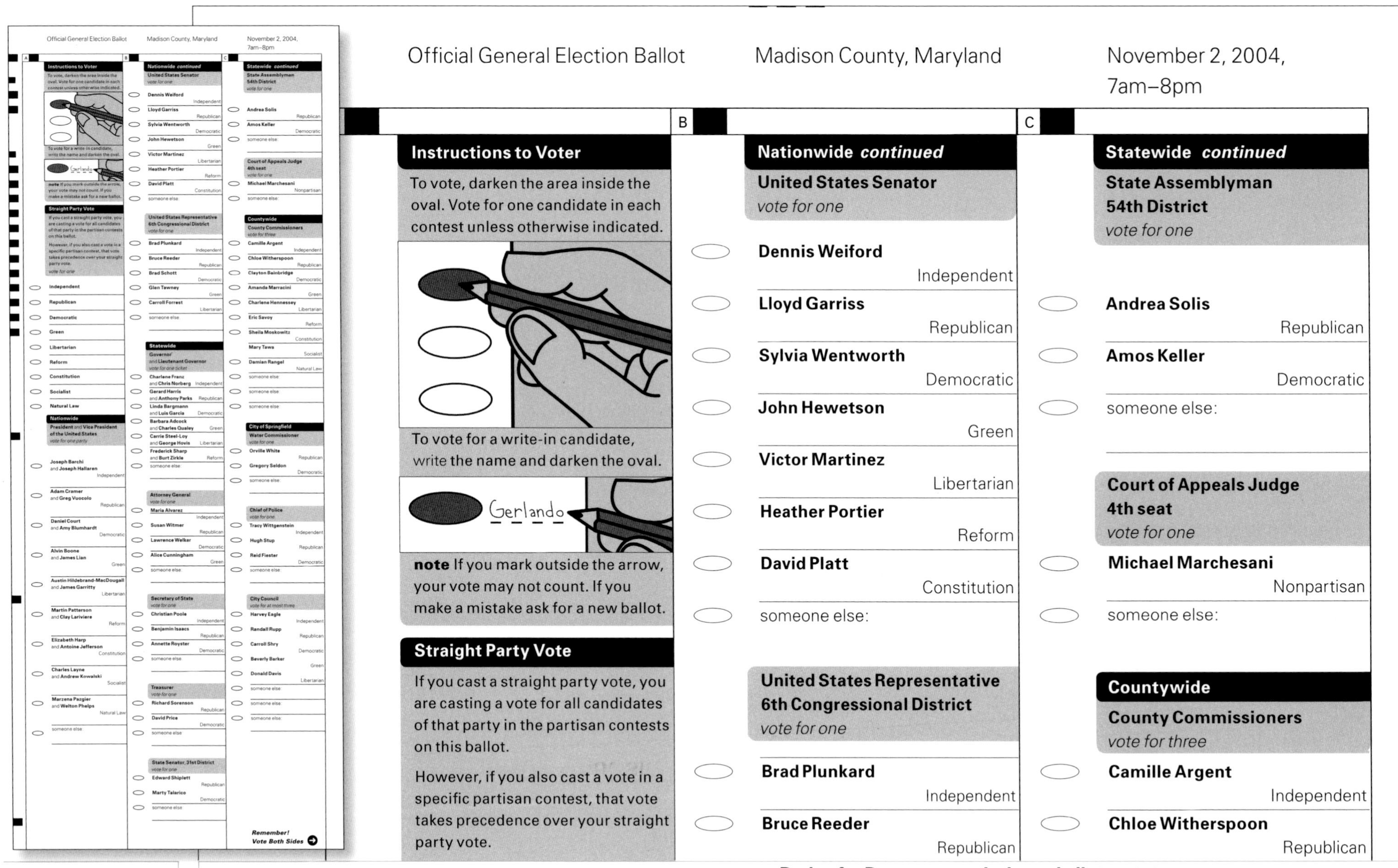
Official General Election Ballot

Madison County, Maryland

November 2, 2004, 7am–8pm

Instructions to Voter

To vote, darken the area inside the oval. Vote for one candidate in each contest unless otherwise indicated.

To vote for a write-in candidate, write the name and darken the oval.

Gerlando

note If you mark outside the arrow, your vote may not count. If you make a mistake ask for a new ballot.

Straight Party Vote

If you cast a straight party vote, you are casting a vote for all candidates of that party in the partisan contests on this ballot.

However, if you also cast a vote in a specific partisan contest, that vote takes precedence over your straight party vote.

B

Nationwide *continued*

United States Senator
vote for one

Dennis Weiford Independent

Lloyd Garriss Republican

Sylvia Wentworth Democratic

John Hewetson Green

Victor Martinez Libertarian

Heather Portier Reform

David Platt Constitution

someone else:

United States Representative 6th Congressional District
vote for one

Brad Plunkard Independent

Bruce Reeder Republican

C

Statewide *continued*

State Assemblyman 54th District
vote for one

Andrea Solis Republican

Amos Keller Democratic

someone else:

Court of Appeals Judge 4th seat
vote for one

Michael Marchesani Nonpartisan

someone else:

Countywide

County Commissioners
vote for three

Camille Argent Independent

Chloe Witherspoon Republican

Design for Democracy optical scan ballot prototype. Shown at actual and reduced size.

optical scan

Optical scan voting systems are highly reliable and widely used. They require the voter to indicate selections by physically marking on a paper ballot. After the ballot is complete, it is inserted into a ballot counting machine, which records the votes.

Many states and counties receiving HAVA funds decided in favor of optical scan voting rather than the still-controversial DRE technologies. Voting by optical scan is intuitive and familiar. The act of filling in an oval shape or completing an arrow is much like that of completing a standardized test. In optical scan voting there is a low percentage of unrecorded votes. Voting errors—most often incorrect ballot markings—are quickly and easily detected by visual inspection or by the ballot counting machine.

The success of optical scan voting can be supported by providing clear and simple voting instructions directly on the ballot and on signs in the polling place. Also, sample ballots and voting instructions can be distributed prior to election day, both online and by mail.

There are a number of optical scan voting system vendors, each with specific features and requirements that affect the design of the ballot. These include the dimensions of the page; the number, length and width of the columns; the ability to print on one or both sides; the choice of typeface; and the nature and position of the marking device. When developing the design of an optical scan ballot, it is crucial to communicate and cooperate with election officials and with the voting system vendor.

At right is a three-column optical scan ballot design. 1] The ballot heading is simple and clear, organized with flush left alignment and one type style (Univers 45). 2] On-ballot instructions, distinguished by a light gray background area, are located at the top of the left column—the place where a voter is most likely to begin reading. 3] Sections for federal, state, and local contests are indicated by headings in a black bar with white type. 4] Candidate names are set in bold type (Univers 65), with lowercase letters printed in high contrast: black on a white background. 5] To distinguish retention questions and ballot measures from contested offices, ballot items with a yes/no vote option are placed on a gray background. 6] Special instructions or warnings are called out with specific icons.

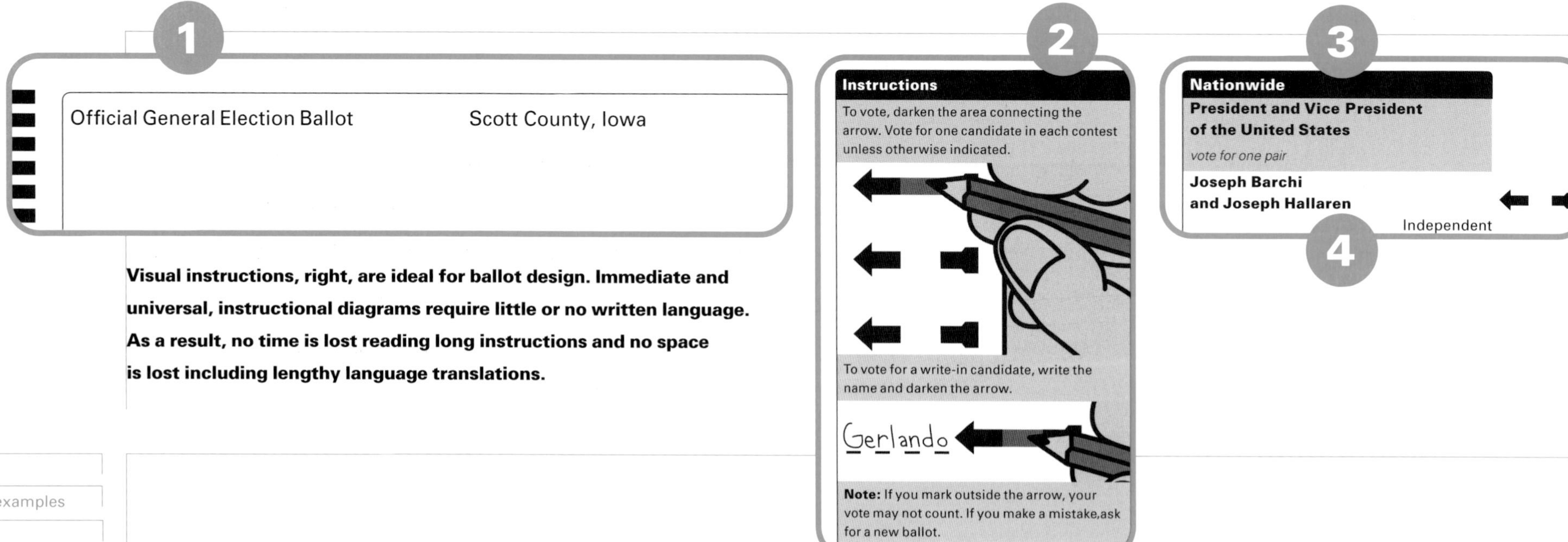

Visual instructions, right, are ideal for ballot design. Immediate and universal, instructional diagrams require little or no written language. As a result, no time is lost reading long instructions and no space is lost including lengthy language translations.

Official General Election Ballot | Scott County, Iowa | Tuesday, November 2, 2004
7am–8pm

Ballot Style 3

Instructions

To vote, darken the area connecting the arrow. Vote for one candidate in each contest unless otherwise indicated.

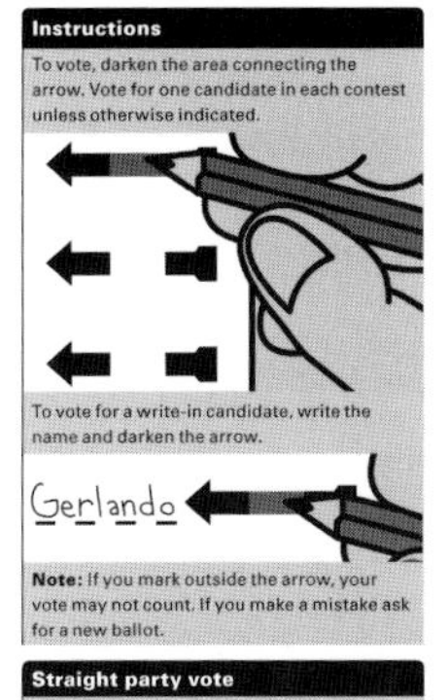

To vote for a write-in candidate, write the name and darken the arrow.

Gerlando

Note: If you mark outside the arrow, your vote may not count. If you make a mistake ask for a new ballot.

Straight party vote

If you cast a straight party vote, you are casting a vote for all candidates of that party in the partisan contests on this ballot. However, if you also cast a vote in a specific partisan contest, that vote will take the place of your straight party vote.

vote for one

- Independent
- Republican
- Democratic
- Green
- Libertarian
- Reform
- Constitution
- Socialist
- Natural Law

Nationwide

President and Vice President of the United States

vote for one pair

- Joseph Barchi and Joseph Hallaren — Independent
- Adam Cramer and Greg Vuocolo — Republican
- Daniel Court and Amy Blumhardt — Democratic
- Alvin Boone and James Lian — Green
- Austin Hildebrand-MacDougall and James Garritty — Libertarian
- Martin Patterson and Clay Lariviere — Reform
- Elizabeth Harp/ and Antoine Jefferson — Constitution
- Charles Layne/ and Andrew Kowalski — Socialist
- Marzena Pazgier/ and Welton Phelps — Natural Law
- someone else:

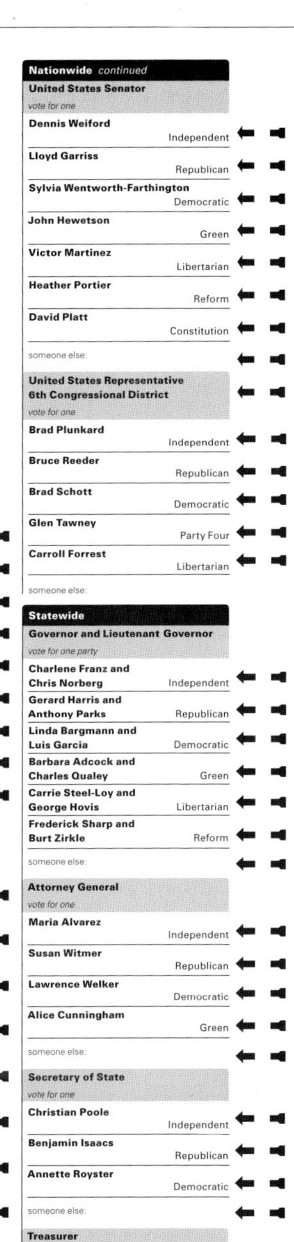

Nationwide *continued*

United States Senator

vote for one

- Dennis Weiford — Independent
- Lloyd Garriss — Republican
- Sylvia Wentworth-Farthington — Democratic
- John Hewetson — Green
- Victor Martinez — Libertarian
- Heather Portier — Reform
- David Platt — Constitution
- someone else:

United States Representative 6th Congressional District

vote for one

- Brad Plunkard — Independent
- Bruce Reeder — Republican
- Brad Schott — Democratic
- Glen Tawney — Party Four
- Carroll Forrest — Libertarian
- someone else:

Statewide

Governor and Lieutenant Governor

vote for one party

- Charlene Franz and Chris Norberg — Independent
- Gerard Harris and Anthony Parks — Republican
- Linda Bargmann and Luis Garcia — Democratic
- Barbara Adcock and Charles Qualey — Green
- Carrie Steel-Loy and George Hovis — Libertarian
- Frederick Sharp and Burt Zirkle — Reform
- someone else:

Attorney General

vote for one

- Maria Alvarez — Independent
- Susan Witmer — Republican
- Lawrence Welker — Democratic
- Alice Cunningham — Green
- someone else:

Secretary of State

vote for one

- Christian Poole — Independent
- Benjamin Isaacs — Republican
- Annette Royster — Democratic
- someone else:

Treasurer

vote for one

- Richard Sorenson — Republican
- David Price — Democratic
- someone else:

Statewide *continued*

State Senator, 31st District

vote for one

- Edward Shiplett — Republican
- Marty Talarico — Democratic
- someone else:

State Assemblyman, 54th District

vote for one

- Andrea Solis — Republican
- Amos Keller — Democratic
- someone else:

Court of Appeals Judge, 4th seat

vote for one

- Michael Marchesani — Nonpartisan
- someone else:

Retention Question 1

Retain Robert Demergue as Chief Justice of the Supreme Court?

- yes
- no

Retention Question 2

Retain Elmer Hull as Associate Justice of the Supreme Court?

- yes
- no

Retention Question 3

Retain Susan Esquer as Associate Justice of the Court of Appeals, 5th Appellate District, Division 2?

- yes
- no

Retention Question 4

Retain Rita Zheng as Associate Justice of Family Court, 3rd District?

- yes
- no

Proposed Constitutional Amendment D

Shall there be an amendment to the State constitution concerning recovery of damages relating to construction of real property improvements, and, in connection therewith, prohibiting laws that limit or impair a property owner's right to recover damages caused by a failure to construct an improvement in a good and workman-like manner; defining "good and workman-like manner" to include construction that is suitable for its intended purposes; and permitting exceptions for laws that limit punitive damages, afford governmental immunity, or impose time limits of specified minimum lengths on filing lawsuits?

- approve
- reject

Remember! Vote Both Sides

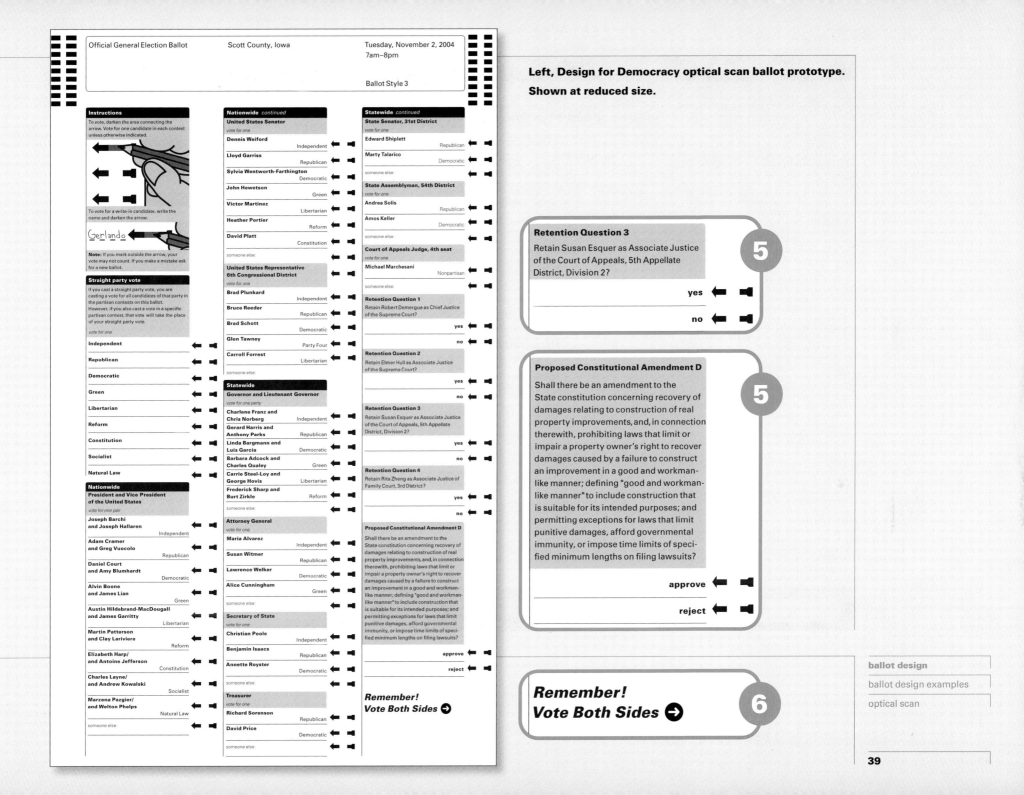

Left, Design for Democracy optical scan ballot prototype. Shown at reduced size.

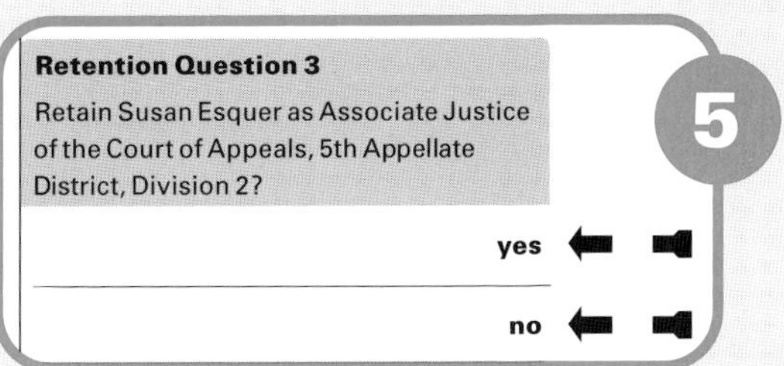

Retention Question 3

Retain Susan Esquer as Associate Justice of the Court of Appeals, 5th Appellate District, Division 2?

- yes
- no

5

Proposed Constitutional Amendment D

Shall there be an amendment to the State constitution concerning recovery of damages relating to construction of real property improvements, and, in connection therewith, prohibiting laws that limit or impair a property owner's right to recover damages caused by a failure to construct an improvement in a good and workman-like manner; defining "good and workman-like manner" to include construction that is suitable for its intended purposes; and permitting exceptions for laws that limit punitive damages, afford governmental immunity, or impose time limits of specified minimum lengths on filing lawsuits?

- approve
- reject

5

Remember! Vote Both Sides

6

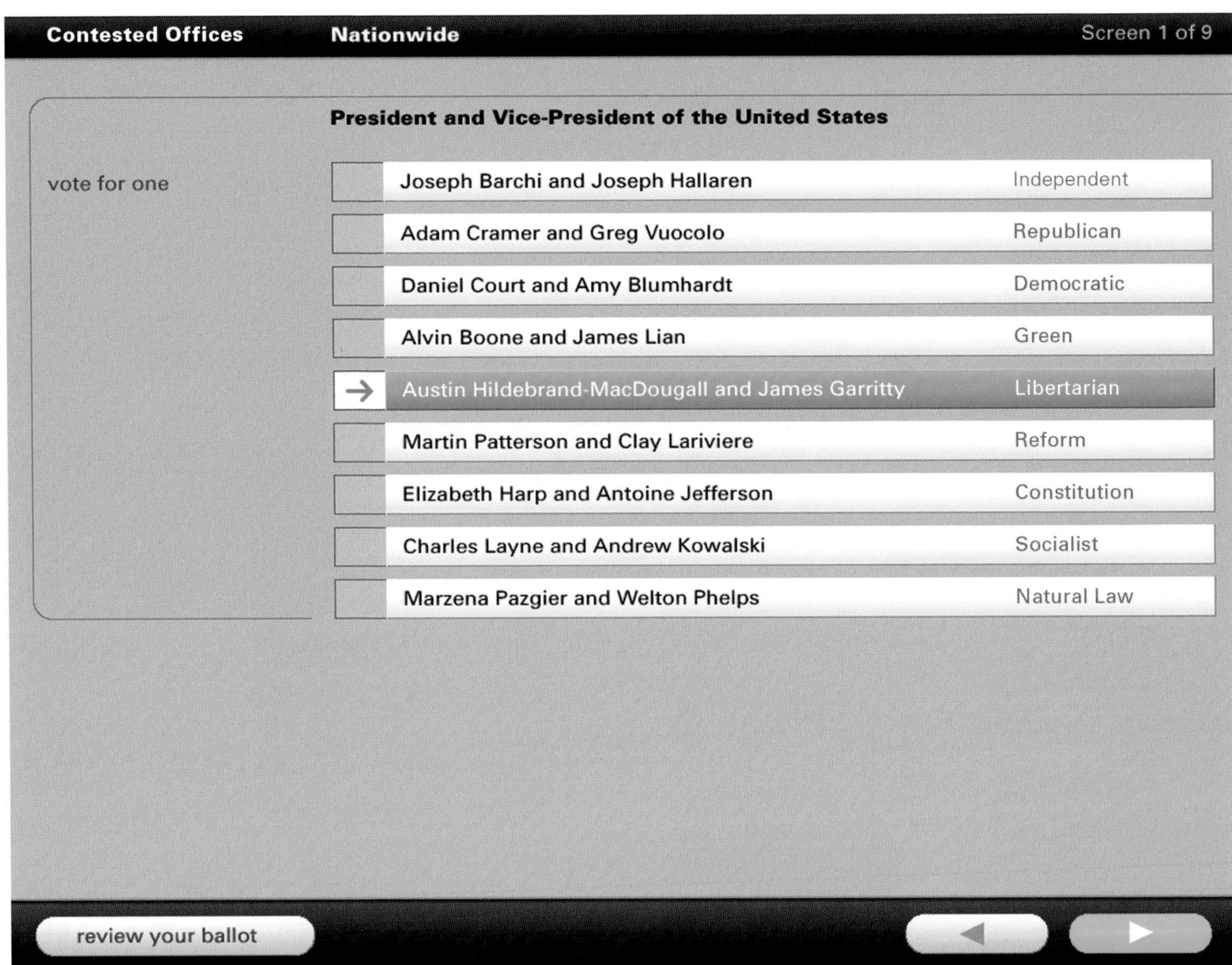

Design for Democracy electronic ballot prototype.

Shown at reduced size.

touch screen

Direct recording electronic voting systems generally require the voter to indicate selections by touching a computer screen. Some voters and voters' rights groups have reacted negatively to DRE systems, based mostly on the potential for programming errors and security breaches, and sometimes on a general distrust of computer technology. From an information design standpoint, though, DRE voting systems can be ideal.

Computer-based voting allows for an unlimited number of sequenced electronic screens. Visual space is not limited to the dimensions of a single sheet of paper. Color, useful for indicating selections and actions, does not add to production costs. And any number of languages can be accommodated, as can modifications for voters with visual and motor impairments. These advantages far exceed the capabilities of other voting systems.

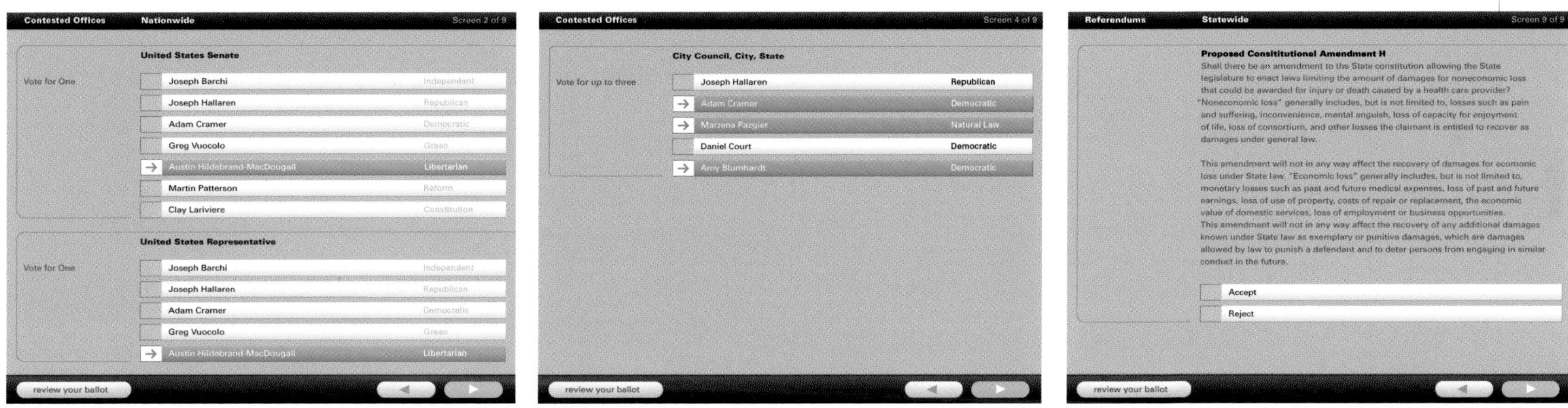

The same design principles apply to electronic ballots. Gray backgrounds allow the names of the candidates to be placed prominently in black type on a white background. Unlike paper ballots, color can be used to indicate selections, as shown here in blue. Green arrow keys instruct the voter to move forward through the screens of the ballot.

A final ballot example is included here to show the importance of good design in new or unusual election formats. The optical scan ballot at right is designed for instant runoff voting (IRV), which has been adopted by several U.S. jurisdictions in recent years.

A runoff election can be required when no candidate in a contested race receives a majority of votes. IRV was created to avoid the expense and inconvenience of runoff elections. In an IRV format, voters rank candidates by preference, selecting one or more additional choices beyond their first choice. If no candidate receives a majority of first-choice votes, candidates are eliminated one by one and the additional choices are used to produce a majority winner.

In ballot design for instant runoff voting, it is crucial to emphasize the rank numbers in the ballot information hierarchy. In the example at right, the rank numbers are set in the largest type on the page, with further emphasis provided by gray background areas of different shades that contain headings, instructions, and the rank numbers. As with the previous ballot examples, the voting instructions are placed in a prominent location directly on the ballot.

Complicating this particular situation is the need for three languages, which is simply too much information for one ballot. In the proposed redesign, this problem is solved by printing two versions of the ballot, one in English and Spanish and the other in English and Chinese.

instant runoff voting

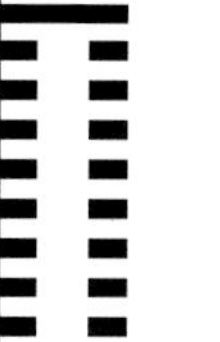

City and County of San Francisco

Demonstration ballot for member and board of supervisors

Instructions for voters

Complete the arrow pointing to your choice. (shown to left)

To vote for qualified write-in candidate, write the person's name on the blank line provided and complete the arrow.

(write name above)

Ranked choice voting

Vote for a different candidate for each choice, or your second and third choice vote will not be counted.

Ciudad y Condado de San Francisco

Boleta de prueba para miembro y mesa directiva de superviso

Instrucciones para electores

Complete la flecha que señala su seleccion, de este modo.

Para votar por un candidato no listado y calificado, escriba el nombre en la linea en blanco y compete la flecha.

(write name above)

Vote ranqueando su seleccion

Vote por un candidato deferente por cada seleccion, de otra manera, su segunda o tercera seleccion no seran tomadas en cuenta.

first choice **primera seleccion** **1**	**second choice** **segunda seleccion** **2**	**third choice** **tercera seleccion** **3**
vote for one vota por uno	vote for one vota por uno	vote for one vota por uno
Nelson W. Aldrich engineer ingenero	**Nelson W. Aldrich** engineer ingenero	**Nelson W. Aldrich** engineer ingenero
Charles Curtis U.S. Senator Senadoro de los Estados Unidos	**Charles Curtis** U.S. Senator Senadoro de los Estados Unidos	**Charles Curtis** U.S. Senator Senadoro de los Estados Unidos
Everett Dirksen attorney abogado	**Everett Dirksen** attorney abogado	**Everett Dirksen** attorney abogado
John Hancock physician medico	**John Hancock** physician medico	**John Hancock** physician medico
Florence Nightingale teacher maestra	**Florence Nightingale** teacher maestra	**Florence Nightingale** teacher maestra
write-in/ no listado (write name above) xxxxxx	**write-in/ no listado** (write name above) xxxxxx	**write-in/ no listado** (write name above) xxxxxx

Below, prior to the redesign, the use of language translations was inconsistent. Chinese was used along with English and Spanish on most of the ballot, but for space reasons was omitted from the rank heading information. A further problem is the visual confusion created by center-aligned typography superimposed over the rank numbers.

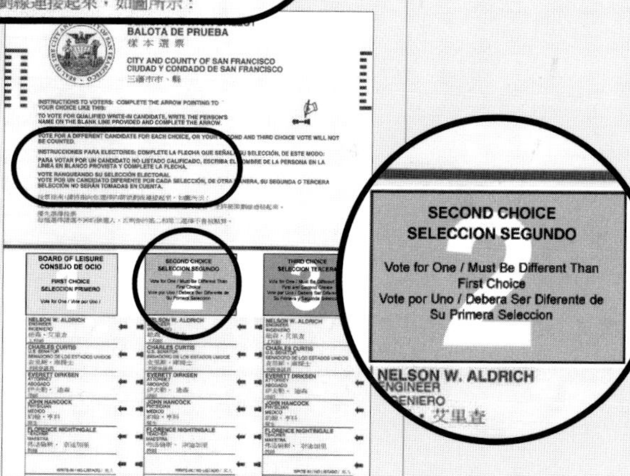

VOTE FOR A DIFFERENT CANDIDATE FOR EACH CHOICE, OR YOUR SECOND
BE COUNTED.
INSTRUCCIONES PARA ELECTORES: COMPLETE LA FLECHA QUE SEÑALA SU SE
PARA VOTAR POR UN CANDIDATO NO LISTADO CALIFICADO, ESCRIBA EL NOMBR
LÍNEA EN BLANCO PROVISTA Y COMPLETE LA FLECHA.
VOTE RANQUEANDO SU SELECCIÓN ELECTORAL
VOTE POR UN CANDIDATO DIFERENTE POR CADA SELECCIÓN, DE OTRA MANERA
SELECCIÓN NO SERÁN TOMADAS EN CUENTA.
BALOTA DE PRUEBA
SECOND CHOICE
SELECCION SEGUNDO
Vote for One / Must Be Different Than First Choice
Vote por Uno / Debera Ser Diferente de Su Primera Seleccion
NELSON W. ALDRICH

Left, Design for Democracy optical scan ballot prototype for instant runoff election. Developed for the Center of Voting and Democracy (www.fairvote.org). Shown at reduced size.

in this section

registering

Participation begins with registration

getting information

Using information design principles to provide voters with what they need to know

voting

Beyond ballot design: polling place signs, setup, and wayfinding

Casting votes on a ballot represents only a fraction of the total voting experience. Each stage of the election process involves distinct procedures with unique communication and design requirements.

Eligible citizens must to be made aware of their right to vote and must be informed about fair voting practices. Information on the whens, wheres, and hows of registering and voting must be easy to find and easy to understand. The same is true for candidate and issue information that some jurisdictions provide before elections. On election day, registered voters need to find their polling place, be directed to navigate the voting environment, understand the required interactions with pollworkers, and be provided with instruction and assistance for using voting equipment.

From voter outreach to election data entry, the Design for Democracy system applies established design principles to the communication materials involved in all three stages of the voting process: registering, getting information, and voting.

2 design + the voting experience

registering

With 150 million registered voters, registration is a massive and complex system fraught with potential errors and obstacles. The National Voter Registration Act (NVRA) of 1993 introduced reforms to make registration easier for all voters. Commonly known as the Motor Voter Act, NVRA allows for voter registration at the time of driver's license application or renewal.[1] It also increases the number of state agencies that can supply voter registration forms; provides for the acceptance of mail-in voter registration; and places limitations on the removal of voters from registration lists. Yet despite these reforms, according to one estimate at least 1.5 million citizens were denied the opportunity to vote in the 2000 election because of registration problems.[2] To improve this record, the Help America Vote Act (HAVA) of 2002 required that the states implement and maintain an interactive, centralized statewide computerized voter registration list, accessible to all state election officials.

Design can further improve the voter registration process by:

→ Providing tools and information to encourage voter registration
→ Clearly presenting information on when, where, and how to register
→ Improving the design of the voter registration card to avoid confusion and to eliminate mistakes

[1] For more information on the National Voter Registration Act, see the U.S. Department of Justice website (www.usdoj.gov/crt/voting/nvra/activ_nvra.htm).

[2] Caltech/MIT Voting Technology Project, "Voting: What Is, What Could Be," report, July 2001.

Requisitos

Para ser juez estudiante debes:

→ Ser estudiante del último año de … con buen aprovechamiento

→ Mantener al menos un GPA de … escala de 4.0

→ Ser ciudadano estadounidense … próximas elecciones.

→ Haber completado con éxito un entrenamiento como juez ele… por la oficina del Secretario

→ Ser recomendado por el/la … Director/a de la escuela secu…

→ Tener la recomendacion esc… padres o guardian legal

Responsabilidades

Los jueces electorales est… las mismas responsabili… misma autoridad y real… que otros jueces elector… cuentan:

→ Abrir el precinto elector… cerrarlo por la noche

→ Preparar el equipo para…

→ Ayudar a los votantes

→ Inscribir a los votantes

→ Verificar que los vota… para votar

→ Distribuir las boletas

→ Operar el equipo de … ularios

Horarios

Como juez electoral, deberás trabajar muchas horas. Debes llegar al precinto electoral a las 5:15 a.m. y permanecer allí hasta que los votos hayan sido contados y transmitidos después de las 7 p.m.

Entrenamiento

Para prepararte para el Día de las Elecciones, debes asistir a una sesión de entrenamiento de dos horas realizada por la oficina del Secretario. Las sesiones se realizan en lugares accesibles en todo el condado.

El entrenamiento, diseñada para prepararte a cumplir tus responsabilidades en el precinto electoral, incluye instrucción práctica centrada en procedimientos electorales y el equipo de votación.

Compensacion

…os jueces electorales reciben $150 por su …abajo. Eso incluye $100 por trabajar todo …Día de las Elecciones y $50 por asistir …na sesión de entrenamiento antes de las …cciones. Tienes que hacer ambas cosas …a ganar los $150.

Election

…g a mock electio…

…ección

…n de

…simuladas

First Voter

Learning how to register voters

Primer Votante

Aprendiendo a registrar votantes

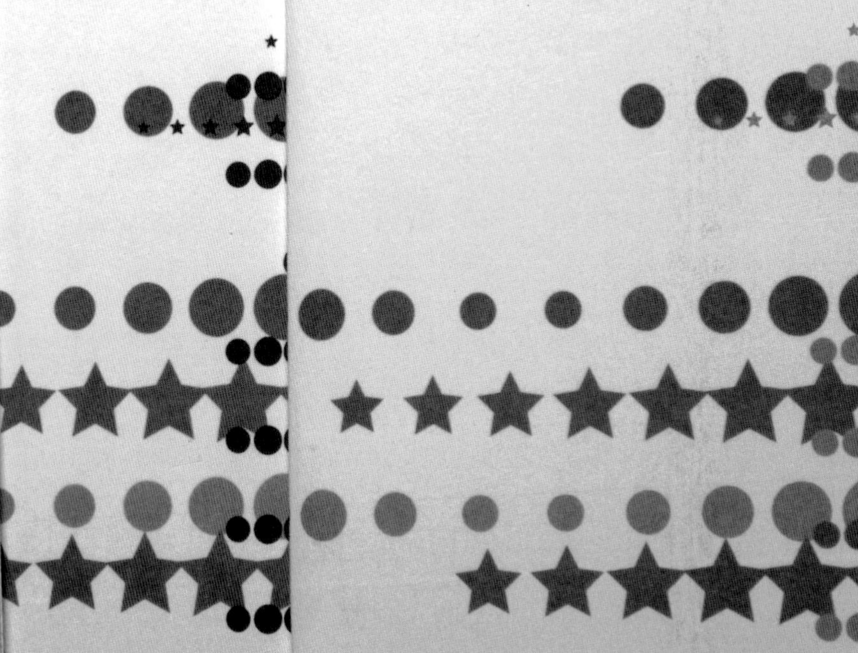

recruiting registrants

Once registered, people are likely to vote, at least in major elections. In general elections in 1996, 2000, and 2004, turnout of registered voters was 82.3, 85.5, and 88.5 percent, respectively. These are historically high levels of presidential-year voting.[3]

Materials designed to provide information and to encourage voter registration and participation should take into account the need to encourage younger citizens to register and vote. Younger citizens are relatively less likely to register to vote, possibly because they are more transient or because they have less of a stake in society than older citizens.[4] Shown at left and below is a series of brochures developed by Design for Democracy and the Office of the Cook County Clerk to provide younger citizens with information on ways to become more involved in the registration and election process.

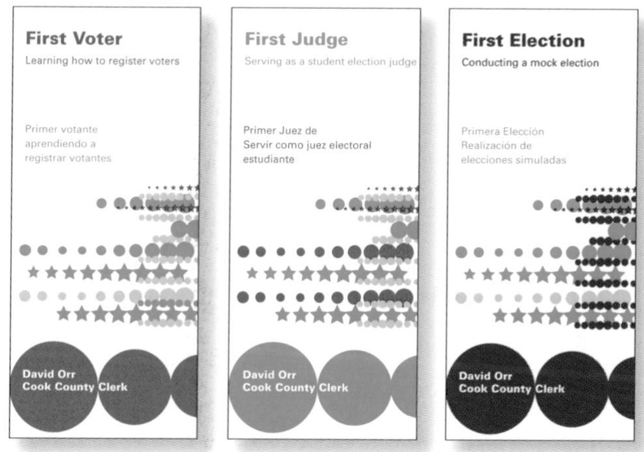

At left, Cook County First Voter brochure series. Shown at reduced size. Below, Design for Democracy *"vote!"* buttons.

[3] U.S. Census Bureau, "Voting and Registration in the Election of November 2004," report, March 2006.

[4] Ibid.

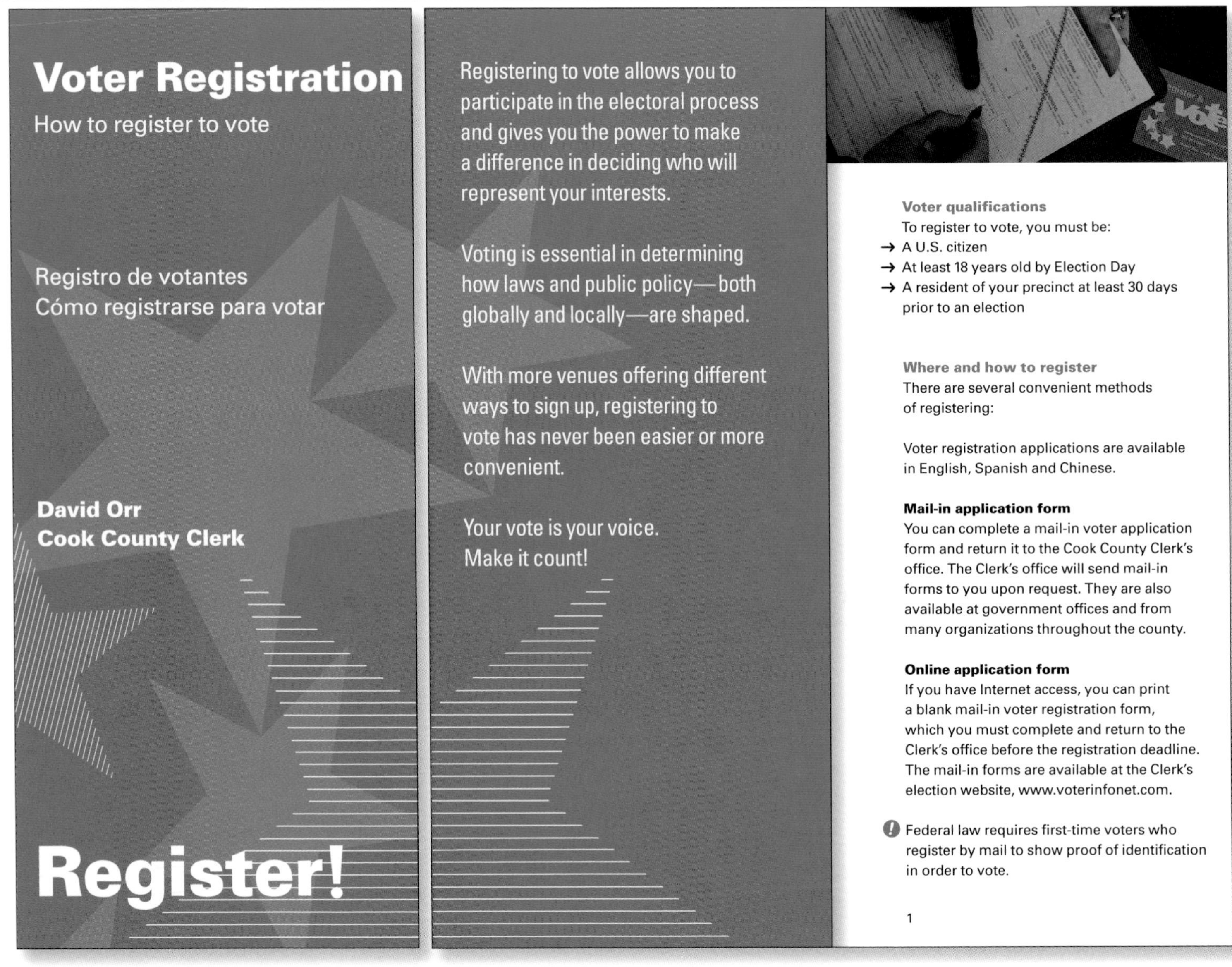

Voter Registration
How to register to vote
Registro de votantes
Cómo registrarse para votar
David Orr
Cook County Clerk
Register!
Registering to vote allows you to participate in the electoral process and gives you the power to make a difference in deciding who will represent your interests.
Voting is essential in determining how laws and public policy—both globally and locally—are shaped.
With more venues offering different ways to sign up, registering to vote has never been easier or more convenient.
Your vote is your voice.
Make it count!
Voter qualifications
To register to vote, you must be:
→ A U.S. citizen
→ At least 18 years old by Election Day
→ A resident of your precinct at least 30 days prior to an election
Where and how to register
There are several convenient methods of registering:
Voter registration applications are available in English, Spanish and Chinese.
Mail-in application form
You can complete a mail-in voter application form and return it to the Cook County Clerk's office. The Clerk's office will send mail-in forms to you upon request. They are also available at government offices and from many organizations throughout the county.
Online application form
If you have Internet access, you can print a blank mail-in voter registration form, which you must complete and return to the Clerk's office before the registration deadline. The mail-in forms are available at the Clerk's election website, www.voterinfonet.com.
Federal law requires first-time voters who register by mail to show proof of identification in order to vote.
1

To encourage registration and provide information about the registration process, Design for Democracy and the Office of the Cook County Clerk, David Orr, developed a voter registration brochure available in five languages. *"Register!"* is one of a series of eight brochures that provide voter education information.

Visit any of the Cook County Clerk's six office locations:

→ Downtown Chicago
69 W. Washington St., 5th floor
312 603 0906

→ North suburbs/Skokie
5600 W. Old Orchard Road, Room 149
847 470 7233

→ Northwest suburbs/Rolling Meadows
2121 Euclid Ave., Room 238
847 818 2850

→ West suburbs/Maywood
1311 Maybrook Square, Room 109
708 865 6010

→ South suburbs/Markham
16501 S. Kedzie Ave., Room 238
708 210 4150

→ Southwest suburbs/Bridgeview
10220 S. 76th Ave., Room 238
708 974 6150

Village, city and township hall offices
Visit your local village, city or township clerk's office.

Drivers license facilities and State agencies
You can register to vote when you obtain or renew your drivers license or state identification at any of the Illinois Secretary of state's drivers license facilities.

Registration is also available at other state government offices, including public assistance offices and military recruitment offices.

2

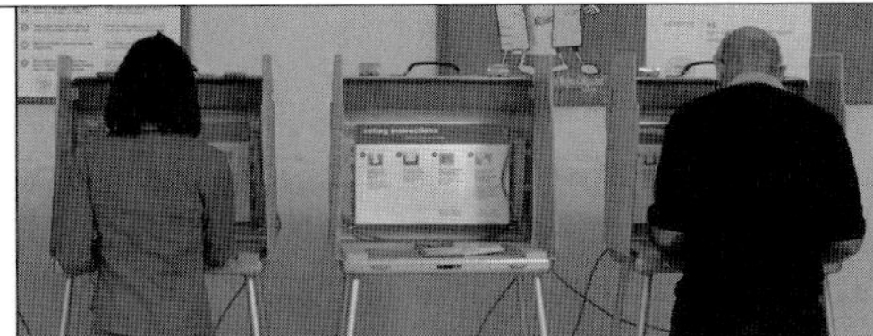

Deputy registrars
Volunteer deputy registrars trained by the Clerk's office and sponsored by specific groups and organizations may register you to vote. You must show the registrar two forms of identification. Both forms must include your name, and one must include your current address.

For more information about the Clerk's deputy registrar program:
call 312 603 0992
e-mail depreg@cookcountygov.com

Registration deadlines
You must register no later than 28 days before each election.

Party declaration
Illinois does not require you to register by political party or declare a political party membership or preference. However, you may select a specific political party's ballot when voting in a primary election.

Voter identification card
After approving and processing your application, the Clerk's office will mail you an identification card. The card lists your precinct information and voting districts.

3

When to re-register
Your registration is permanent unless you move or change your name.

Change of address
If you have moved to a different address within suburban Cook county, you must notify the clerk's office to transfer your registration.

If you have moved into suburban Cook County from another county or from the city of Chicago, you must re-register with the Clerk's office.

Change of name
If you legally change your name, you must re-register with the Clerk's office.

David Orr, Cook County Clerk
69 W. Washington Street, 5th floor
Chicago IL 60602

www.voterinfonet.com

4

Since November of 2000, AIGA, the professional association for design, has sponsored a nonpartisan "Get out the vote" initiative. Every four years AIGA members from around the country create posters to encourage voter registration and participation. At right are three examples of these posters.

Central to voter outreach efforts are communities of potentially disenfranchised voters who may feel excluded from the voting process because of language or cultural barriers. "Get out the vote" offerings include posters designed specifically for such communities. For example, the poster at the far right on the facing page was developed for Latino voters in Chicago. The simplicity and white space allow the poster to stand out in a visually energetic and colorful urban neighborhood. Stating that "A small action can make a big difference," this poster compares the impact of the eñe, an important letter in Spanish, with the potential impact of casting a vote.

"Get out the vote" **posters are available for free download on the AIGA website (www.aiga.org/getoutthevote).**

Speak louder.
Good design makes choices clear.
AIGA

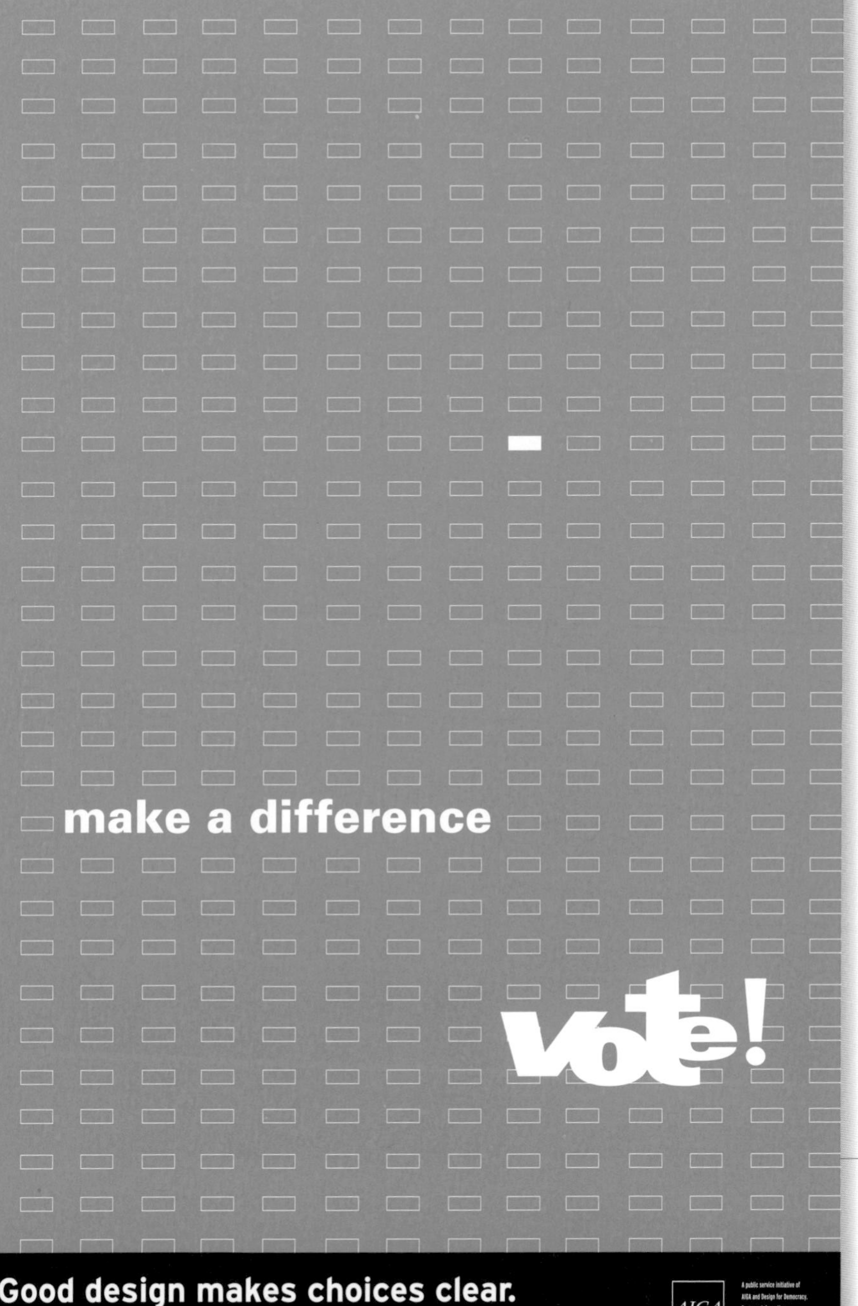
make a difference
vote!
Good design makes choices clear.
This initiative was made possible by the generous support of more than 16,000 AIGA members in 47 chapters and 150 student groups nationwide; Yupo Corporation, Chesapeake, Va., www.yupo.com; and designers everywhere who believe in the power of design for the public good.
AIGA
A public service initiative of AIGA and Design for Democracy. For more information visit www.aiga.org and www.electiondesign.org.

[eñe]

Una pequeña acción hace una gran diferencia.

¡vota!

Good design makes choices clear.

This initiative was made possible by the generous support of more than 16,000 AIGA members in 47 chapters and 150 student groups nationwide; Yupo Corporation, Chesapeake, Va., www.yupo.com; and designers everywhere who believe in the power of design for the public good.

AIGA

A public service initiative of AIGA and Design for Democracy. For more information visit www.aiga.org and www.electiondesign.org.

voter registration form

The voter registration form is used not only for first-time registrants but also for voter change-of-address information. And U.S. citizens move a lot. In March 2000 the Census Bureau estimated that more than 15 percent of eligible voters had moved in the previous year. Accurate address information is critical to successful voter registration and, in turn, to high turnout on election day.

The 2002 Help America Vote Act (HAVA) mandated improvements in the accuracy of voter registration information systems. Voter registration data is now required to be centralized in each state, which helps to ensure that more accurate voter information reaches the polling place. Additional accuracy can be achieved by improving the design of voter registration application forms. The following pages illustrate the application of basic information design principles to an actual registration form used in the state of Oregon, and proposed improvements to a national voter registration application.

Guidelines for voter registration application form design:

→ Use capital and lowercase letters rather than all capital letters
→ Prioritize information for registrants over information for administrators
→ Keep type font, size, weight, and width variations to a minimum
→ Do not center-align text or headings
→ Use contrast and graphics to support hierarchy and aid legibility
→ Do not use decorative art or illustration

Prior to its redesign, the Oregon voter registration form, shown below, had a complex and confusing layout on a letter-size card that was to be folded in half for mailing. Heavy black bars—by far the most dominant graphic device on the page—were used for data entry codes rather than for registrant instructions. The bars also created oddly shaped divisions of information that were confusing to registrants.

The form was further complicated by perforated areas that suggested folds for mailing but were actually for reducing the form to small-card size for placement in a specific file drawer. Usability for the registrant was sacrificed for storage considerations.

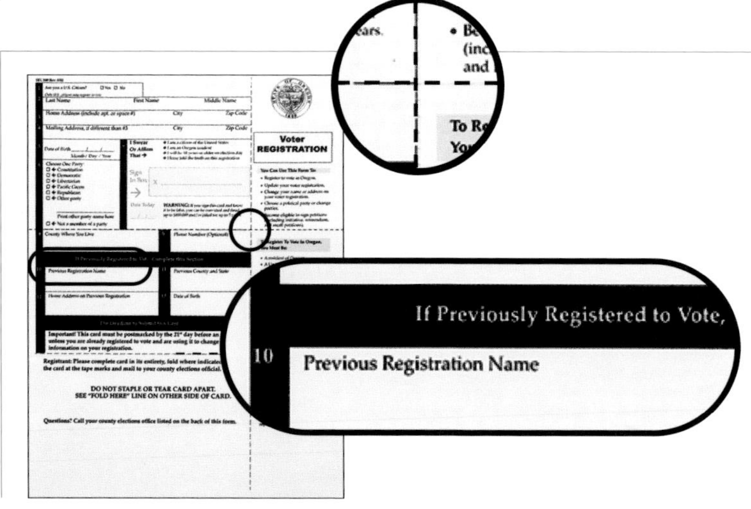

Voter REGISTRATION

If Previously Registered to Vote,

10 Previous Registration Name

DO NOT STAPLE OR TEAR CARD APART.
SEE "FOLD HERE" LINE ON OTHER SIDE OF CARD.

Above is the old version of the Oregon voter registration form, with a layout driven by administrative needs and constraints.

Instructions

you may use this form to:

- Register to vote in Oregon.
- Change your name, mailing address, residence address or political party affiliation on your voter registration.
- Become eligible to sign petitions, including initiative, referendum and recall petitions.

how to register to vote

- Use blue or black ink to fill out the form.
- Sign the form.
- Mail the completed form to your county by following the instructions below.

selecting a political party

Some political parties require you to be registered in their party to vote for their candidates in a primary election.

how to mail this registration card

- Fold the card in half at the center crease. ***Do not tear off the envelope.***
- Seal the envelope. ***Do not staple.***
- Stamp and mail the card to your county.

Addresses are on the backside of this form and envelope.

Your county elections office will mail you a card to let you know that your registration was received.

If the form is incomplete, it may be rejected.

Secretary of State
Bill Bradbury

Elections Division
141 State Capitol
Salem OR 97310-0722

www.sos.state.or.us

phone 503 986 1518
fax 503 373 7414
TTY 503 986 1521

place only identification materials in this envelope

Oregon Voter Registration SEL 500 rev. 1/04

qualifications ***If you check no in response to either of these questions, do not complete this form.***

Are you a citizen of the United States of America? ○ yes ○ no

Will you be at least 18 years of age on or before election day? ○ yes ○ no

personal information ***please print***

name (required) last | first | middle

home address (required, include apt. or space number) | city | zip code

date of birth (required, month/day/year) | phone number (optional) | county of residence

mailing address (required if different from home address)

political party ***choose one of the following:***

○ Constitution ○ Democratic ○ Libertarian ○ Pacific Green

○ Republican ○ Not a member of a party ○ Other________

signature ***I swear or affirm that I am qualified to be an elector, and I have told the truth on this registration.***

sign here________ date today________

warning: If you sign this card and know it to be false, you can be fined up to $100,000 and/or jailed for up to 5 years.

identification ***with mailed registration only***

Identification is requested **only** if you are a new registrant in this county and are mailing this form via the United States Postal Service. Identification is not required for updates within the same county or new registrations delivered in person or by means other than mail.

Sufficient identification is a **copy** of one of the following showing your current name and address:

- → valid photo identification (such as a driver's license)
- → a paycheck stub
- → a utility bill
- → a bank statement
- → a government document

← ***If you submit a copy of a valid form of identification, please enclose it in the attached envelope.***

If previously registered and changing personal information, fill out this section ***please print***

previous registration name | previous county and state

home address on previous registration | date of birth (month/day/year)

The redesigned, voter-friendly Oregon voter registration form, shown at left, provides clear instructions to users. The document itself, with a single center fold, opens up to reveal a simplified form, instructions to voters, and a built-in envelope (lined in red) for enclosing a copy of valid identification.

Red is used throughout the form to indicate instructions and warnings. In addition, the step-by-step data entry codes have been eliminated. This gives priority to information needed by registrants, who may be unfamiliar with the form, rather than to information needed for administrative purposes. The form is simple enough that data entry clerks can quickly become familiar with the categories of information without needing numbered steps.

This voter registration form has been used by the state of Oregon since 2002. Shown at actual size.

Below is the original version of a national voter registration application. While straightforward and relatively easy to use, this design can be further improved through careful analysis of space requirements and application of basic information design principles.

A reconceived form, at right, provides additional and more flexible space for name and address. Red type indicates instruction, and headings in black bars clearly indicate the steps of the process.

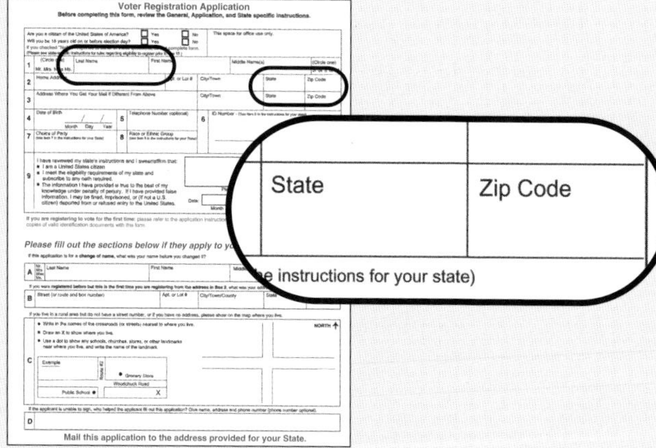

Right, redesign of a national voter registration form. Shown at reduced size.

Voter Registration Application

Before completing this form, review the General, Application and State specific instruction. If you are registering to vote for the first time, please refer to the Application instructions for information on submitting copies of valid identification documents with this form.

1 qualifications *If you mark "no" in response to either of these questions, do not complete this form.*

Are you a citizen of the United States of America? ☐ yes ☐ no

Will you be 18 years of age on or before election day? ☐ yes ☐ no

Please see state-specific instructions regarding eligibility to register prior to age 18.

2 personal information *If you mark no in response to either of these questions, do not complete this form.*

Mr/Mrs/Miss/Ms/Dr last name	first name	middle name(s)	Jr/Sr/I/II/III
home address (include apt. or space number)	city/town	state	zip code
address where you get mail (if different from above)	city/town	state	zip code
date of birth (month/day/year)	phone number (optional)	email address (optional)	

3 political party *See instructions for your state.*

4 race/ethnic group *See instructions for your state.*

5 ID number *See instructions for your state.*

6 signature

I have reviewed my state's instructions and I swear/affirm that:

→ I am a U.S. citizen

→ I meet the eligibility requirements of my state and subscribe to any oath required

The information I have provided is true to the best of my knowledge under penalty of perjury. If I have provided false information, I may be fined, imprisoned, or (if not a U.S. citizen) deported from or refused entry to the United States.

signature — date today (month/day/year)

Please fill out the sections below if they apply to you.

7 updating personal information *If you are using this application to update your voter registration, please provide your previous information.*

Mr/Mrs/Miss/Ms/Dr last name	first name	middle name(s)	Jr/Sr/I/II/III
home address on previous registration	city/town	state	zip code

8 rural address *If you live in a rural area and have no street number, or you have no address, please illustrate where you live on the map below.*

→ Write the names of the crossroads (or streets) nearest to where you live.

→ Draw an **X** to show where you live.

→ Use a dot to show any schools, churches, stores or other landmarks near where you live and write the name of the landmark.

example

Route 2 • Grocery Store **Woodchuck Road** Public School• **X**

North

9 registration assistance *If the applicant is unable to sign, list the name and address of the person who provided assistance.*

name	phone number (optional)		
address	city/town	state	zip code

Mail this application to the address provided for your state.

for office use only

States have different requirements for voting eligibility and for registration deadlines. In addition to the registration forms that are provided by state and local agencies, the EAC provides a national form that includes instructions specific to each state. Design for Democracy analyzed the EAC application and found it to be more effective than most of the registration forms that we examined. Yet by conducting usability tests and by applying basic information design principles, improvements can be made.

A simple usability test for form design can be conducted by completing the form. Often the spaces provided for filling in name and address information are sufficient only for the shortest entries, whereas the space provided for entering the state information, a two-letter acronym, is often larger than necessary. Space is at a premium on a voter registration form. It is important to test and analyze space requirements and to allocate the amount of space needed for each category of information.

Analysis of the existing EAC application provided these suggestions for improvement: **1**] increase length of spaces for last name, first name, middle name, street address, and city/town; **2**] eliminate the use of center-aligned type; **3**] lessen the visual impact of lines and boxes that divide areas of information; **4**] minimize the number of different type sizes and weights; and **5**] use fewer capital letters, reserving initial caps only for the main title and proper nouns. The redesigned form, at left, incorporates these suggestions and illustrates that even an effective application can benefit greatly from design improvements.

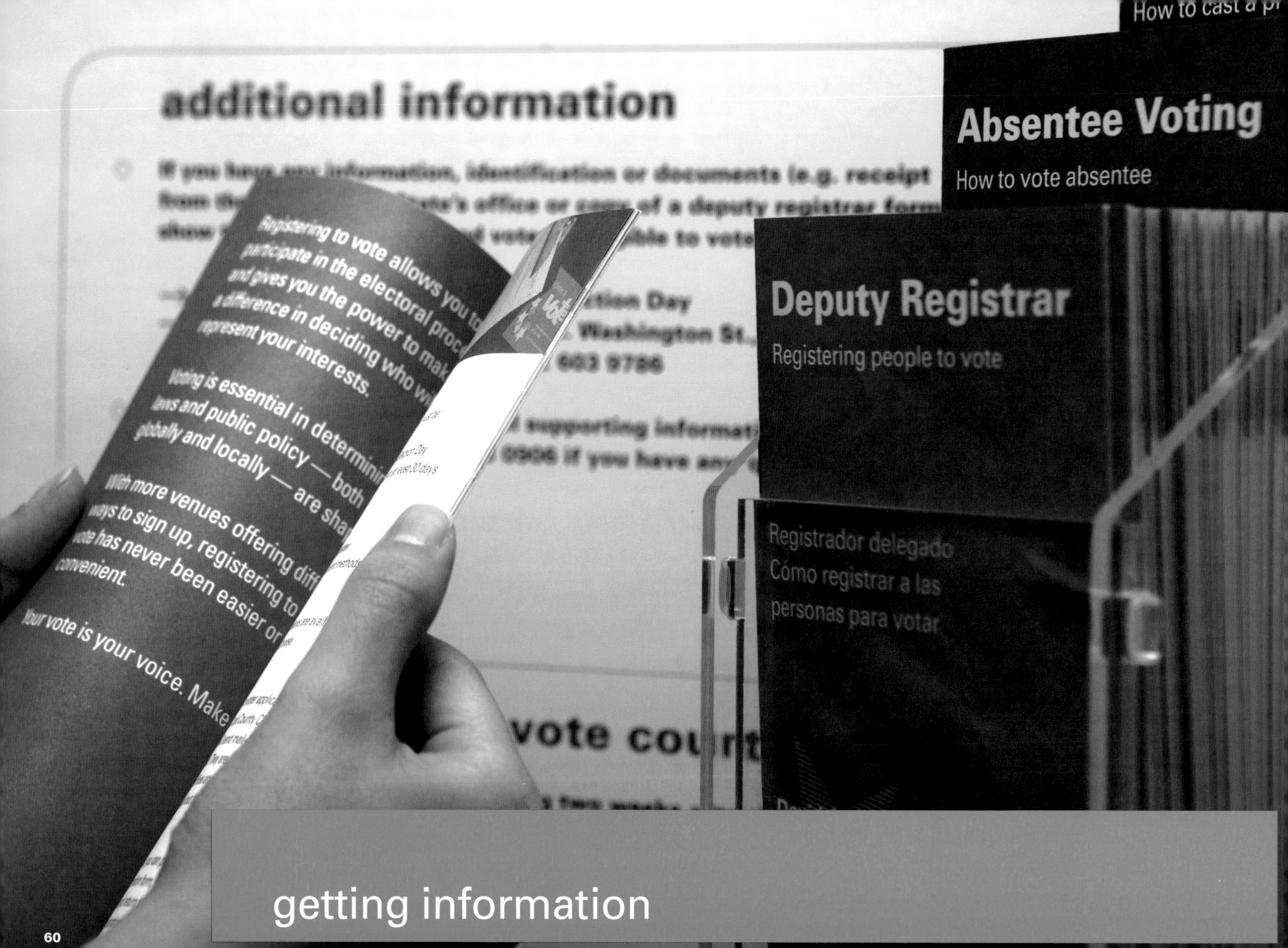

getting information

To prepare for entering the polling place on election day, voters need information and guidance. Voting information can come from a variety of public and private sources. Unfortunately, the sources may be inconsistent or even suspect, and the amount of information available can range from insufficient to overwhelming. State and local governments must give the highest priority to providing clear, neutral, and accessible information relevant to all stages of the voting process.

In the weeks prior to an election, voters are seeking information about election procedures, locations, candidates, and issues. Most states and counties provide print and online information on when, where, and how to vote, and on how to get help if a voter needs it. In addition, some states produce pamphlets that provide voters with detailed information on candidates and ballot measures.

Design can improve the information gathering process by:

→ Providing information services that encourage voter registration and participation
→ Advertising the election agency as the first place to turn for reliable election information
→ Presenting information in a clear, accessible, and inviting form
→ Improving the design and usability of informational brochures, websites, and voters' pamphlets
→ Providing tools to help voters to determine the background and credibility of outside sources

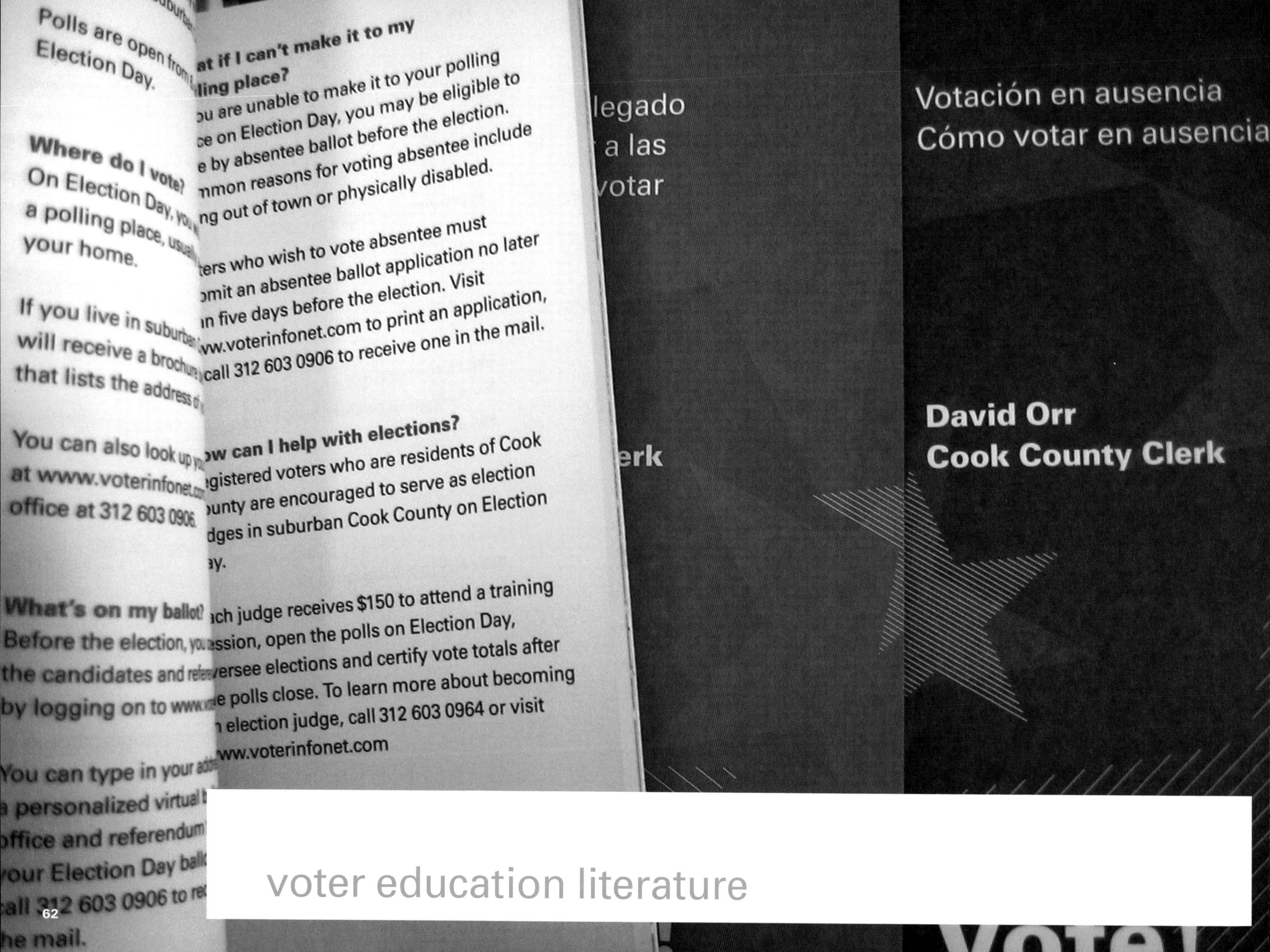

voter education literature

Small educational brochures, each devoted to a topic relevant to the voting process, provide voters with easy access to election information. Topics can be grouped into four categories: *register!*, *vote!*, *learn!*, and *serve!* Adding an exclamation point to the category titles reinforces the importance of participatory activity. The use of a single color on each cover helps to distinguish different topics, and patterns of stars and stripes provide additional visual interest.

Although it is important to include contact information for the election agency, and perhaps to indicate endorsement by placing the state or county seals on the back cover, official graphics on brochure covers are more likely to remind citizens of taxes and parking tickets than of the power of their vote and the pride of their participation. Use government graphics only as an official "seal of approval" and not as primary artwork on election communications.

To encourage voter registration and to provide information about the voting process, Design for Democracy and the Office of the Cook County Clerk developed a series of single-topic informational brochures and voter information cards. Economically printed in two colors, the series is designed to be enthusiastic and inviting. Shown at reduced size. Note: the Cook County seal was left off of voter education literature.

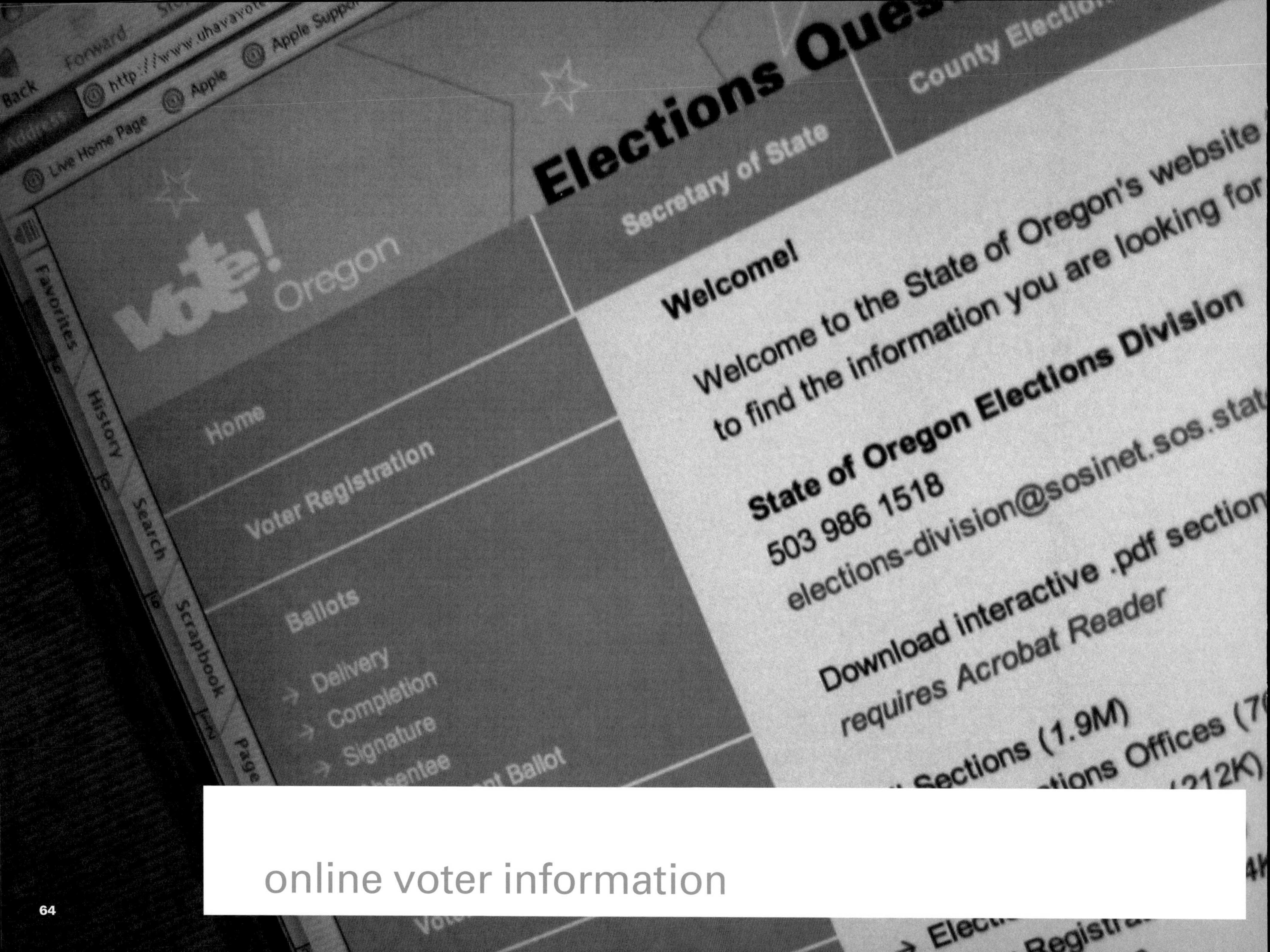

online voter information

Voter education information should be made available through electronic media as well as in print. Access to online election information is convenient for many voters and can be less costly to provide than print materials. Electronic resources may include voter registration forms and registration verification, schedules of elections, absentee ballot applications, demonstration ballots, directories of candidates and elected officials, polling place locations, information about serving as a pollworker, and archived election results.

Below, two different interpretations of the Design for Democracy system are used in voter information websites for Cook County (Illinois) and the state of Oregon.

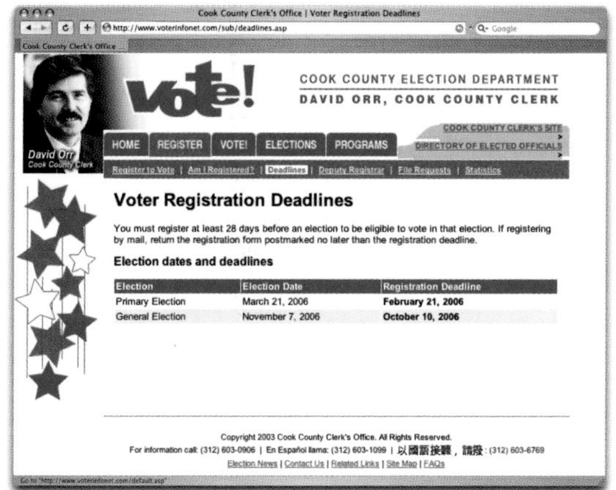

www.voterinfonet.com.

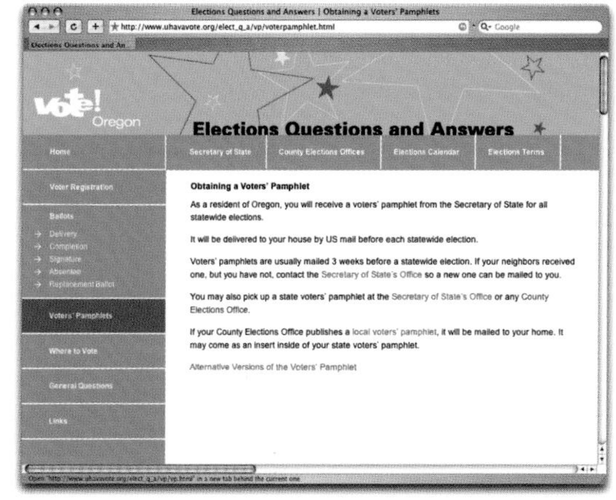

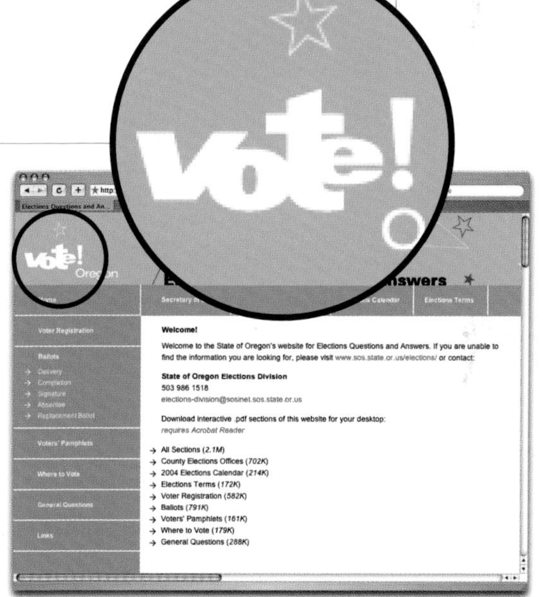

www.uhavavote.org/elect_q_a/main.html.

voters' pamphlets

Some states prepare pamphlets to distribute information to voters. Besides providing registration, schedule, and location information, these voters' pamphlets contain detailed information on candidates and ballot measures. The amount of information in a single voters' pamphlet can be so voluminous that the end product is more like a book than a pamphlet.

Voters in Oregon receive their pamphlets by mail in two volumes. One volume covers state ballot measures; the other covers candidates, political parties, and local measures. The two volumes often arrive on different days prior to the election. In comparing the existing and redesigned covers shown below, note how substantial improvement in clarity is achieved by simply adding and emphasizing volume numbers.

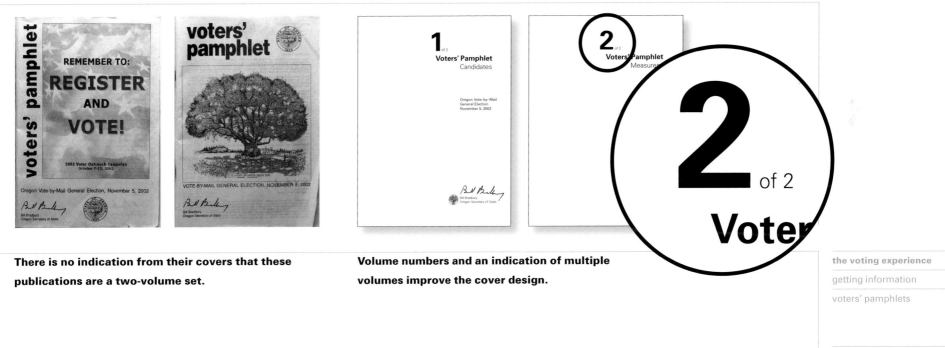

There is no indication from their covers that these publications are a two-volume set.

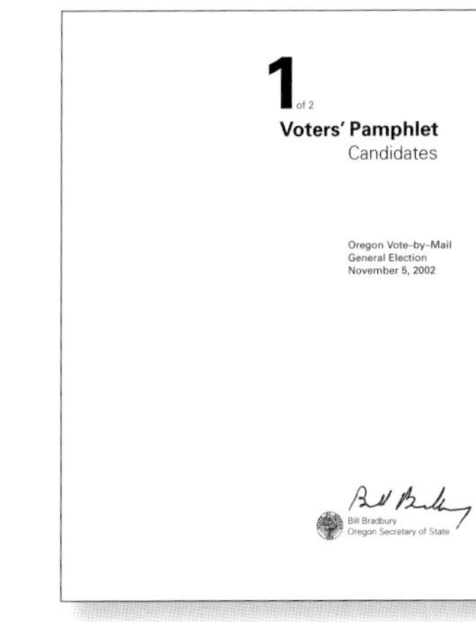

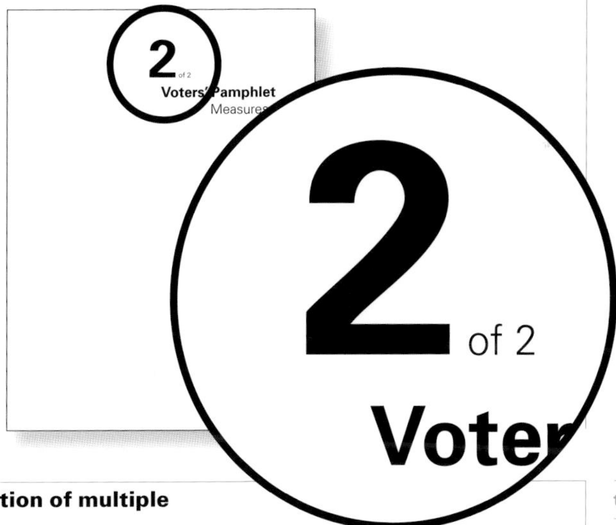

Volume numbers and an indication of multiple volumes improve the cover design.

voters' pamphlet

REMEMBER

REGIST

AND

VOT

2002 Voter Outreach C
October 7-15, 20

voters' pamphlet

Owen's Cherry Tree

VOTE-BY-MAIL GENERAL ELECTION, NOVEMBER 5, 2002

Another point of confusion in the existing cover design is the completely different artwork and layout used for each volume. As shown below in redesigned form, each volume in a multiple-volume set should use the same image on its cover. This provides an obvious visual connection, especially helpful when different volumes arrive on different days.

Voters' pamphlet cover recommendations:

→ Number each volume and indicate the total number of volumes
→ State the category or categories of information contained within
→ Use the same artwork for each volume in a set
→ Use the same layout grid consistently over time, changing only the artwork

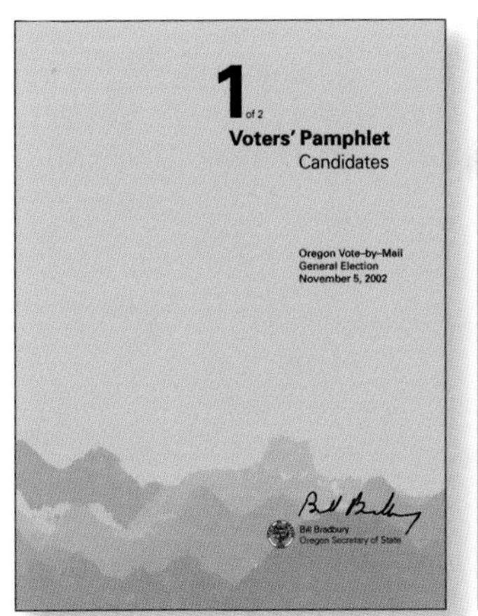

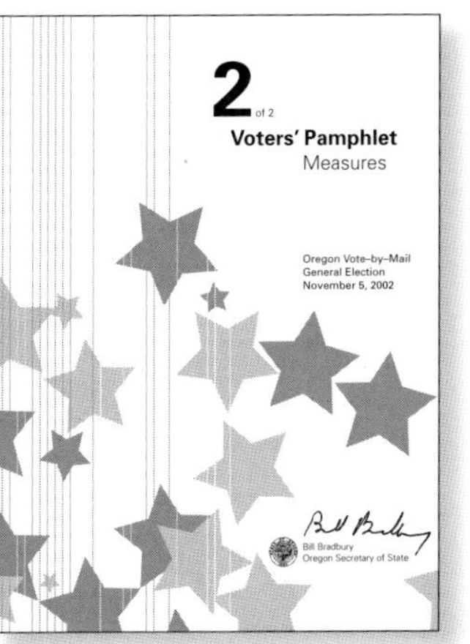

To make an immediate visual connection, identical artwork should be used on pamphlet volumes that are mailed to voters at different times prior to each election. Cover artwork can be printed in two colors or in black only. Artwork can change for each election.

As seen in the illustrations below and on the facing page, the opportunities for design improvements in the pamphlet are not limited to its covers. For instance, the table of contents, which is the primary navigation tool for the pamphlet, is squeezed onto the bottom of the fourth page rather than placed in a separate, more prominent location that would allow for easier access. It is important to use space efficiently to prevent paper waste and to keep costs low, but not at the risk of causing users to become confused or frustrated.

Voters' pamphlets can also be improved to eliminate problems discussed in the previous section, including center alignment, overuse of all capital letters, numerous type variations, and an unclear information hierarchy. Other improvements can result from eliminating unnecessary illustrations and increasing the clarity and simplicity of graphics such as district maps.

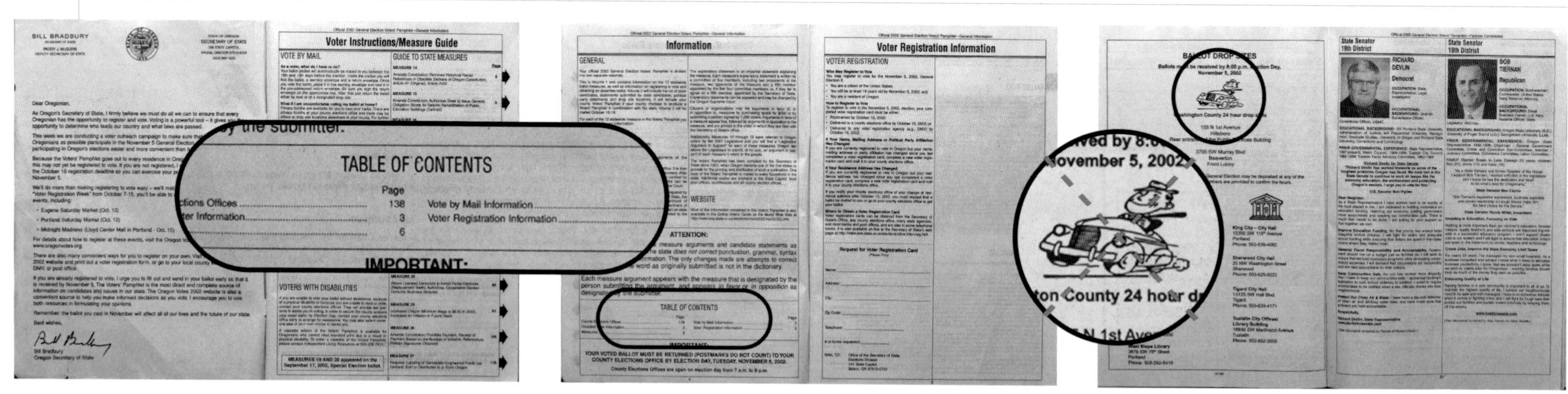

Above, inside the November 2000 Oregon voters' pamphlet, there are many opportunities for design improvement, including a more prominent table of contents.

Illustrations should be used sparingly and only in the form of instructional diagrams or photographs that provide needed information.

In addition to providing candidate statements and background information, the Oregon pamphlets include summaries of all ballot measures and arguments for or against each measure. Along with official arguments prepared by the state legislature, arguments of up to 500 words in length are included from any individual or group that pays a set fee. This can lead to an overwhelming amount of information, especially for voters who are looking simply to access and understand a short summary of each measure and a sampling of the supporting and opposing arguments.

To keep costs low, it is important to maximize the amount of information per page in the pamphlet. A redesign must embrace this density of information and find ways to reorganize and resize the measure numbers, summaries, and pro/con argument headings. As shown on the following pages, all can be enlarged, visually strengthened, and positioned for greater prominence and clarity.

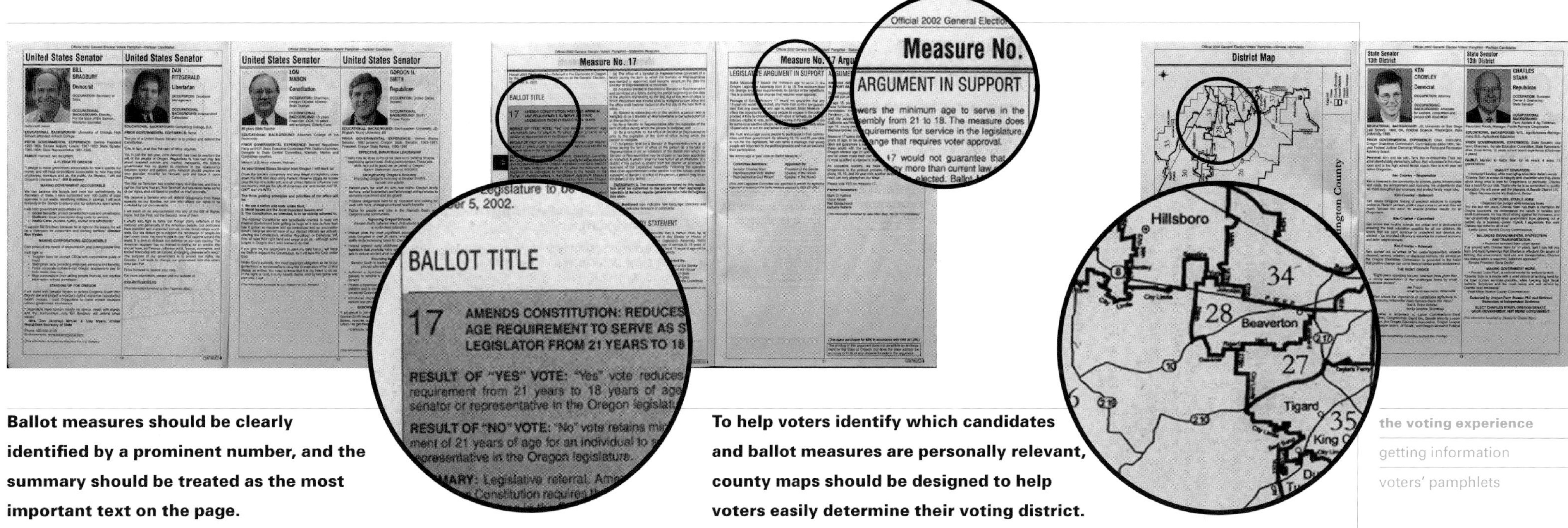

Ballot measures should be clearly identified by a prominent number, and the summary should be treated as the most important text on the page.

To help voters identify which candidates and ballot measures are personally relevant, county maps should be designed to help voters easily determine their voting district.

Most voters are interested in reading the summary of a given ballot measure. By placing the measure number and the summary text in black type on a white background, this key information is the highest contrast and most legible on the page.

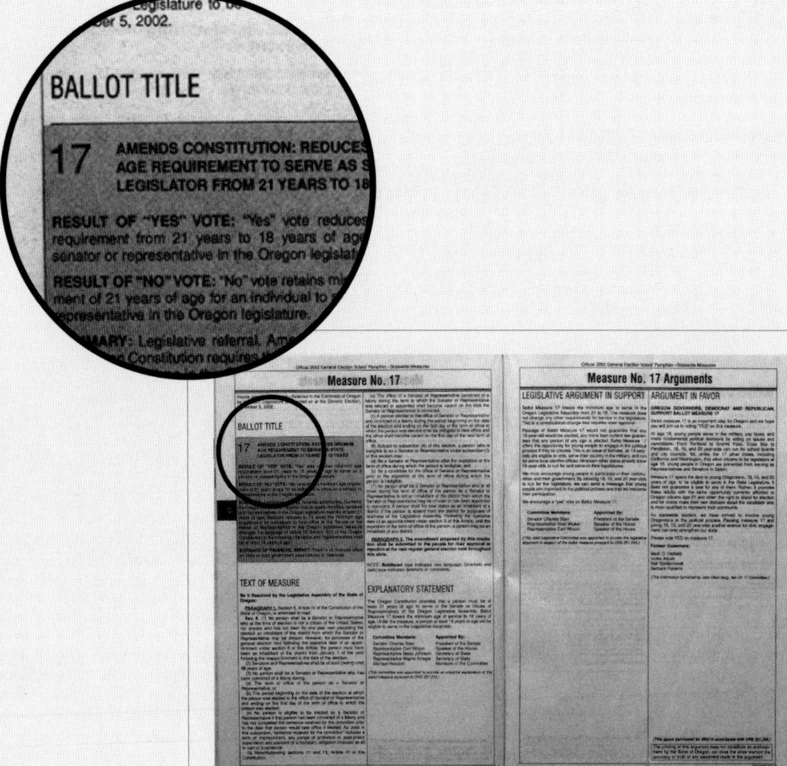

In the existing design, above, the number and summary of each ballot measure are insufficiently emphasized. The proposed redesign, right, emphasizes both by increasing the size of the measure number and by using high contrast. Shown at reduced size.

Measures | Statewide

8 **House Joint Resolution 16—Referred to the Electorate of Oregon by the 2001 Legislature to be voted on at the General Election, November 5, 2002.**

17

Ballot Title
Amends constitution: reduces minimum age requirement to serve as state legislator from 21 years to 18 years.

Result of "yes" vote:
"Yes" vote reduces minimum age requirement from 21 years to 18 years of age to serve as a senator or representative in the Oregon legislature.

Result of "No" vote:
"No" retains minimum age requirement of 21 years of age for an individual to serve as a senator or representative in the Oregon legislature.

Summary:
Legislative referral. Amends constitution. Currently, the Oregon Constitution requires that, to qualify for office, senators and representatives in the Oregon legislature must be at least 21 years of age. Measure reduces to 18 years the minimum age requirement for individuals to hold office in the Senate or the House of Representatives on the Oregon legislature. Measure changes to the language of Article IV, Section 8(2) of the Oregon Constitution to the following: "Senators and Representatives shall be at least 18 years of age."

Estimate of financial impact:
There is no financial effect on state or local government expenditures or revenues.

Text of Measure

Be it resolved by the Legislative Assembly of the State of Oregon:

Paragraph 1

Section 8, Article IV of the Constitution of the State of Oregon, is amended to read:

Sec. 8

1 No person shall be a senator or Representative who at the time of election is not a citizen of the United States; nor anyone who has not been for one year next preceding the election an inhabitant of the district from which the Senator or Representative may be chosen. However, for purposes of the general election next following the operative date of an appointment under section 6 of this Article, the person must have been an inhabitant of the district from January 1 of the year following the reappointment to the date of the election.

2 Senators and Representatives shall be at least 18 years of age.

3 No person shall be a Senator or Representative who has been convicted of a felony during:
- **a** The term of office of the person as a Senator or Representative; or
- **b** The period beginning on the date of the election at which the person was elected to the office of the Senator or Representative and ending on the first day of the term of office to which the person was elected.

4 No person is eligible to be elected as Senator or Representative if that person has been convicted of a felony and has not completed the sentence received for the conviction prior to the date that person would take office if elected. As used in this subscription, "sentence received for the conviction" includes a term imprisonment, any period of probation or post-prison supervision and payment of a monetary obligation imposed as all or part of a sentence.

5 Notwithstanding sections 11 and 15, Article IV of this Constitution:
- **a** The office of a Senator or Representative convicted of a felony during the term to which the Senator or Representative was elected or appointed shall become vacant on the date the Senator or Representative is convicted.
- **b** A person elected to the office of Senator or Representative and convicted of a felony during the period beginning on the date of the election and ending on the first day of the term of office to which the person was elected shall be ineligible to take office and the office shall become vacant on the first day of the next term of office.

6 Subject to subsection (4) of this section, a person who is ineligible to be a Senator or Representative under subsection (3) may:
- **a** Be a Senator or Representative after the expiration of the term of office during which the person is ineligible; and
- **b** Be a candidate for the office of the Senator or Representative prior to the expiration of the term of office during which the person is ineligible.

continued...

Official 2000 General Election Voters' Pamphlet

Design for Democracy's proposed redesign of the Oregon voters' pamphlet utilizes a series of templates that designate areas of a given page to have a light background color (or a light screen of black to make areas of gray), allowing information to be grouped and organized. General information and detailed text are printed in black on the color background fields. The white background areas, which provide the highest contrast and legibility, hold the most important information: page numbers; candidate information; measure numbers, summaries and arguments; and action items.

Clear designation of information hierarchy, highly visible page numbers, and headings in tab shapes at the top of each page all help voters to access and navigate the dense volumes of information.

Shown above at reduced size are five types of page templates for various sections of the redesigned voters' pamphlet.

In the proposed redesign, two additional pages are added to the front matter. Although this increases the page count, it also allows space for a more organized entry to the dense material. The table of contents, shown on the facing page, receives its own page immediately following an introductory letter from the secretary of state.

The most important information on these two pamphlet pages—the secretary's letter, the page number, and the voting deadline—appears with the highest contrast: black type on a white background.

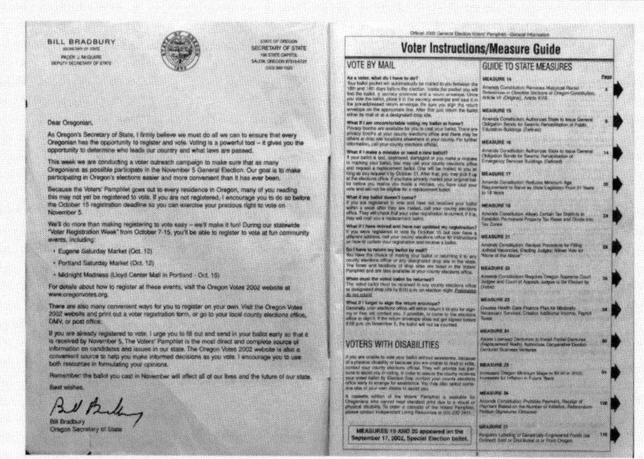

BILL BRADBURY
SECRETARY OF STATE
PADDY J. McGUIRE
DEPUTY SECRETARY OF STATE

STATE OF OREGON
SECRETARY OF STATE
136 STATE CAPITOL
SALEM, OREGON 97310-0722

Dear Oregonian,

As Oregon's Secretary of State, I firmly believe we must do all we can to ensure that every Oregonian has the opportunity to register and vote. Voting is a powerful tool – it gives you the opportunity to determine who leads our country and what laws are passed.

This week we are conducting a voter outreach campaign to make sure that as many Oregonians as possible participate in the November 5 General Election. Our goal is to make participating in Oregon's elections easier and more convenient than it has ever been.

Because the Voters' Pamphlet goes out to every residence in Oregon, many of you reading this may not yet be registered to vote. If you are not registered, I encourage you to do so before the October 15 registration deadline so you can exercise your precious right to vote on November 5.

We'll do more than making registering to vote easy – we'll make it fun! During our statewide "Voter Registration Week" from October 7-15, you'll be able to register to vote at fun community events, including:

- Eugene Saturday Market (Oct. 12)
- Portland Saturday Market (Oct. 12)
- Midnight Madness (Lloyd Center Mall in Portland - Oct. 15)

For details about how to register at these events, visit the Oregon Votes 2002 website at www.oregonvotes.org.

There are also many convenient ways for you to register on your own. Visit the Oregon Votes 2002 website and print out a voter registration form, or go to your local county elections office, DMV, or post office.

If you are already registered to vote, I urge you to fill out and send in your ballot early so that it is received by November 5. The Voters' Pamphlet is the most direct and complete source of information on candidates and issues in our state. The Oregon Votes 2002 website is also a convenient source to help you make informed decisions as you vote. I encourage you to use both resources in formulating your opinions.

Remember: the ballot you cast in November will affect all of our lives and the future of our state.

Best wishes,

Bill Bradbury
Oregon Secretary of State

Voter Instructions/Measure Guide

VOTE BY MAIL

GUIDE TO STATE MEASURES

VOTERS WITH DISABILITIES

MEASURES 19 AND 20 appeared on the September 17, 2002, Special Election ballot.

Like the existing design, above, the proposed redesign, right, includes an official introductory letter from the secretary of state. Shown at reduced size.

Bill Bradbury
Secretary of State

Paddy J. McGuire
Deputy Secretary of State

State of Oregon
Secretary of State
136 State Capitol
Salem, Oregon 97310–0722
503.986.1523

Dear Fellow Oregonian:

This is volume 2 of a two volume 2002 General Election Voter's Pamphlet. This volume contains information about candidates. Volume 1 with information about state ballot measures was mailed earlier.

If you did not receive a copy of volume 1, please call my office at 503.986.1518 and we will send you one.

This volume contains:
— A list of state candidates,
— Statements filed by individual candidates,
— Congressional and district maps,
— Voter registration information,
— Political party statements, and
— Your county voter's pamphlet with information about local measure and candidates.

The voter's pamphlet has been an important tool for Oregonians since Secretary of State Frank I. Dunbar produced the nation's first voters' pamphlet in 1903. It remains today the single most important tool that Oregonians use in deciding how to vote.

I urge you not to be turned off by the record length of the two volume Voters' Pamphlet. Please take the time to study the candidates and measures on the ballot. The decisions we Oregonians make together in this election will have a profound effect on our state for many years to come.

With this election Oregon will make history. Ours will be the first presidential election ever conducted entirely by mail. I am challenging Oregonians to make history in another way: to have the highest voter turnout of any state in the nation this fall. We are consistently among the highest, but I want Oregon to be the highest.

To promote effort, I have launched a web site (www.oregonvotes.com) as a clearinghouse for election information. If you need different information beyond what is in this publication, www.oregonvotes.com is an excellent place to begin looking.

To participate in this election, there are some important dates to remember: October 20 to 24 is the period when ballots will be mailed to registered voters–if you are registered and you do not received a ballot in the mail, call your county election office for assistance and November 7 at 8:00pm is the deadline for your ballot drop-off site nearest you.

Thank you for taking the time to study the candidates and measures on the ballot and for participating in the election.

Sincerely,

Oregon Secretary of State

Official 2000 General Election Voters' Pamphlet

Information

3

Table of Contents

Your local country's measures and candidate statements have been inserted in the center of this pamphlet. This section can be identified by the page numbers including the first letter of the county.

Your voted ballot must be returned (postmarks do not count) to your county elections office by election day, Tuesday, November 7, 2002.

County Elections Offices are open on election day from 7am to 8pm.

Official 2000 General Election Voters' Pamphlet

As in ballot design, the proposed redesign of the voters' pamphlet avoids the use of only capital letters and centered alignment. Any change in size or weight of type indicates a change in meaning or hierarchy. There is little variation in the size, width, and weight of type.

The entire voter pamphlet is typeset in the Univers font family. Selected for its legibility in ballot design, Univers is a flexible typographic system with 21 variations in weight, width, and slant, all designed to work together.

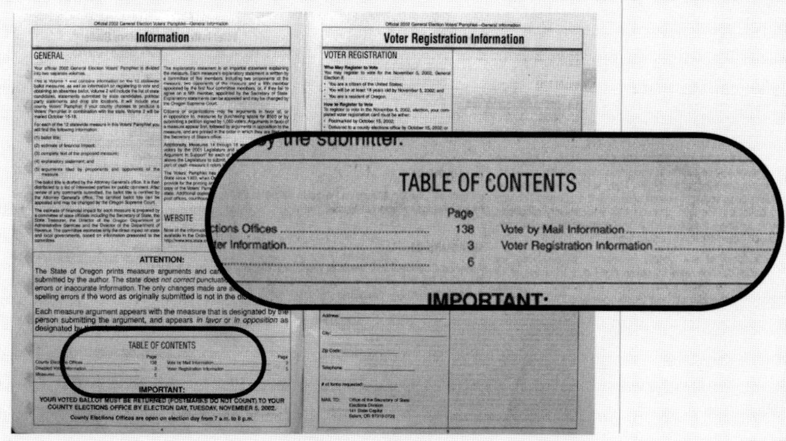

The table of contents is the primary navigational tool for the voters' pamphlet. In the existing design, above, the table is buried in dense information at the bottom of page four. The proposed redesign, left, moves the table of contents to a more prominent and accessible location.

In the proposed redesign, shown at right and on the facing page (green background), small page numbers, previously centered and located at the bottom of the page, have been enlarged and moved up to a more prominent position. Putting the numbers on the outer edges allows users to locate information quickly and efficiently.

Two sizes and two weights of the Univers font family are the only typographic variations required to present the varied information on these two pages.

Main heading:	**Subheading:**
Univers 75: 13	**Univers 75: 8/13**
Text	**Page number:**
Univers 45: 8.5/13	**Univers 45: 14**

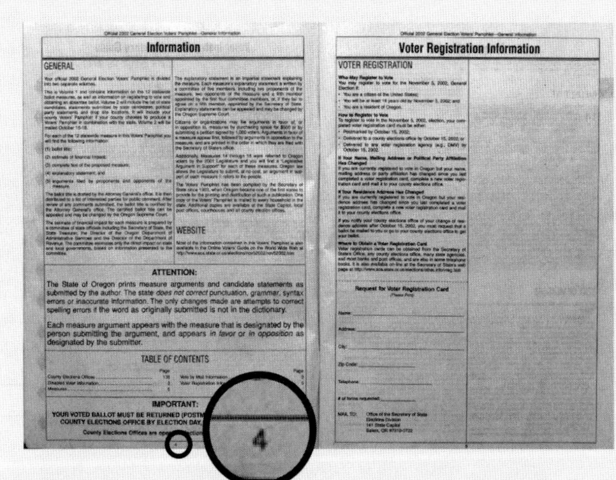

Information

GENERAL

WEBSITE

ATTENTION:

The State of Oregon prints measure arguments and candidate statements as submitted by the author. The state *does not correct* punctuation, grammar, syntax errors or inaccurate information. The only changes made are attempts to correct spelling errors if the word as originally submitted is not in the dictionary.

Each measure argument appears with the measure that is designated by the person submitting the argument, and appears *in favor* or *in opposition* as designated by the submitter.

TABLE OF CONTENTS

IMPORTANT:

YOUR VOTED BALLOT MUST BE RETURNED (POSTM... COUNTY ELECTIONS OFFICE BY ELECTION DAY, ...

4

Voter Registration Information

VOTER REGISTRATION

In the existing voters' pamphlet, above, the page numbers are located dangerously close to the lower page trim. The proposed redesign, right, places numbers near the top of the page in a clearly designated position.

Information

4

General

Your official 2000 General Election Voters' Pamphlet is divided into two separate volumes. This was necessary because there are 26 statewide measures and 607 arguments filed in support of or in opposition to these measures. The amount of information is too large to be bound into one book in a cost-effective manner. This is Volume 2 and contains information on candidates only. You should have already received Volume 1, containing on statewide measures. If you have not received Volume 1, please call the Oregon Elections Division at 503.986.1518. In this Volume, partisan candidates appear before nonpartisan candidates.

All space is purchased; statements and photographs are submitted by the candidates or their designated agents. The information required by law—pertaining to occupation, occupational background, educational background and prior governmental experience—has been certified by each candidate. Volume 2 also includes other voting aids, such congressional and district maps, drop site locations and a complete list of the state candidates. If your county has chosen to produce a Voters' Pamphlet in conjunction with the state, drop site locations will appear in your county Voters' Pamphlet. The Voters' Pamphlet has been produced by the Secretary of State since 1903, when Oregon became one of the first states to provide for the printing and distribution of such a publication. One copy of the Voters' Pamphlet is mailed to every household in the state. Additional copies are available at the Elections Division in the State Capitol, post offices, courthouses, and all election offices.

Random Alphabet

While the candidates' statements appear in alphabetical order by their last name in this Voters' Pamphlet, you will notice that they appear in a different order on our ballot Pursuant to ORS254.155, the Secretary of State is required to complete a random order of the letters of alphabet to determine the order in which the names of candidates appear on the ballot.

The alphabet for the 2000 General Election is:
Z, O, D, E, B, J, M, L, C, K, R, W, F, N, T, Y, H, S, I I, P, U, G, A, Q, V, X

Website

Most of the information contained in this Voters' Pamphlet is also available in the Online Voters' Guide on-line at:
www.sos.state.or.us/elections/nov72000/nov72000.htm

Attention: The State of Oregon prints measure arguments and candidate statements as submitted by the author. The state does not correct punctuation, grammar, syntax errors or inaccurate information. The only charges made are attempts to correct spelling errors if the word as originally submitted is not in the dictionary.

Official 2000 General Election Voters' Pamphlet

Voter Registration Information

5

Eligibility

You may register to vote for the November 5, 2002 General Election if:

- You are a citizen of the United States
- You will be at least 18 years old by November 2, 2002, and
- You are a resident of Oregon

How to Register

The deadline to register to vote for the November 5, 2002 General Election is October 15, 2002. If you register after that date, you will be entitled to vote only in future elections. You may obtain a voter registration card at any county elections office, most banks and post offices, and many state agencies. The card is also available online at: **www.sos.state.or.us/elections/other.info/vreg.htm.**

Change of information

If you are currently registered to vote in oregon but your name, mailing address or party affiliation has changed, complete a new voter registration application and mail to your county elections office.

If you notify your county elections office of your change of residence address after October 15, 2002, you must request that a ballot be mailed to you or go to your county elections office to get your ballot.

Request for Voter Registration Card please print

name __________

address __________

zip code __________

telephone __________

number of forms requested __________

Mail to: Office of Secretary of State
Elections Division 141 State Capitol
Salem, OR 97310–0722

Official 2000 General Election Voters' Pamphlet

Large bold headings appear in the designated tabs at the top of each page.

Page numbers are easily seen and referenced.

Subheadings, embedded within text in the existing design (shown in insets below and on the facing page), need to be oversized and set in aggressive capital letters to be seen. The proposed redesign (green background) provides a separate column to the left of the text for bold subheadings that politely direct users to the related information.

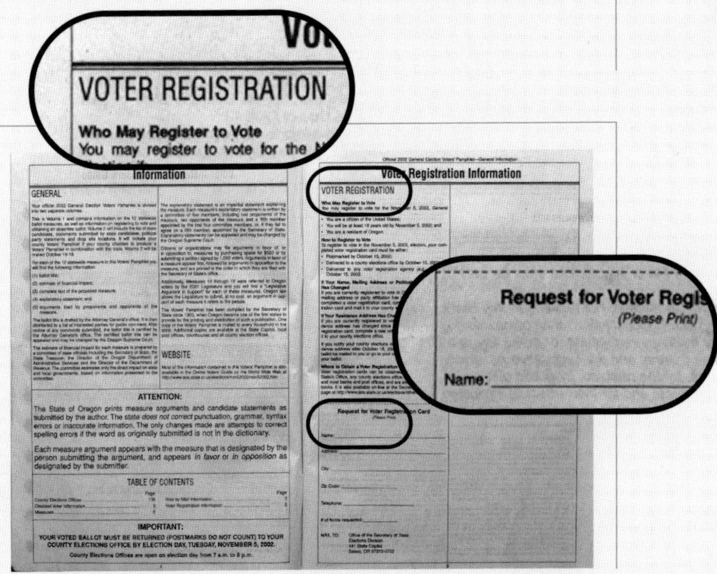

A mail-in request for a voter registration card is included in the voters' pamphlet. The proposed redesign, left, is more visible and usable than the existing version, above.

In the proposed redesign (green accent color), legislative arguments, and arguments sponsored by individuals and groups, are presented on page templates with a white background.

Voters are first interested in the position of the argument: whether it is in favor or in opposition. The redesign places this information in a clearly designated and prominent location. Of secondary interest are the names of the parties who wrote the argument. This information is indicated in bold at the base of the argument.

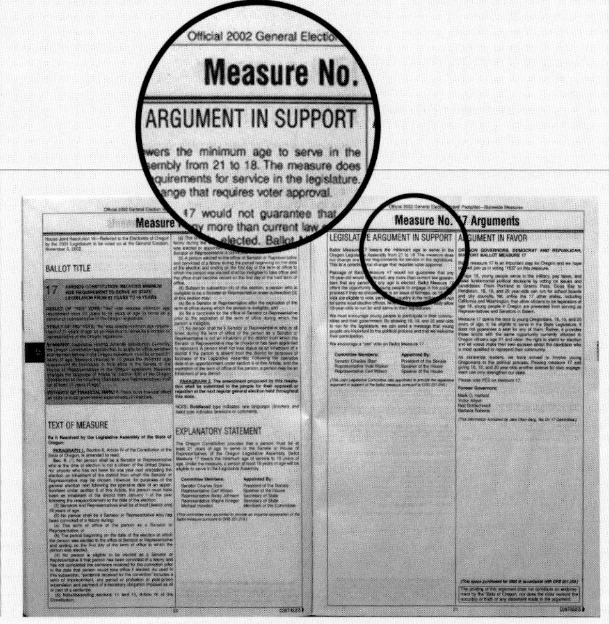

Above, in the existing voters' pamphlet, the heading for the argument position (for or against a ballot measure) is embedded in the text, making it difficult to access. In the proposed redesign, at right, argument positions are placed more prominently.

Arguments | Measure 17

8

Legislative Argument In Support

Ballot measure 17 lowers the minimum age to serve in the Oregon Legislative Assembly from 21 to 18. The measure does not change any other requirements for service in the legislature. This is a constitutional change that requires voter approval.

Passage of Ballot Measure 17 would not guarantee that any 18-year-old would be elected, any more than the current law guarantees that any person of any age is elected. Ballot measure 17 offers the opportunity for young people to engage in the political process if they so choose. This is an issue of fairness, as 18-year-olds are eligible to vote, serve their country in the military, and run for some local elective offices. Nineteen other states already allow 18-year-olds to run for and serve in their legislatures.

We must encourage young people to participate in their communities and their government. By allowing 18, 19, and 20 year-olds to run for legislature, we can send a message that young people are important to the political process and that we welcome their participation.

We encourage a "yes" vote on Ballot Measure 17.

Committee Members	**Appointed by**
Senator Charles Starr	President of the Senate
Representative Vicki Walker	Speaker of the House
Representative Carl Wilson	Speaker of the House

This joint Legislative Committee was appointed to provide the legislative argument in support of the ballot measure pursuant to ORS251.245.

In Favor

Oregon Governors, Democrat and Republican, Support Ballot Measure 17

Ballot Measure 17 is an important step for Oregon and we hope you will join us in voting "YES" on this measure.

At age 18, young people serve in the military, pay taxes, and make fundamental political decision by voting on issues and candidates. From Portland to Grant Pass, Coos Bay to Pendleton, 18, 19, and 20 year-olds can run for school boards and city councils. Yet, unlike that 17 other states, including California and Washington, that allow citizens to be legislators at age 18, young people in Oregon are prevented from serving as Representatives and Senators in Salem.

Measure 17 opens the door to young Oregonians, 18, 19, and 20 years of age, to be eligible to serve in the State Legislature. It does not guarantee a seat for any of them. Rather, it provides these adults with the same opportunity currently afforded to Oregon citizens age 21 and older: the right to stand for elections and let voters make their own decision about the candidate who is most qualified to represent their community.

As statewide leaders, we have strived to involve young Oregonians in the political process. Passing measure 17 and giving 18, 19 and 20 year-olds another avenue for civic engagement that can only strengthen our state.

Please vote YES on measure 17.

Former Governors
Mark O. Hatfield
Victor Atiyeh
Neil Goldschmidt
Barbara Roberts

This information furnished by Jake Oken–Berg, Yes on 17 Committee.

This space purchased for $500 in accordance with ORS251.255
The printing of this argument does not constitute an endorsement by the State of Oregon, nor does the state warrant the accuracy or truth of any statement made in the argument.

Official 2000 General Election Voters' Pamphlet

District Map

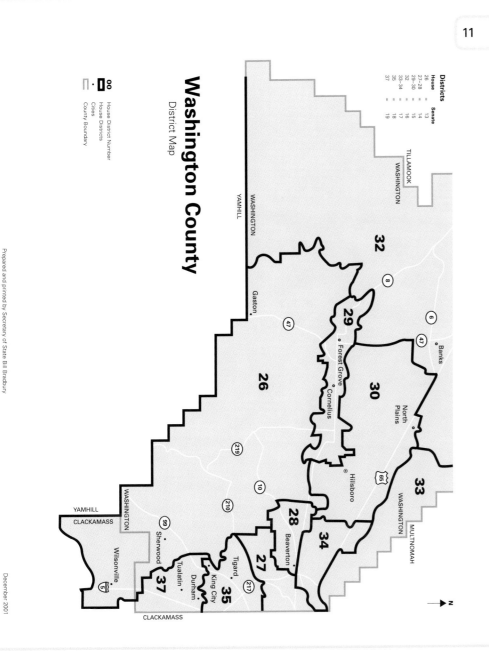

11

Washington County

District Map

Districts

House		Senate
26	=	13
27–28	=	14
29–30	=	15
32	=	16
33–34	=	17
35	=	18
37	=	19

00 House District Number
House Districts
Cities
County Boundary

Prepared and printed by Secretary of State Bill Bradbury

December 2001

Official 2000 General Election Voters' Pamphlet

County maps help voters identify their voting district numbers. However, maps can be difficult to decipher (see the map in existing pamphlet, below). Roads and boundary lines require distinct visual treatment, as do numbers with different meanings.

In the proposed redesign, left, roads are drawn in thin white lines, while district boundaries are drawn in thick black lines. Road numbers are enclosed in shapes that suggest familiar state and interstate road signs. District numbers, in black to match the boundary lines, are the most prominent information on the map.

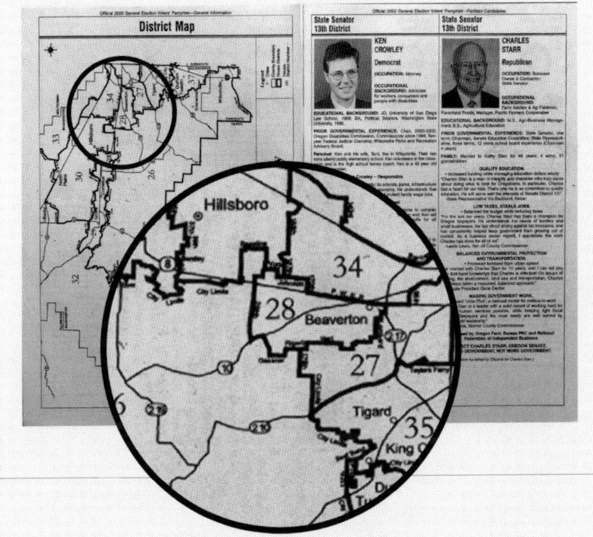

security sleeve
if the ballot counter rejects your ballot:
FOR MEMBERS OF THE BOARD OF EDUCATION (FULL 4-YEAR TERM)
Marco Corsi
Samira J. Abbasi
Insert this side up.
Place holes over the red pins.
Inserte este lado hacia arriba.
Asegurese de que los agujeros encajen sobre los broches rojos.
If you make a mistake, please ask an election judge for a new ballot.

voting

Clear communication is required to get voters to the polls, to help them understand the voting process and the roles of pollworkers, to navigate the space and information encountered in the polling place, and to mark and cast an error-free ballot in privacy.

The methods and mechanisms of voting can be confusing and intimidating. Most citizens have limited experience with the voting process, in which they participate only once every two to four years. The polling place, a temporary environment often at odds with its surroundings, only adds to the confusion. Upon entering a polling place, often a functioning public building assigned to multiple precincts, even experienced voters might feel unsure about where to go or what to do. Encounters with information should be well-planned and immediate—and as simple and self-explanatory as possible.

Design can improve the voting process by:

→ Planning and evaluating the complete polling place environment
→ Helping voters to orient themselves and find their way through both the space and the information
→ Explaining the roles of pollworkers
→ Providing information on voting rules, regulations, rights, and responsibilities
→ Providing instruction for voting and for submitting a ballot

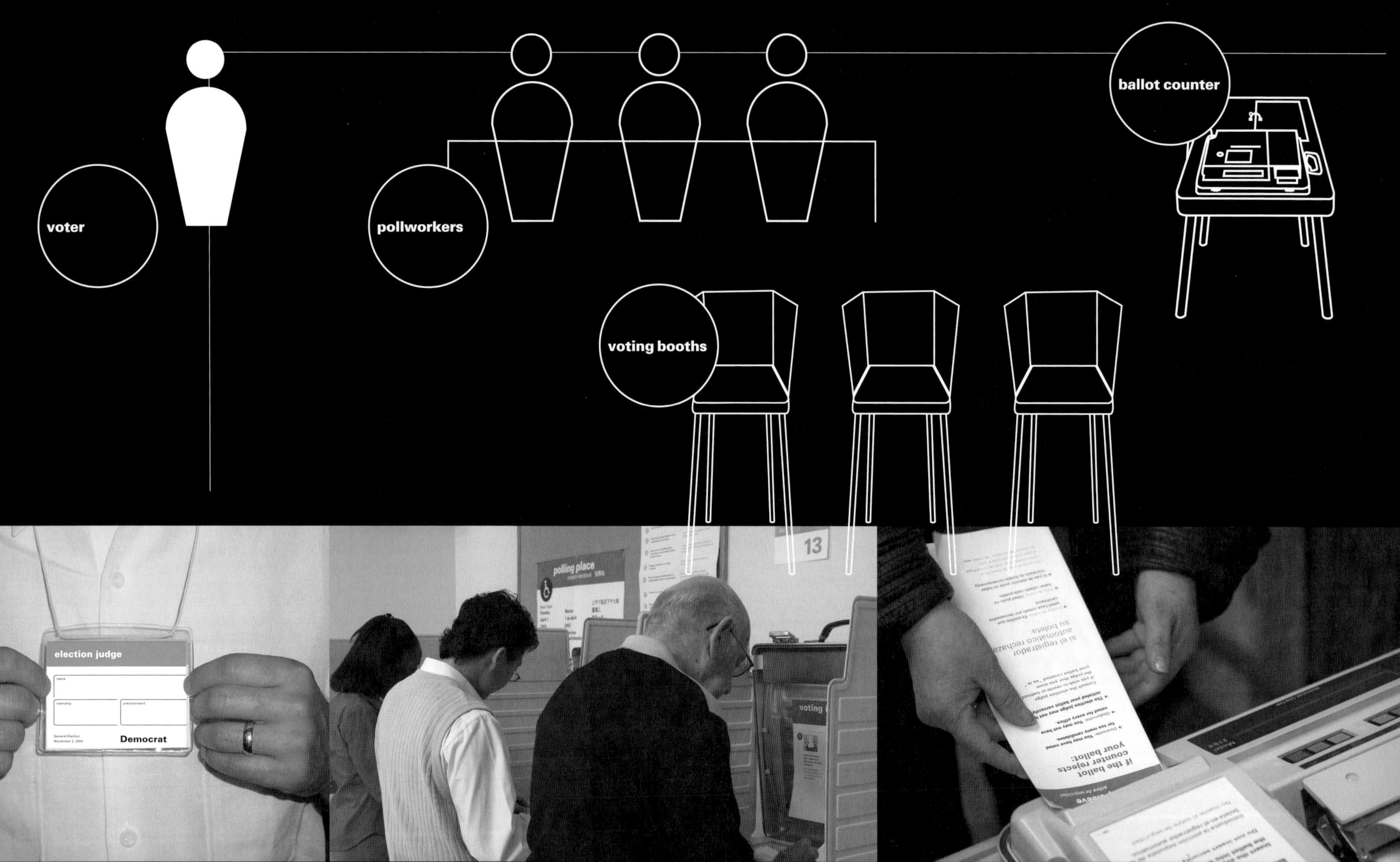
voter
pollworkers
ballot counter
voting booths
election judge
Democrat
polling place
13
if the ballot
counter rejects
your ballot:
si el registrador
automatico rechaza
su boleta:

An election in the United States is a massive production. On a federal election day in the U.S. there are approximately 200,000 polling places staffed by 700,000 employees who are hired just for the day. A typical polling place handles 400 to 500 voters.[5] While there are different types of voting systems and equipment, the stages of the voting process and the issues of orientation and communication are universal. Voters need to find their polling places, navigate the voting environment, and feel confident that they have effectively participated in an important civic process.

The presentation of information in a polling place should anticipate and answer the questions that might go through a voter's mind: *Where do I begin? What are my rights? What is the role of the pollworker? How do the mechanisms function? Who can help me if I have a question?*

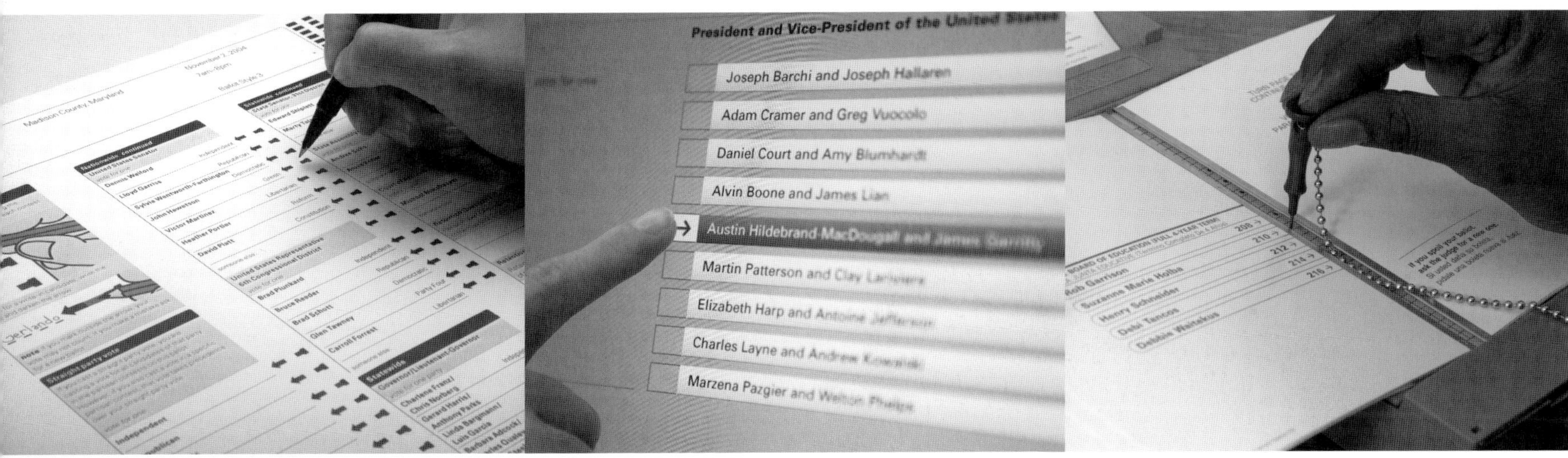

[5] CalTech/MIT Voting Technology Project, "Voting."

polling place setup

Professional space planners from the Environments Group created layout templates for polling places in Chicago and Suburban Cook County, Illinois. The templates provide recommended configurations for traffic flow and equipment setup.

Polling place setup is a logistical challenge involving space planning, equipment assembly and testing, posting of informational and instructional signs, and distribution and arrangement of administrative materials. A polling place is typically a busy public space never intended to be used for voting, such as the lobby of an apartment or office building; a school auditorium, gymnasium, or library; the corridor of an administrative building; or a church basement. Access to the space prior to election day is not always possible. During an average of only 45 minutes allotted prior to the opening of the polls, this space must be rapidly transformed into a fully functional voting service center.[6]

In our work with Cook County and the City of Chicago, Design for Democracy engaged a professional space planning firm to recommend layouts for typical polling place environments. Pollworkers follow the space planning template best suited for the configuration of their location.

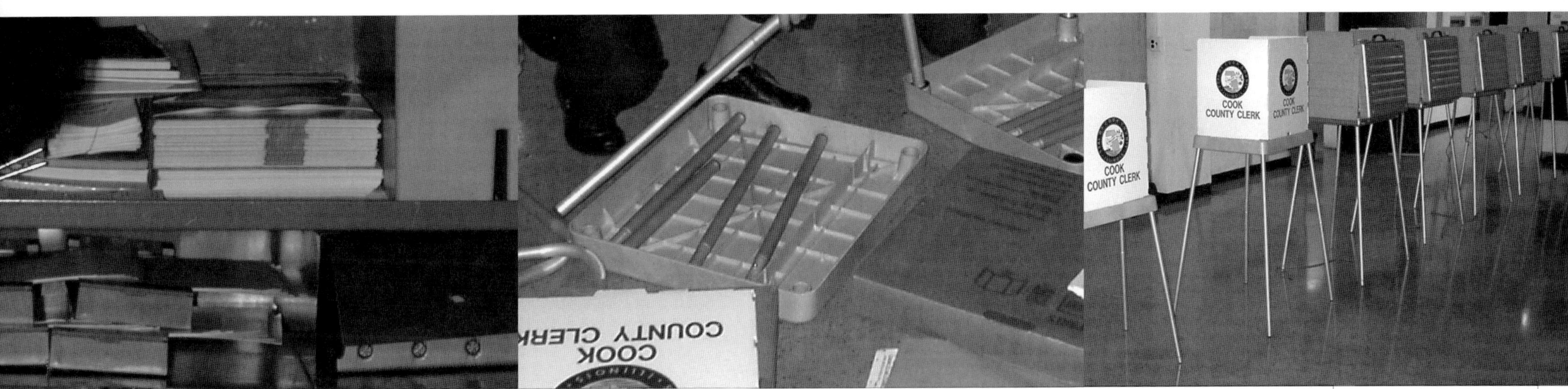

[6] CalTech/MIT Voting Technology Project, "Voting."

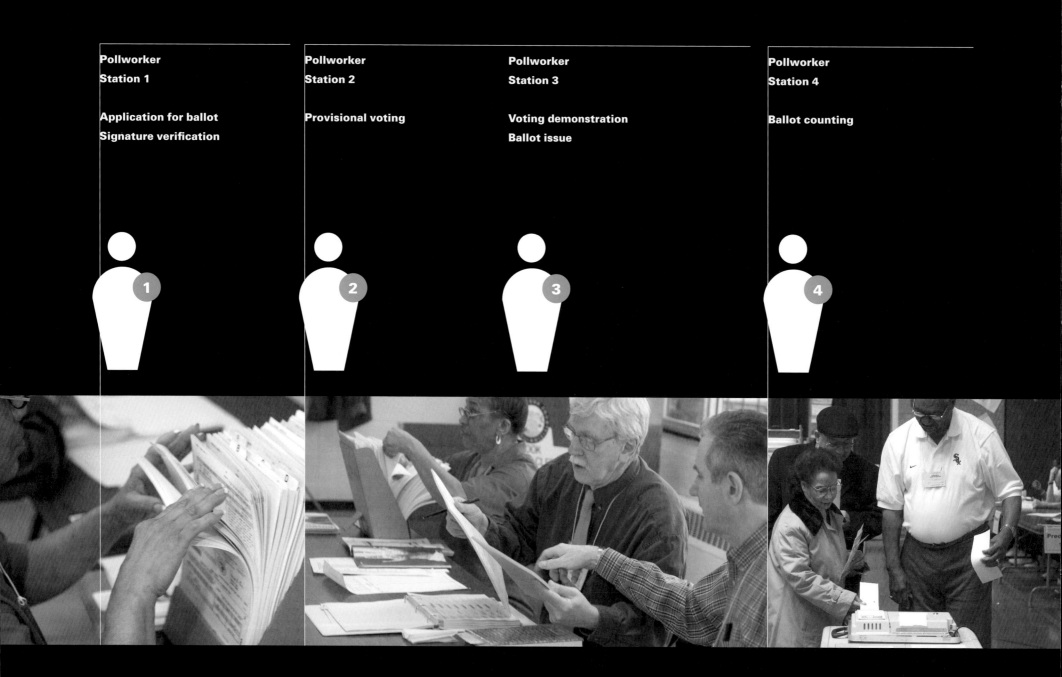

Pollworker
Station 1

Application for ballot
Signature verification

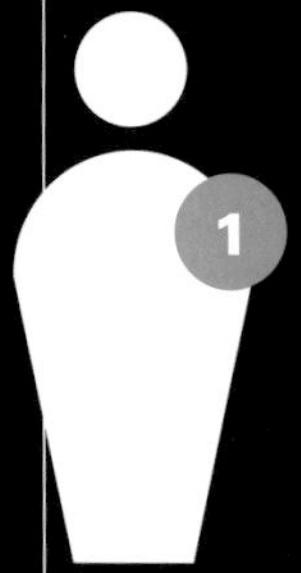

1

Pollworker
Station 2

Provisional voting

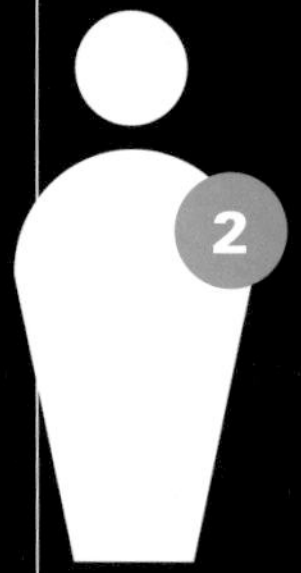

2

Pollworker
Station 3

Voting demonstration
Ballot issue

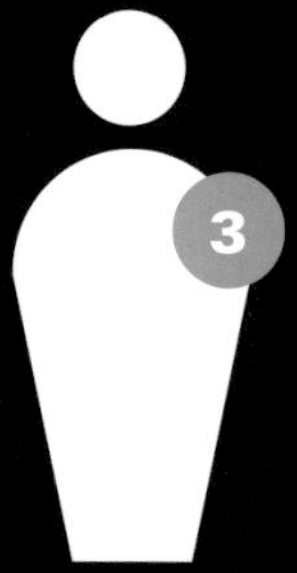

3

Pollworker
Station 4

Ballot counting

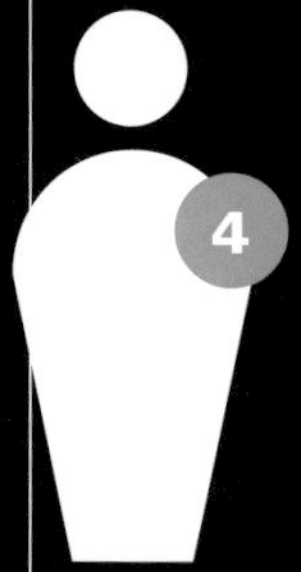

4

Some voters think that a pollworker's job is simply to hand them a ballot. They can become frustrated with the administrative steps and the amount of interaction required to complete the voting process. The more voters know about the polling place environment, the more likely they are to trust the people and the processes encountered. Increased understanding can be achieved by providing information on the roles, responsibilities, and political affiliations of pollworkers. Identification badges with visible names provide personalization. Numbering the badges by station indicates order of encounter. Information on pollworkers can also be included in voter information literature and in polling place signage.

Similar identification badges and posted descriptions can be used to clarify the roles of others who have the credentials to be in the polling place on election day, such as state and county election staff, law enforcement officials, pollwatchers, media representatives, and exit pollsters.

election judge
1
name
township
precinct/ward
General Election
November 2, 2004
Democrat

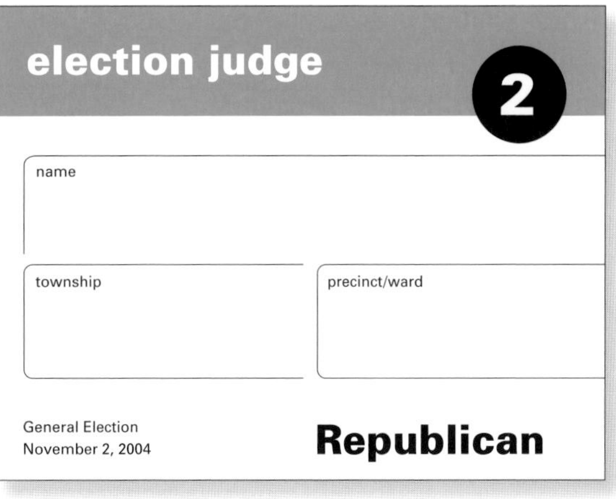

election judge
2
name
township
precinct/ward
General Election
November 2, 2004
Republican

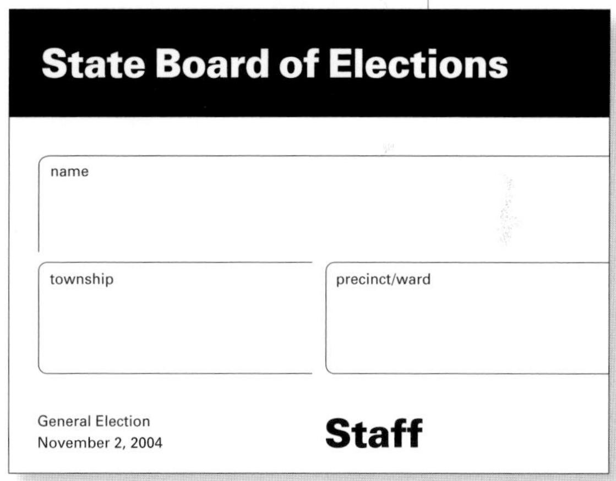

State Board of Elections
name
township
precinct/ward
General Election
November 2, 2004
Staff

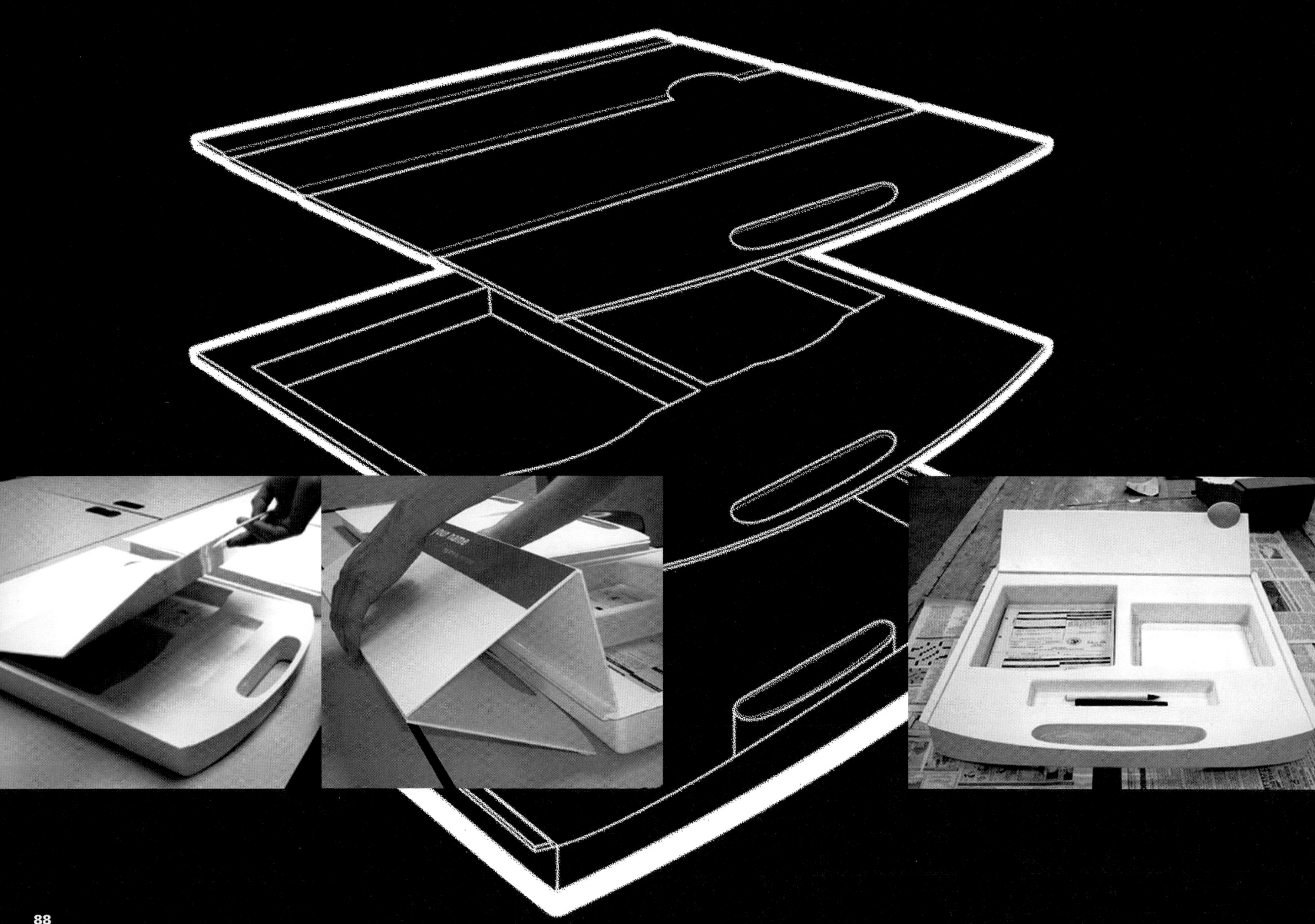

One of the great difficulties of polling place setup is configuring the pollworker stations. A variety of records and administrative forms and envelopes that arrive at the polling place in disorder must be sorted out and assembled into workable stations before the polls open. This is a time-consuming process on a day when time pressures are severe.

Design for Democracy has designed a prototypical cost-efficient pollworker station tray system. With a universal molded base, custom configurations can be developed for the interior of each station tray. Time can be saved by pre-loading the administrative materials at the warehouse in the days and weeks prior to an election. In testing this proposed design solution, we were able to reduce the setup time of the pollworker stations in the polling place from nearly an hour to less than one minute.

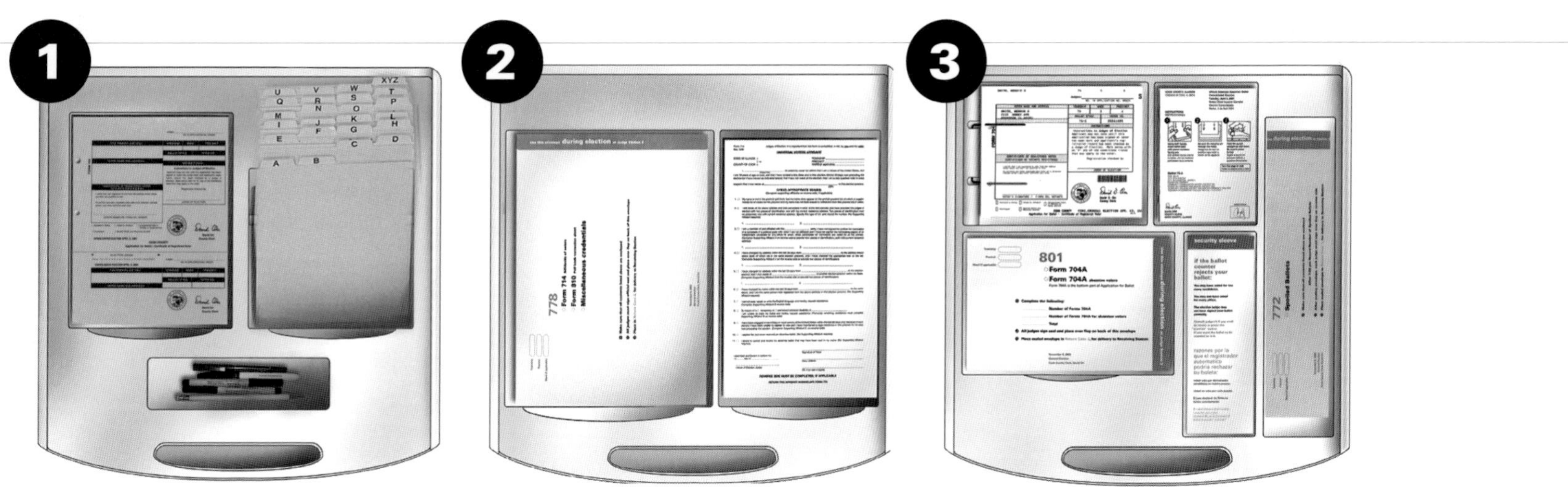

Left and above, proposed numbered pollworker station trays for simplified polling place setup. Design for Democracy prototypes include a common exterior carrying case that folds open to form a base for customizable injection molded interior compartments.

Pollworker station trays provide an opportunity for instructional signs that can help both voters and pollworkers. Numbered signs that describe the activities performed at each station tell voters what to expect at each step of the process.

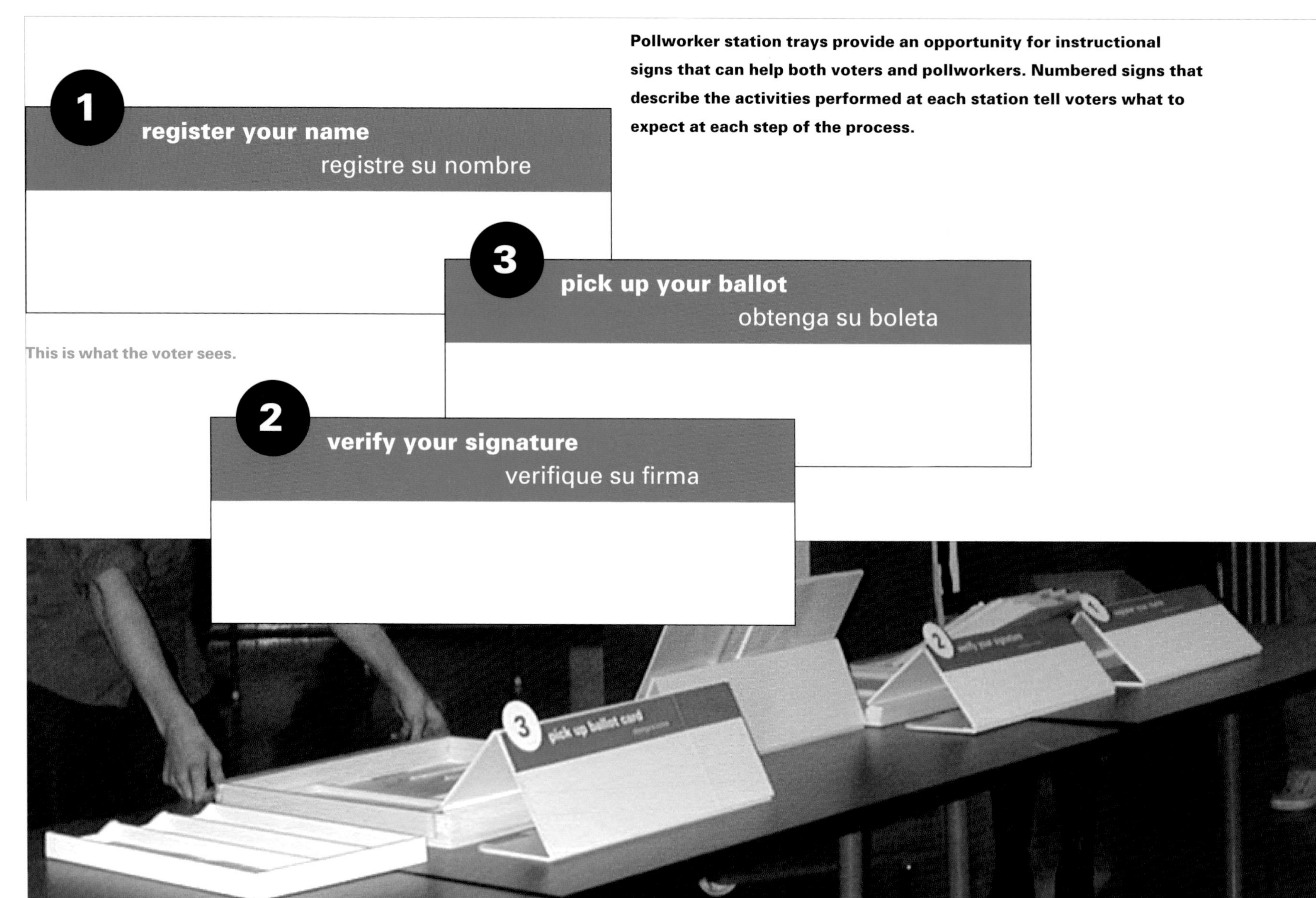

1
register your name
registre su nombre
3
pick up your ballot
obtenga su boleta
2
verify your signature
verifique su firma

This is what the voter sees.

The instructional signs can also provide each pollworker with station-specific troubleshooting information. Particularly in jurisdictions that require pollworkers to rotate stations throughout the day, this information can help orient pollworkers as they assume different roles.

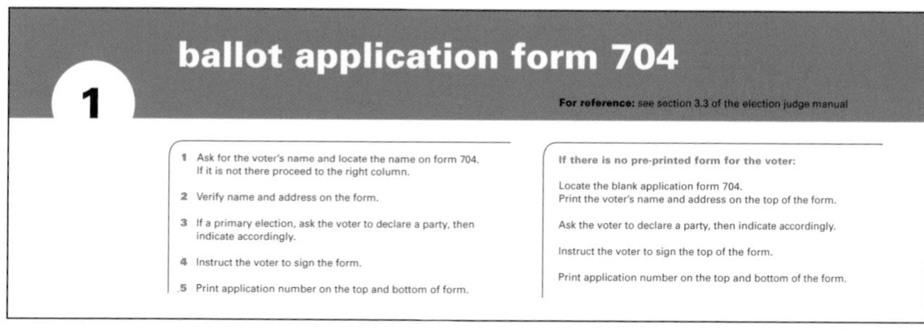

1
ballot application form 704
For reference: see section 3.3 of the election judge manual
1 Ask for the voter's name and locate the name on form 704. If it is not there proceed to the right column.
2 Verify name and address on the form.
3 If a primary election, ask the voter to declare a party, then indicate accordingly.
4 Instruct the voter to sign the form.
5 Print application number on the top and bottom of form.
If there is no pre-printed form for the voter:
Locate the blank application form 704. Print the voter's name and address on the top of the form.
Ask the voter to declare a party, then indicate accordingly.
Instruct the voter to sign the top of the form.
Print application number on the top and bottom of the form.

This is what the pollworker sees.

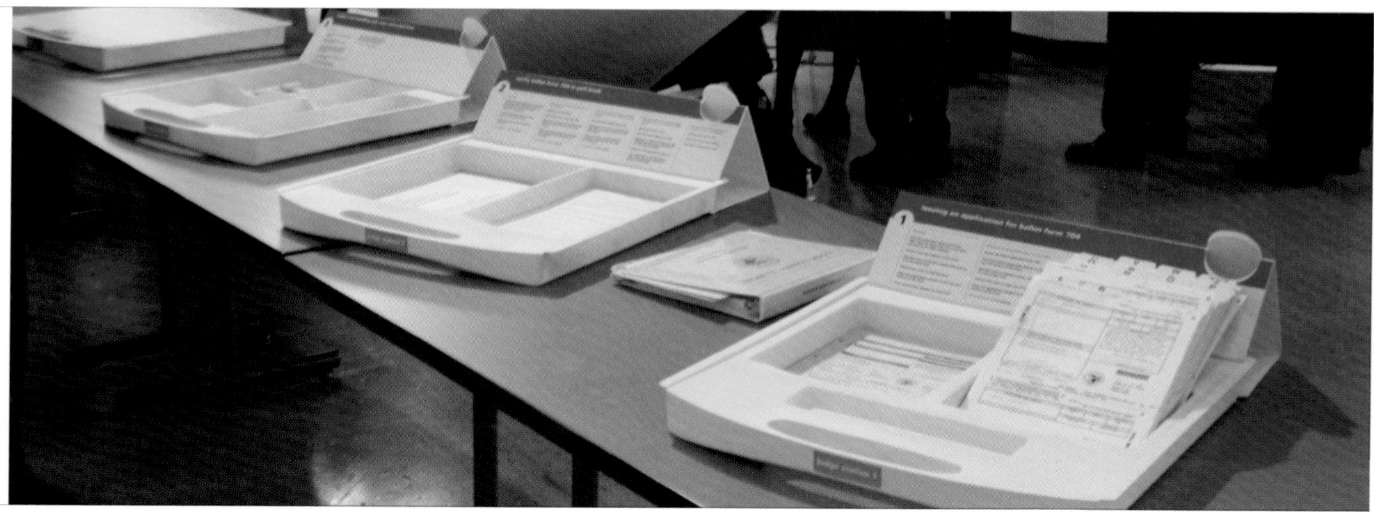

signage + wayfinding

Signs are needed on election day to help voters locate their polling places, navigate their way through unfamiliar spaces, and receive information and instruction related to the voting process. Often posted in the haste of early morning setup, election signs must compete for attention with existing signs and postings and other distractions that relate to the day-to-day activities of the polling place location.

The larger the signs, the better. Big signs with white backgrounds, simple layouts, distinct areas of color, straightforward language, and large type work best to draw attention away from surrounding clutter. Signs should clearly mark the polling place entryway and provide directional indicators for any alternate entrances. Accessibility indicators and smoking restrictions can be identified with bold symbols, and simple directional arrows can be used to help voters find their way.

Polling place signs should be used to:

→ Make the polling place visible from a distance
→ Indicate the main entry and any alternate entry required for wheelchair access
→ Provide election date; hours of operation; and ward, township, and/or precinct designation
→ Help voters find their way
→ Present information and provide instruction

precinct
precinto
13
polling place
precinto electoral
6am–7pm
Tuesday
April 1
2003
Consolidated
Election
Martes
1 de abril
2003
Comicios
Consolidados
上午六點至下午七點
星期二
四月一日
2003 年
全部選舉
voter bill of rights
servicios para los votantes
voting services
servicios para los votantes
voting instructions
instrucciones para voter
voting instructions
instrucciones para voter

The Design for Democracy system for signs recommends the use of blue bands for headings that provide general information and red bands for headings that require activity, provide instruction, or indicate warning. At a minimum there should be exterior signs marking the polling place location and indicating the building entrance and interior signs that provide information on voters' rights and services and voting instructions. Polling places serving multiple precincts need to have signs that clearly label each precinct and indicate direction.

Use visual symbols or instructional diagrams to provide posted information whenever possible. Pictures are straightforward and powerful. If designed correctly they require no language translations. When multiple languages are needed on polling place signs in a given precinct, it is best to use signs that are limited to English plus one other language.

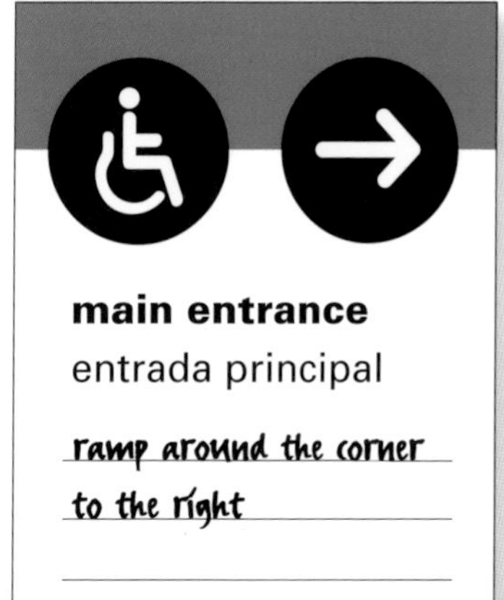

22"

22"

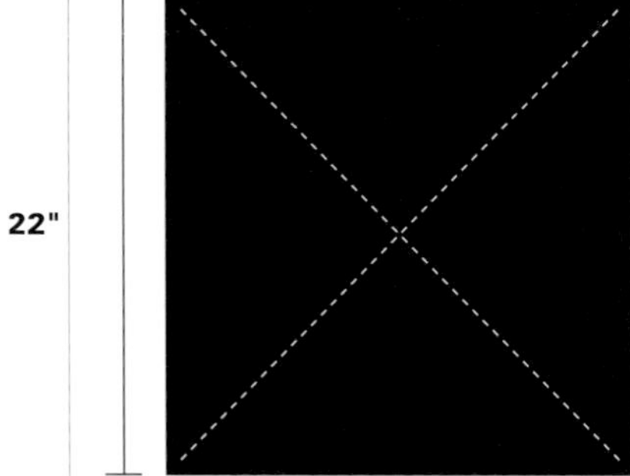

Sign system measurements are based on the dimensions of the voting supply carrier.

34"

polling place
precinto electoral

6am–7pm

Tuesday	martes
November 7	2 de noviembre
2006	del 2004
General Election	Elección General

Large signs should clearly mark the polling place entry and provide directional indicators for any alternate entrances.

22"

22"

66"

6am–7pm

Tuesday
November 7
2006
General Election

martes
2 de noviembre
del 2006
Elección General

vote!

22"

ramp around the corner
to the right

la rampa esta a la
vuelta de la esquina a
mano derecha

18"

Large banners can be used to clearly identify a polling place location from a distance. Such banners should label the polling place and indicate hours of access. Single-color graphic patterns draw attention and add visual interest.

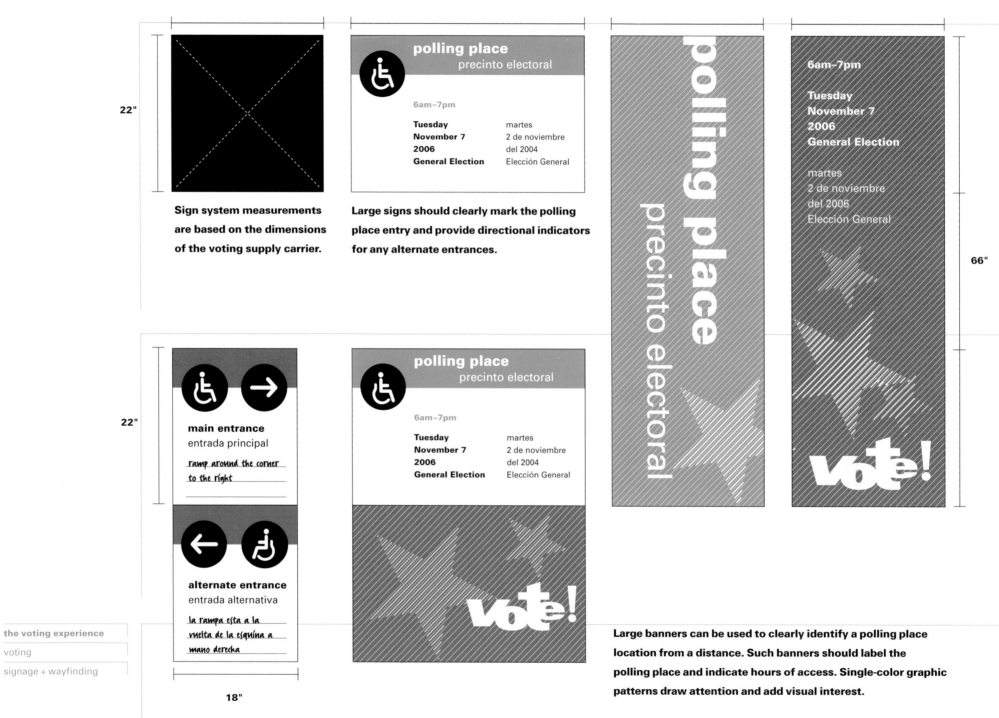

11"

22"

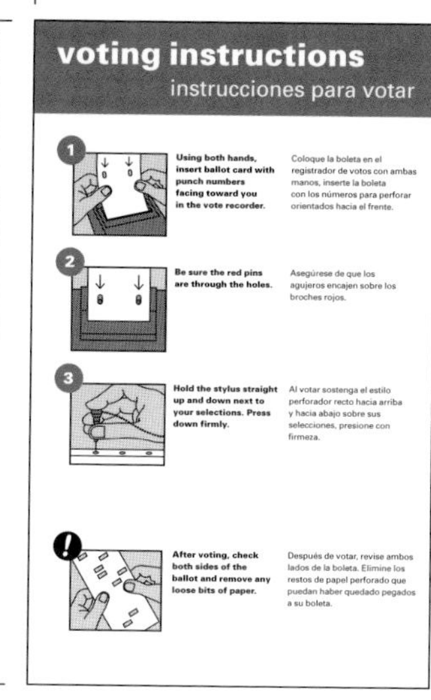

34"

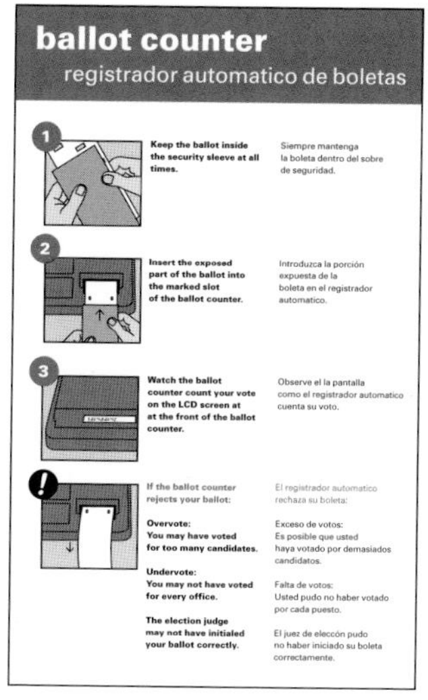

The polling place sign system designed and implemented for Cook County (Illinois) uses modular sizing based on the interior dimensions of the county's voting supply carrier.

To keep signs from becoming too cluttered, the information is presented in single-topic posters: voting instructions, language assistance, information and services, voting rights, etc.

Signs should contain no more than two languages: English as the primary language in bold type, and the second language in a lighter-weight type. To allow for more space and greater clarity, the second-language headings may also be set at a smaller type size.

election assistance
asistencia de la elección
assistance in english
312 603 0906
Voters who need election assistance in English can call the County Clerk's voter information hotline.
asistencia en español
312 603 6767
Los votantes que necesiten asistencia en español pueden llamar a la línea directa del Secretario para información a los votantes.

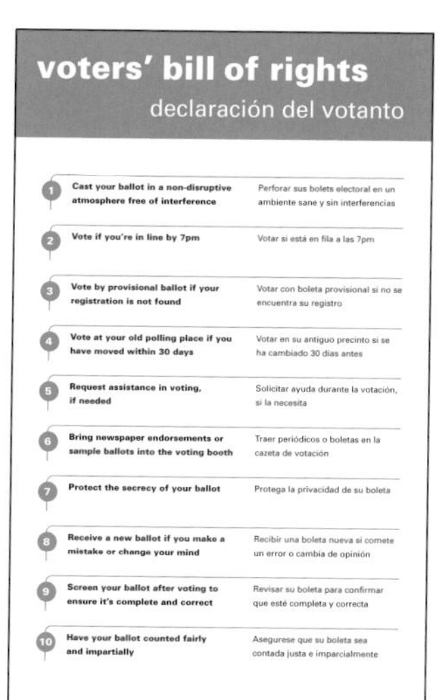

34"

22"

Signs with red bands indicate instruction; signs with blue bands indicate information.

In these examples, Univers 75 Bold is used for English and Univers 55 for Spanish. Text type is set at the same point size for both languages. English headings are set in 120pt, Spanish headings in 60pt.

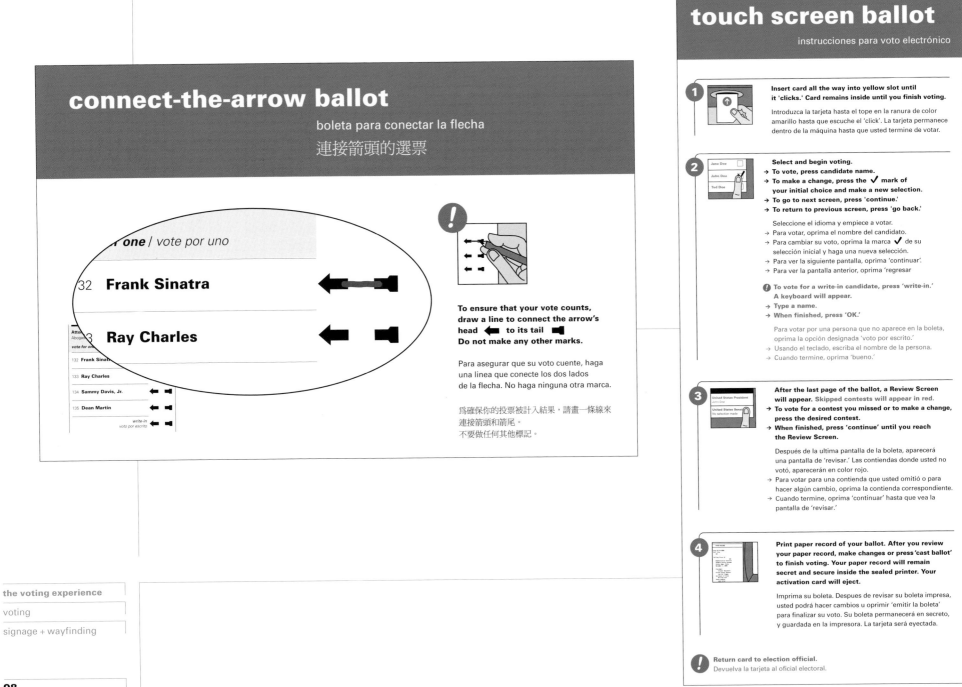

connect-the-arrow ballot

boleta para conectar la flecha

連接箭頭的選票

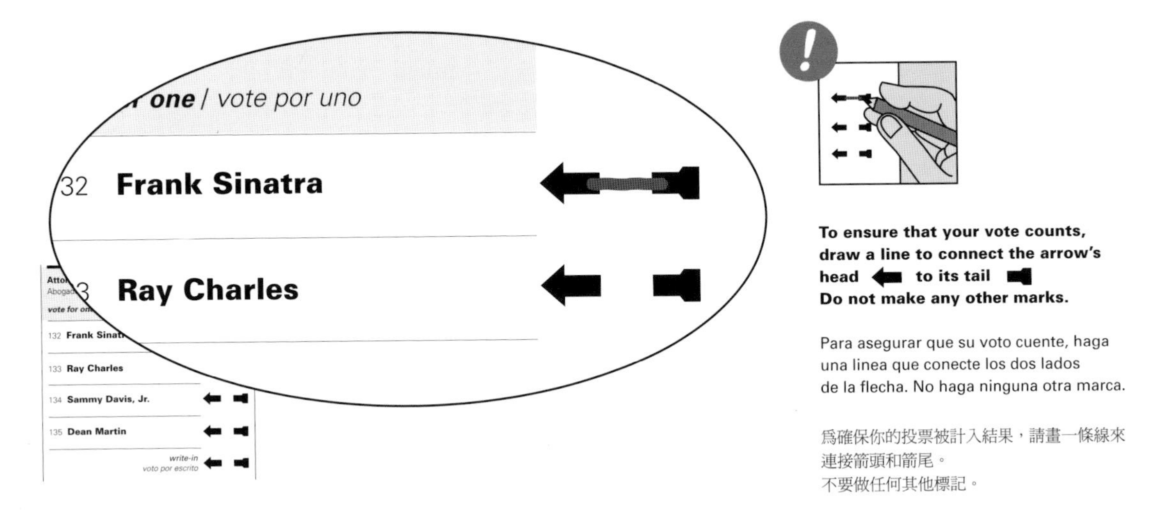

To ensure that your vote counts, draw a line to connect the arrow's head ⬅ to its tail ▬ Do not make any other marks.

Para asegurar que su voto cuente, haga una linea que conecte los dos lados de la flecha. No haga ninguna otra marca.

爲確保你的投票被計入結果，請畫一條線來連接箭頭和箭尾。
不要做任何其他標記。

touch screen ballot

instrucciones para voto electrónico

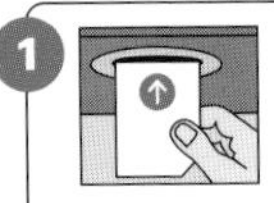

1 **Insert card all the way into yellow slot until it 'clicks.' Card remains inside until you finish voting.**

Introduzca la tarjeta hasta el tope en la ranura de color amarillo hasta que escuche el 'click'. La tarjeta permanece dentro de la máquina hasta que usted termine de votar.

2 **Select and begin voting.**

- **To vote, press candidate name.**
- **To make a change, press the ✓ mark of your initial choice and make a new selection.**
- **To go to next screen, press 'continue.'**
- **To return to previous screen, press 'go back.'**

Seleccione el idioma y empiece a votar.

- Para votar, oprima el nombre del candidato.
- Para cambiar su voto, oprima la marca ✓ de su selección inicial y haga una nueva selección.
- Para ver la siguiente pantalla, oprima 'continuar'.
- Para ver la pantalla anterior, oprima 'regresar

! To vote for a write-in candidate, press 'write-in.' A keyboard will appear.

- **Type a name.**
- **When finished, press 'OK.'**

Para votar por una persona que no aparece en la boleta, oprima la opción designada 'voto por escrito.'

- Usando el teclado, escriba el nombre de la persona.
- Cuando termine, oprima 'bueno.'

3 **After the last page of the ballot, a Review Screen will appear. Skipped contests will appear in red.**

- **To vote for a contest you missed or to make a change, press the desired contest.**
- **When finished, press 'continue' until you reach the Review Screen.**

Después de la ultima pantalla de la boleta, aparecerá una pantalla de 'revisar.' Las contiendas donde usted no votó, aparecerán en color rojo.

- Para votar para una contienda que usted omitió o para hacer algún cambio, oprima la contienda correspondiente.
- Cuando termine, oprima 'continuar' hasta que vea la pantalla de 'revisar.'

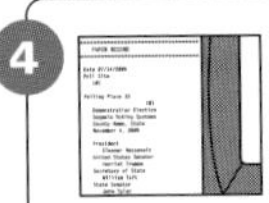

4 **Print paper record of your ballot. After you review your paper record, make changes or press 'cast ballot' to finish voting. Your paper record will remain secret and secure inside the sealed printer. Your activation card will eject.**

Imprima su boleta. Despues de revisar su boleta impresa, usted podrá hacer cambios u oprimir 'emitir la boleta' para finalizar su voto. Su boleta permanecerá en secreto, y guardada en la impresora. La tarjeta será eyectada.

Return card to election official.

Devuelva la tarjeta al oficial electoral.

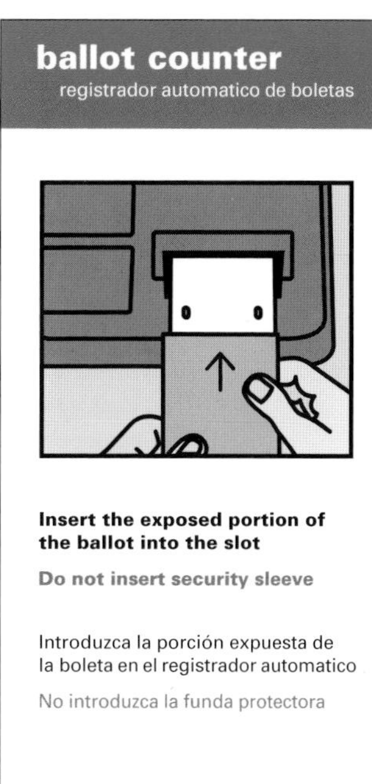

ballot counter
registrador automatico de boletas
Insert the exposed portion of the ballot into the slot
Do not insert security sleeve
Introduzca la porción expuesta de la boleta en el registrador automatico
No introduzca la funda protectora

Instructional signs, indicated by the red band across the top, provide instructions for voting and for casting a ballot. Additional instructions may be provided on a ballot privacy sleeve and on signs posted in voting booths and on ballot counting equipment.

Post instructional signs in or near each voting booth and in areas where voters can review instructions while waiting in line.

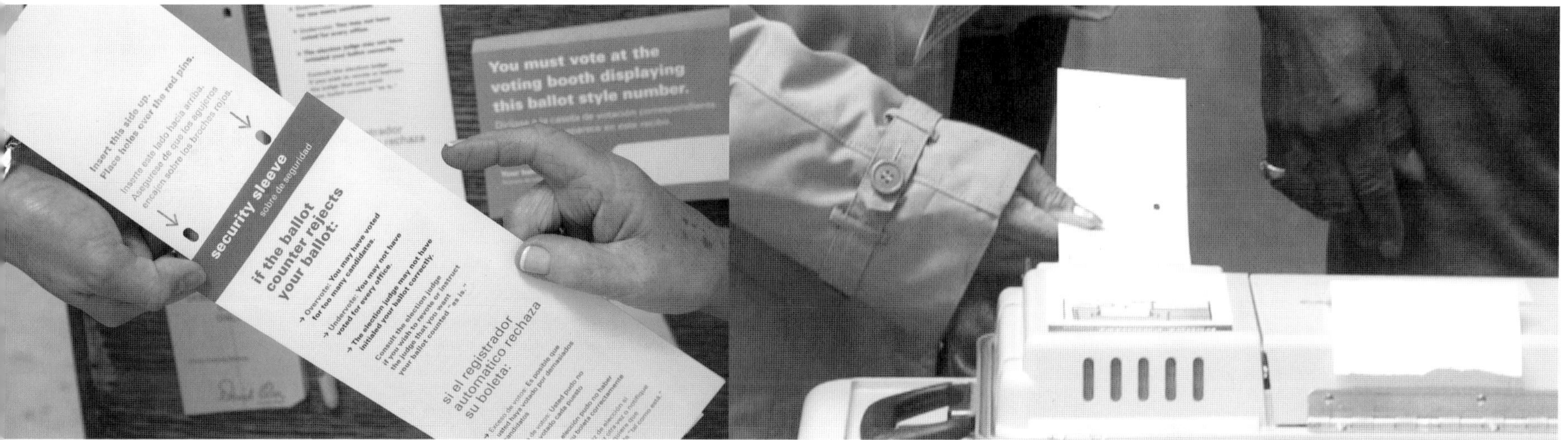

election assistance

asistencia de la elección

assistance in english

312 603 0906 **Voters who need election assistance in English can call the County Clerk's voter information hotline.**

asistencia en español

312 603 6767 Los votantes que necesiten asistencia en español pueden llamar a la línea directa del Secretario para información a los votantes.

voters' bill of rights

declaración del votanto

1	**Cast your ballot in a non-disruptive atmosphere free of interference**	Perforar sus bolets electoral en un ambiente sane y sin interferencias
2	**Vote if you're in line by 7pm**	Votar si está en fila a las 7pm
3	**Vote by provisional ballot if your registration is not found**	Votar con boleta provisional si no se encuentra su registro
4	**Vote at your old polling place if you have moved within 30 days**	Votar en su antiguo precinto si se ha cambiado 30 días antes
5	**Request assistance in voting, if needed**	Solicitar ayuda durante la votación, si la necesita
6	**Bring newspaper endorsements or sample ballots into the voting booth**	Traer periódicos o boletas en la cazeta de votación
7	**Protect the secrecy of your ballot**	Protega la privacidad de su boleta
8	**Receive a new ballot if you make a mistake or change your mind**	Recibir una boleta nueva si comete un error o cambia de opinión
9	**Screen your ballot after voting to ensure it's complete and correct**	Revisar su boleta para confirmar que esté completa y correcta
10	**Have your ballot counted fairly and impartially**	Asegurese que su boleta sea contada justa e imparcialmente

information + services

informacion y servicios

township
municipio ____________

precinct
precinto ____________

ward
distrito ____________

electioneering prohibited

No person shall electioneer or solicit votes on Election Day inside or within ten feet of a polling place.

No person shall interrupt, hinder, or oppose any voter who is approaching the polling place to vote.

está prohibido la campaña electoral/solicitar votos

Ninguna persona hará campaña slectoral o solicitará votos el Día de las Elecciones a menos de 100 pies de distancia del precinto electoral.

Ninguna persona deberá interrumpir, obstruir oponerse a cualquier persona que se aproxime a votar.

identity

You are required to show one of the following forms: photo ID, utility bill, bank statement, government check, paycheck, other government document.

If you do not have any of these forms, you are entitled to cast a provisional ballot.

identidad

Tiene que presentar una de las siguientes formas de identificación actual y válida con su nombre y dirección: documento de identitad com foto, factura de servicio público, estado de cuenta bancario, cheque del gobierno, cheque de paga, otro documento gubernamental.

Si no tiene ninguna de estas formas, tiene derecho a votar con una boleta provisional.

physically disabled

If you are unable to cast your ballot because you are physically disabled or visually impaired, you may receive assistance in voting.

You will be required to complete a sworn affidavit Form 61 and the person or persons who assist you will also have to complete the affidavit.

incapacidaded físicas

So no esta en condiciones de depositar su boleta debido a una incapacidad física o visual, usted puede recibir ayuda para votar.

Se le pedirá que complete el formulario de declaración jurada 714 y la persona o personas que le ayuden también tendrán que completarla. Asistencia puede ser proveída por dos jueces de elección de ambos partidos políticos o una persona elegida por el votante.

Informational signs, indicated by a blue band across the top, provide voters with rules and regulations as well as information about voters' rights and services. Blue should be used for all signs that provide voting information: precinct numbers, ballot style numbers, and poll-worker identification badges.

Areas where voters queue for check-in, and therefore may have time to read while waiting, are ideal for posting informational signs.

Ballot style number
Número de estilo de boleta
95–15

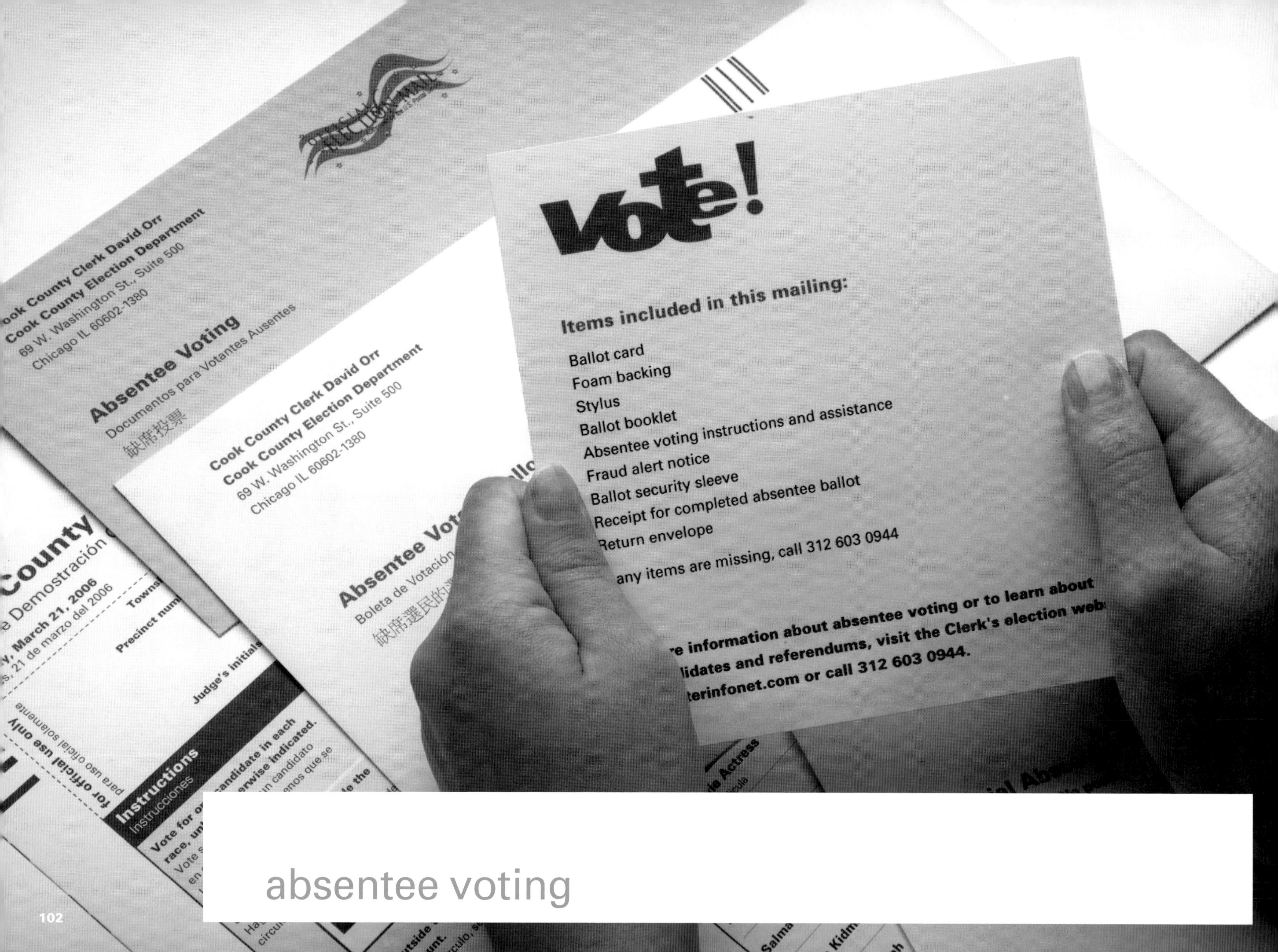

absentee voting

In 1998 the state of Oregon passed an initiative that allows all registered voters to vote by mail. Many U.S. voters cast absentee ballots by mail for reasons such as travel, military service, or physical impairment, but Oregon was the first state to offer vote-by-mail statewide. Design for Democracy worked with Oregon election officials to develop prototype materials to improve the quality of their vote-by-mail program. This work subsequently informed the design and implementation of absentee balloting materials for Cook County, Illinois.

Special design considerations for vote-by-mail include clearly explaining procedures to voters who will not have immediate access to assistance; limiting the quantity and weight of material to keep mailing costs down; and conveying to the absentee voter the same feelings of civic pride and community that should be conveyed on election day in the polling place.

Design can improve the absentee voting process by:

→ Addressing all aspects of the vote-by-mail experience
→ Helping voters to understand the materials received and the order in which they should be used
→ Explaining the voting process and how to get assistance if needed
→ Providing information on rules, regulations, rights, and responsibilities
→ Providing instruction for voting and for submitting a ballot to be counted

Absentee voting materials use the same design principles as polling place signage: black type on white for all critical information, simple instructional diagrams with minimal steps, red to indicate instruction and warning, and blue for general information.

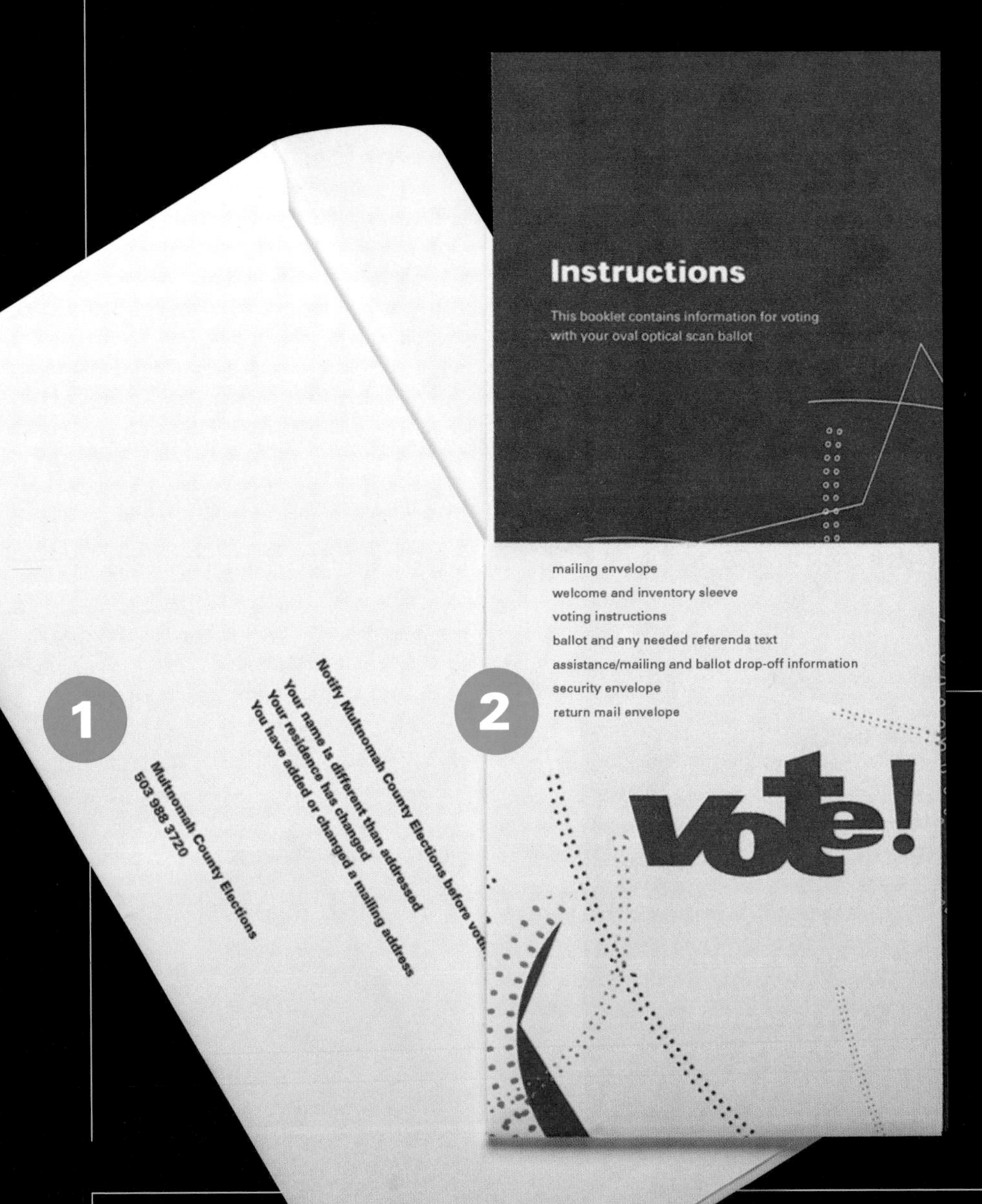

1
Multnomah County Elections
503 988 3720
Notify Multnomah County Elections before
Your name is different than addressed
Your residence has changed
You have added or changed a mailing address
Instructions
This booklet contains information for voting with your oval optical scan ballot
2
mailing envelope
welcome and inventory sleeve
voting instructions
ballot and any needed referenda text
assistance/mailing and ballot drop-off information
security envelope
return mail envelope
vote!

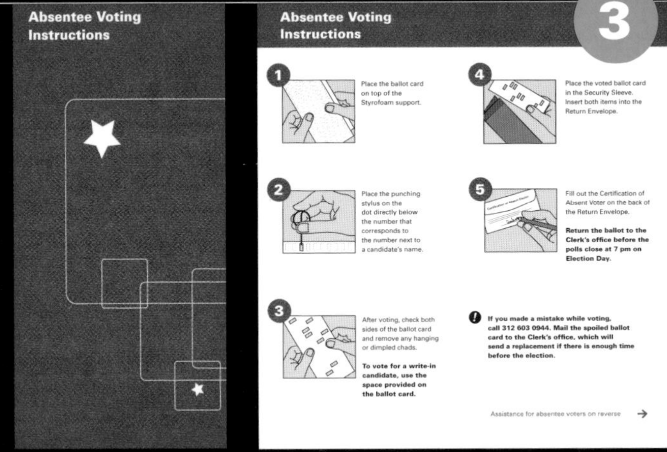

The same level of planning and consideration given to polling place voting should be applied to the absentee voting process. From the moment a ballot packet is received by mail, the voter should be welcomed and guided through the information provided. Voting instructions should be clearly presented. A small sleeve that contains all mailed materials, which the voter sees upon opening the outer envelope, is a useful device. The sleeve provides introductory language and a complete listing of contents.

Components of an absentee ballot package include 1] mailing envelope, 2] welcome and inventory sleeve, 3] voting instructions, 4] ballot and referenda text, 5] information on obtaining assistance and on ballot drop-off, 6] security envelope for completed ballot, and 7] return mail envelope.

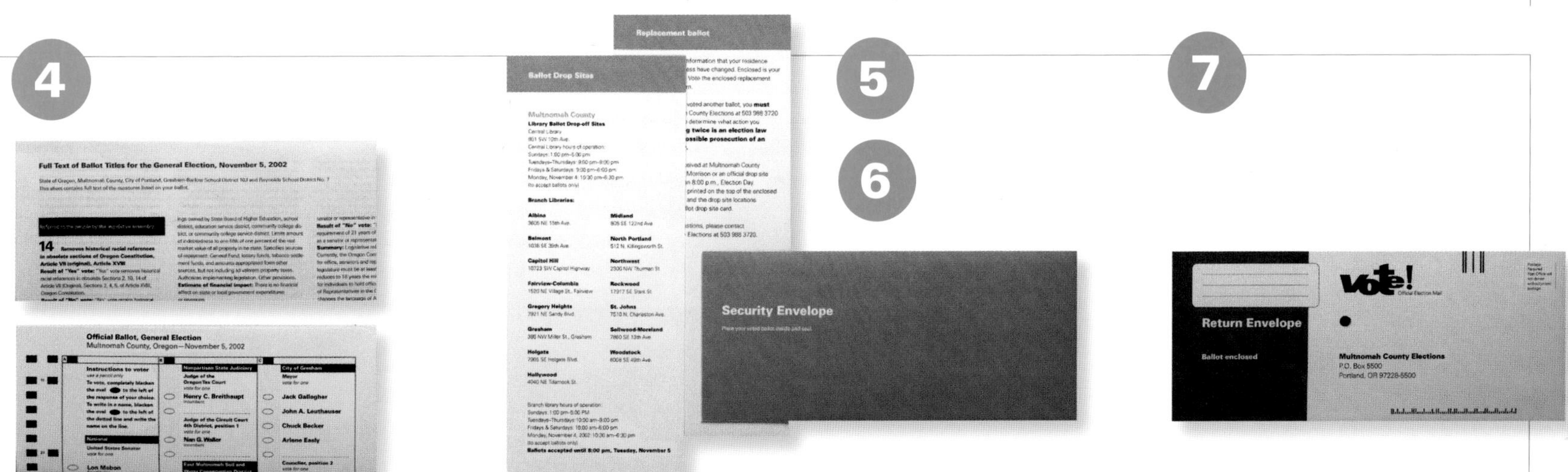

Above and left, prototypes of a redesigned Oregon vote-by-mail ballot packet. Shown at reduced size.

in this section

behind the scenes
What the voters can’t see can hurt them

pollworker support
Providing needed tools for those who control the voting experience

document management
From chaos to clarity and consistency

provisional voting
Adapting the design system to meet HAVA requirements

The administration of elections is a highly complex undertaking involving many people and personalities; systems, processes, and procedures; and physical equipment, materials, and facilities. Elections are not federally administered. They are overseen at the state level and are produced locally by individual counties or municipalities.

The permanent staff of an election division is supplemented during elections by a massive temporary workforce—many working for a single day. This workforce of election officials and pollworkers is responsible for the efficiency and accuracy of our nation's elections.

Job responsibility and pressure are severe for those who work in elections. Both permanent and temporary participants need to be recruited, trained, and supported with tools that make their jobs easier and more enjoyable. Design can play a crucial role in the development of materials used behind the scenes of election production.

3 design + election administration

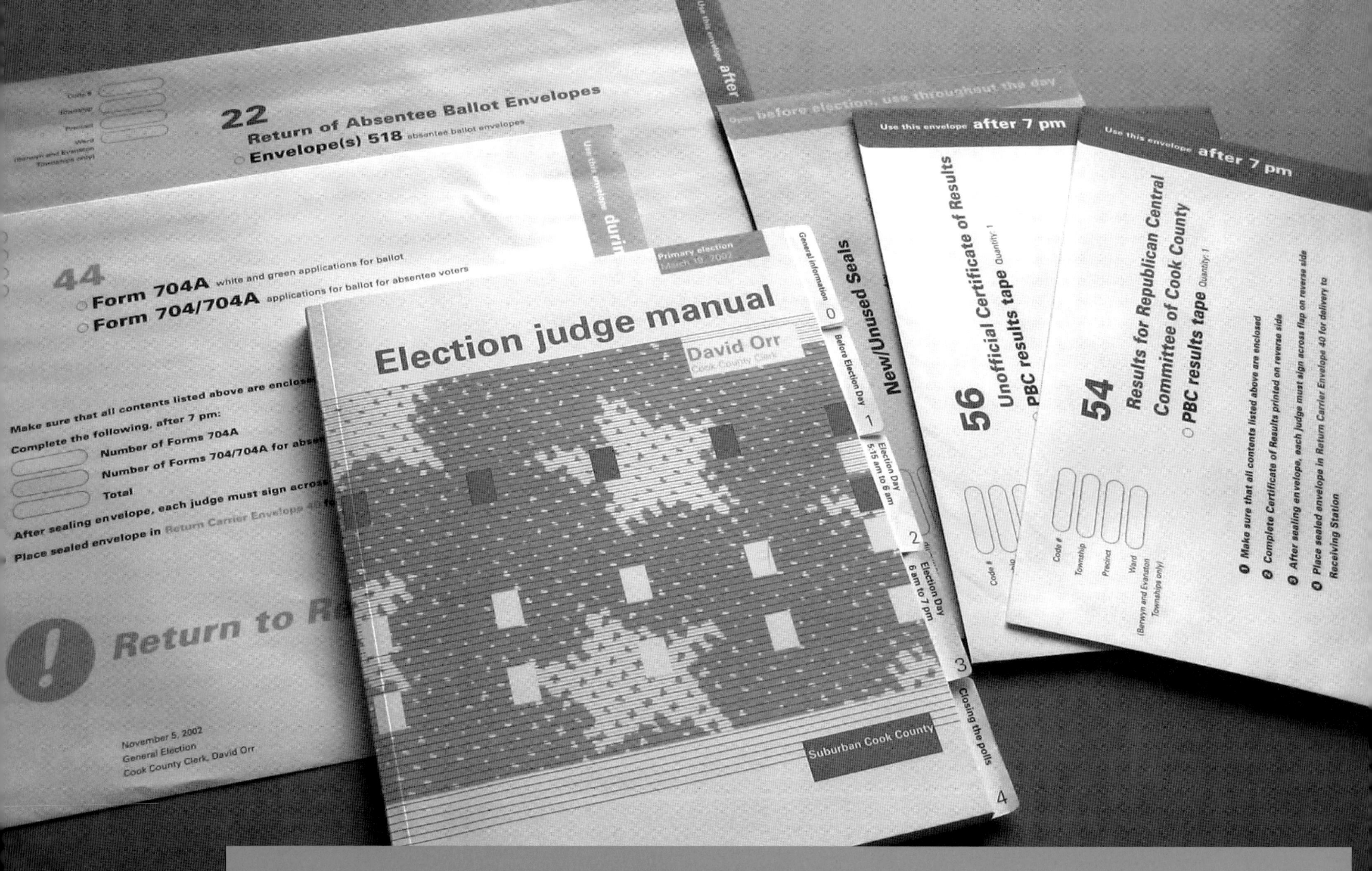

behind the scenes

Most of the activities involved in running an election are not seen by the voter. Yet the accuracy and efficiency of behind-the-scenes administrative activities do have a direct effect on the voting experience. A great deal of information, most of which changes with each election, must be provided to voters, news organizations, voters' rights groups, pollworkers, legislators, candidates, and political parties. Schedules must be made and calendars kept. Materials for communication, education, and administration must be updated, ordered, processed, and distributed. Procedures are often complex, and constant changes are the norm.

By streamlining processes and by designing systems and guidelines to emphasize clarity and efficiency, time and money are saved and there is less opportunity for error.

Design can help to improve election administration by

→ Reevaluating procedures, information, and the presentation of information
→ Introducing a design system that applies information design principles to all election materials
→ Providing tools and resources for training and supporting pollworkers
→ Evaluating and redesigning administrative forms and envelopes
→ Extending the design system into new administrative areas like provisional voting

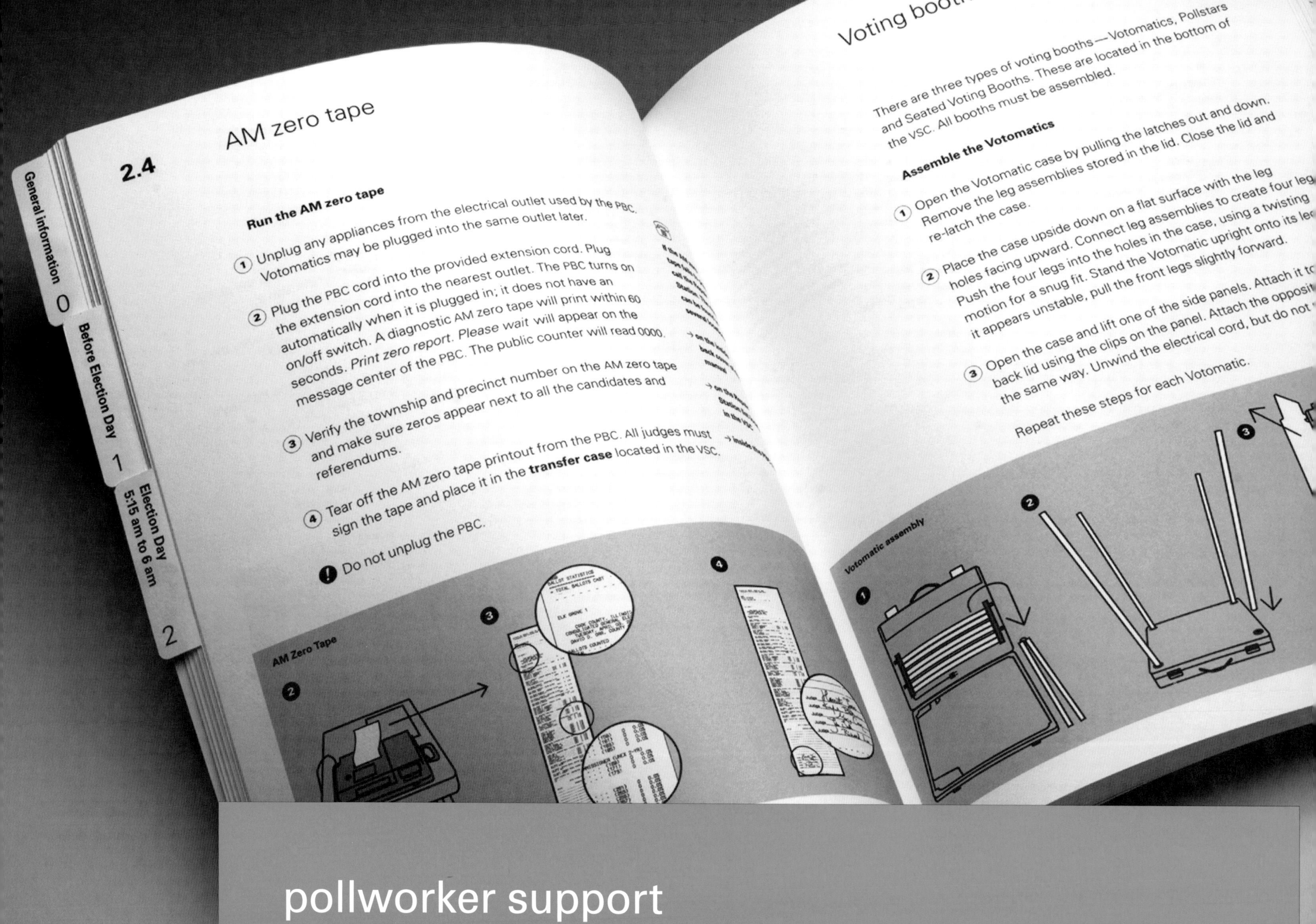
General information
0
Before Election Day
1
Election Day
5:15 am to 6 am
2
2.4
AM zero tape
Run the AM zero tape
1 Unplug any appliances from the electrical outlet used by the PBC. Votomatics may be plugged into the same outlet later.
2 Plug the PBC cord into the provided extension cord. Plug the extension cord into the nearest outlet. The PBC turns on automatically when it is plugged in; it does not have an on/off switch. A diagnostic AM zero tape will print within 60 seconds. Print zero report. Please wait will appear on the message center of the PBC. The public counter will read 0000.
3 Verify the township and precinct number on the AM zero tape and make sure zeros appear next to all the candidates and referendums.
4 Tear off the AM zero tape printout from the PBC. All judges must sign the tape and place it in the transfer case located in the VSC.
Do not unplug the PBC.
AM Zero Tape
2
3
4
Voting booth
There are three types of voting booths—Votomatics, Pollstars and Seated Voting Booths. These are located in the bottom of the VSC. All booths must be assembled.
Assemble the Votomatics
1 Open the Votomatic case by pulling the latches out and down. Remove the leg assemblies stored in the lid. Close the lid and re-latch the case.
2 Place the case upside down on a flat surface with the leg holes facing upward. Connect leg assemblies to create four leg
Push the four legs into the holes in the case, using a twisting motion for a snug fit. Stand the Votomatic upright onto its le
it appears unstable, pull the front legs slightly forward.
3 Open the case and lift one of the side panels. Attach it t
back lid using the clips on the panel. Attach the opposit
the same way. Unwind the electrical cord, but do not
Repeat these steps for each Votomatic.
Votomatic assembly
1
2
3

pollworker support

Stories, both good and bad, shared among voters on election day often involve the workers they encounter in the polling place. Pollworkers, sometimes called election judges, are in direct control of the voting experience. They are often underpaid and overworked and can be resistant to change. They are also dedicated citizens who want to do the right thing and who are willing to assume a great deal of responsibility—under tremendous time pressure—to work amidst the mechanics of democracy. Often preoccupied with their duties on election day, pollworkers do not always focus on their personal communication skills. The 2001 Caltech/MIT joint report on voting recommended that pollworkers be trained as service agents, to view their job as being in the polling place to assist voters in casting their votes with accuracy, privacy, and dignity.[1] Design can help to promote this professional service mentality by providing tools that simplify the tasks to be performed, and by developing professional educational and reference materials that can be used to train and support pollworkers.

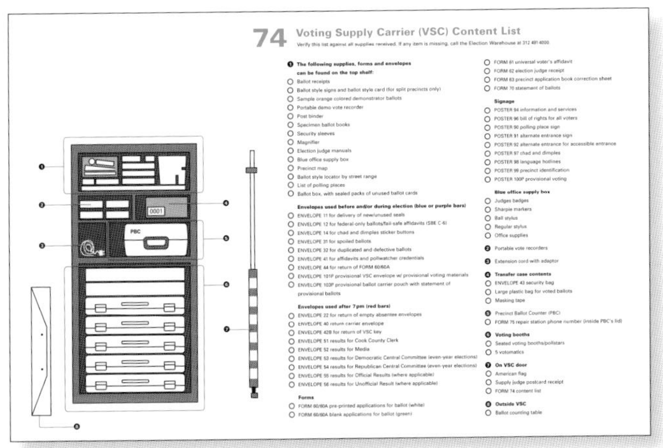

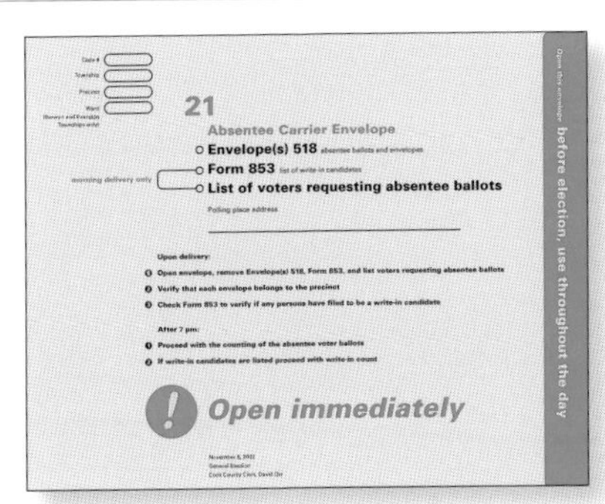

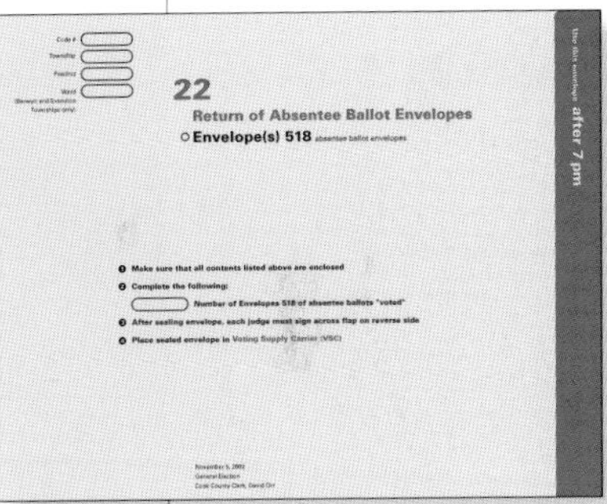

[1] Caltech/MIT Voting Technology Project, "Voting: What Is, What Could Be," report, July 2001.

The materials and equipment needed to conduct an election are delivered to each polling place in a voting supply carrier immediately prior to election day (and sometimes the same day if earlier access is not possible). A pollworker assigned to the location reviews the contents of the carrier to be certain that all items are accounted for. This pollworker is likely faced with a confusing array of materials and an intimidating supply checklist. As a result, this task is generally performed by an experienced worker who has completed the supply checklist in the past.

Activities that depend upon past experience create a barrier to improving elections and can make it difficult to recruit new pollworkers. If the materials in the supply carrier are thoughtfully organized, and if the checklist is designed to be user-friendly, a newly trained pollworker can easily do the work.

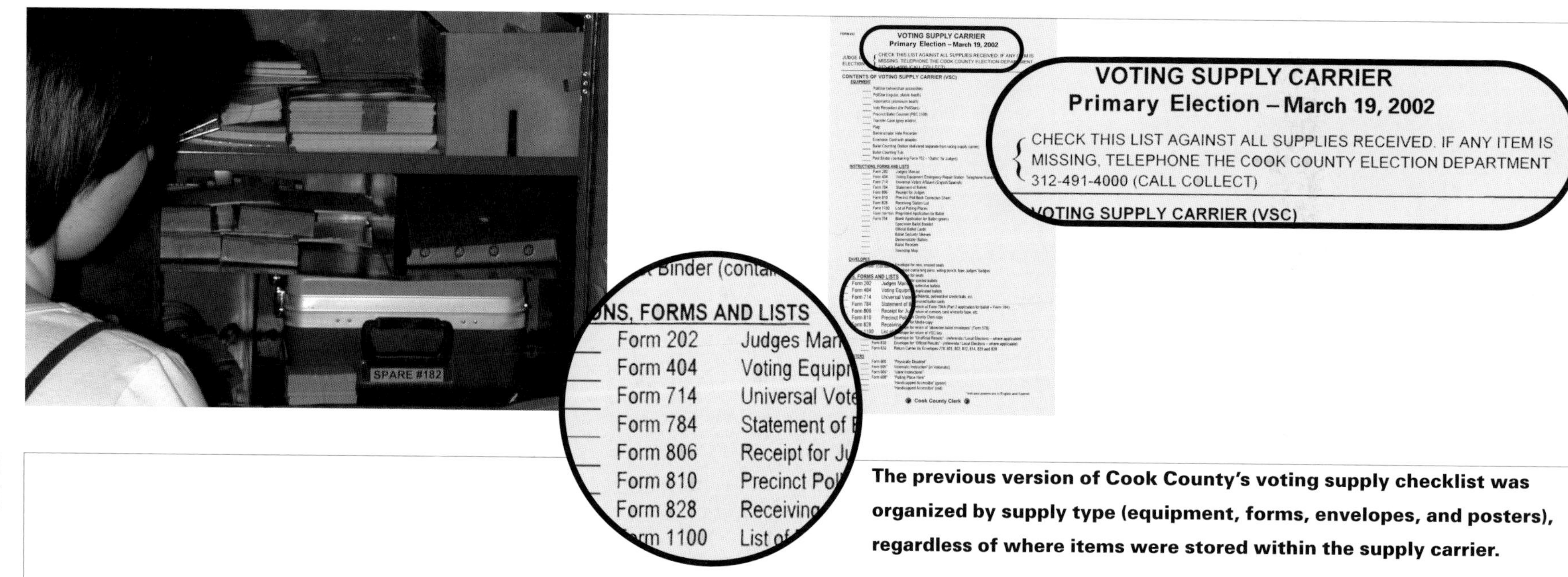

The previous version of Cook County's voting supply checklist was organized by supply type (equipment, forms, envelopes, and posters), regardless of where items were stored within the supply carrier.

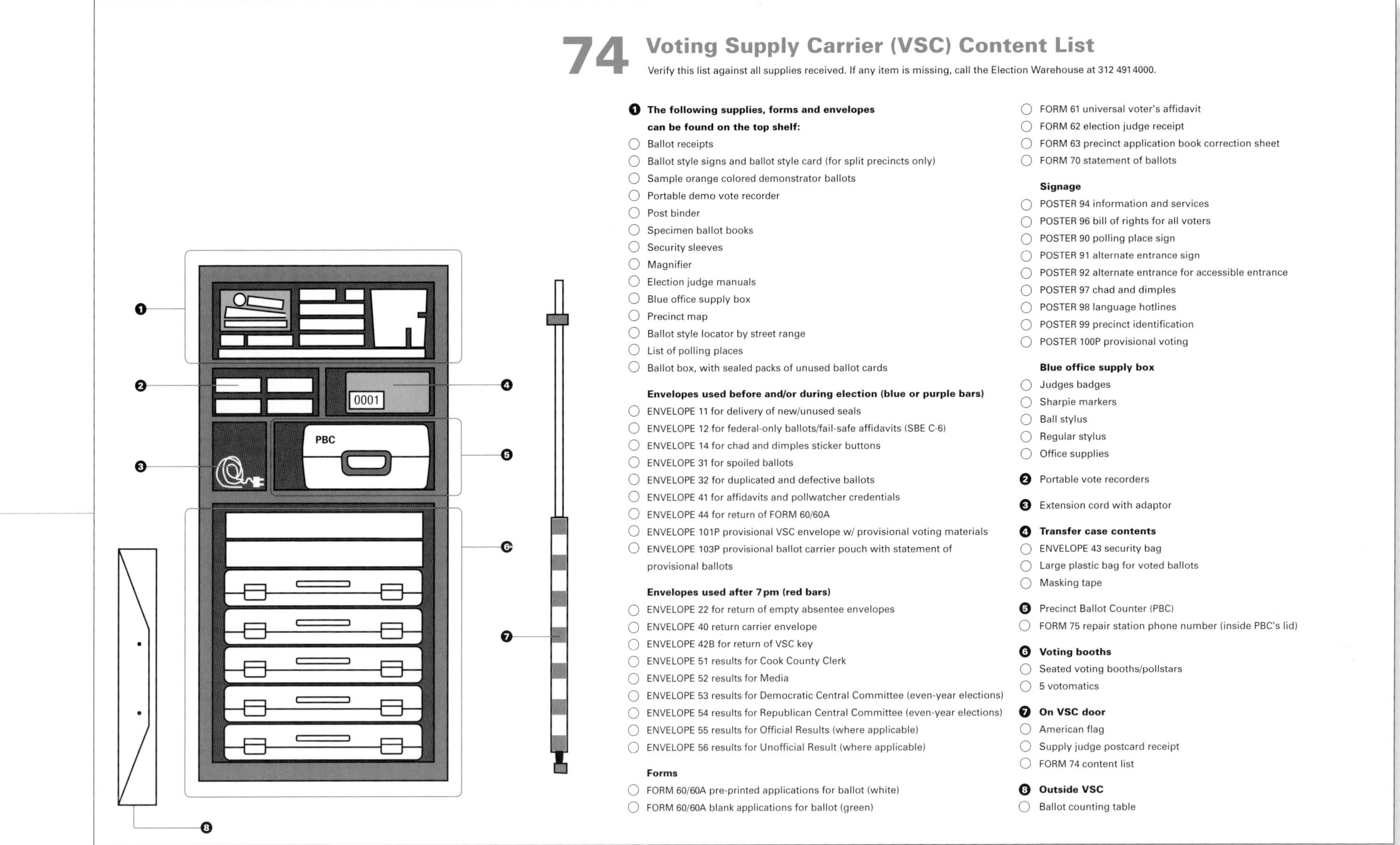

74 Voting Supply Carrier (VSC) Content List

Verify this list against all supplies received. If any item is missing, call the Election Warehouse at 312 491 4000.

1 The following supplies, forms and envelopes can be found on the top shelf:

- ○ Ballot receipts
- ○ Ballot style signs and ballot style card (for split precincts only)
- ○ Sample orange colored demonstrator ballots
- ○ Portable demo vote recorder
- ○ Post binder
- ○ Specimen ballot books
- ○ Security sleeves
- ○ Magnifier
- ○ Election judge manuals
- ○ Blue office supply box
- ○ Precinct map
- ○ Ballot style locator by street range
- ○ List of polling places
- ○ Ballot box, with sealed packs of unused ballot cards

Envelopes used before and/or during election (blue or purple bars)

- ○ ENVELOPE 11 for delivery of new/unused seals
- ○ ENVELOPE 12 for federal-only ballots/fail-safe affidavits (SBE C-6)
- ○ ENVELOPE 14 for chad and dimples sticker buttons
- ○ ENVELOPE 31 for spoiled ballots
- ○ ENVELOPE 32 for duplicated and defective ballots
- ○ ENVELOPE 41 for affidavits and pollwatcher credentials
- ○ ENVELOPE 44 for return of FORM 60/60A
- ○ ENVELOPE 101P provisional VSC envelope w/ provisional voting materials
- ○ ENVELOPE 103P provisional ballot carrier pouch with statement of provisional ballots

Envelopes used after 7 pm (red bars)

- ○ ENVELOPE 22 for return of empty absentee envelopes
- ○ ENVELOPE 40 return carrier envelope
- ○ ENVELOPE 42B for return of VSC key
- ○ ENVELOPE 51 results for Cook County Clerk
- ○ ENVELOPE 52 results for Media
- ○ ENVELOPE 53 results for Democratic Central Committee (even-year elections)
- ○ ENVELOPE 54 results for Republican Central Committee (even-year elections)
- ○ ENVELOPE 55 results for Official Results (where applicable)
- ○ ENVELOPE 56 results for Unofficial Result (where applicable)

Forms

- ○ FORM 60/60A pre-printed applications for ballot (white)
- ○ FORM 60/60A blank applications for ballot (green)
- ○ FORM 61 universal voter's affidavit
- ○ FORM 62 election judge receipt
- ○ FORM 63 precinct application book correction sheet
- ○ FORM 70 statement of ballots

Signage

- ○ POSTER 94 information and services
- ○ POSTER 96 bill of rights for all voters
- ○ POSTER 90 polling place sign
- ○ POSTER 91 alternate entrance sign
- ○ POSTER 92 alternate entrance for accessible entrance
- ○ POSTER 97 chad and dimples
- ○ POSTER 98 language hotlines
- ○ POSTER 99 precinct identification
- ○ POSTER 100P provisional voting

Blue office supply box

- ○ Judges badges
- ○ Sharpie markers
- ○ Ball stylus
- ○ Regular stylus
- ○ Office supplies

2 Portable vote recorders

3 Extension cord with adaptor

4 Transfer case contents

- ○ ENVELOPE 43 security bag
- ○ Large plastic bag for voted ballots
- ○ Masking tape

5 Precinct Ballot Counter (PBC)

- ○ FORM 75 repair station phone number (inside PBC's lid)

6 Voting booths

- ○ Seated voting booths/pollstars
- ○ 5 votomatics

7 On VSC door

- ○ American flag
- ○ Supply judge postcard receipt
- ○ FORM 74 content list

8 Outside VSC

- ○ Ballot counting table

Now organized by numbered storage location, the checklist includes a diagram of supply carrier contents for easy visual reference. Shown at reduced size.

A pollworker training and reference manual provides indispensable information to help pollworkers: descriptions of roles and responsibilities, step-by-step instructions for polling place set-up, important phone numbers and emergency contacts, administrative procedures, advice for handling unexpected or difficult situations, issues of accessibility and assistance, a glossary of election terminology, an index of forms, and troubleshooting tips.

In the redesigned version of Cook County's pollworker manual, the contents are organized in chronological order and presented in five tabbed sections: General Information, Before Election Day, Election Day 5:15am to 6am (before the polls open), Election Day 6am–7pm (while the polls are open), and Closing the Polls. The same organization and design approach is used in presentation slides for training support, as shown below.

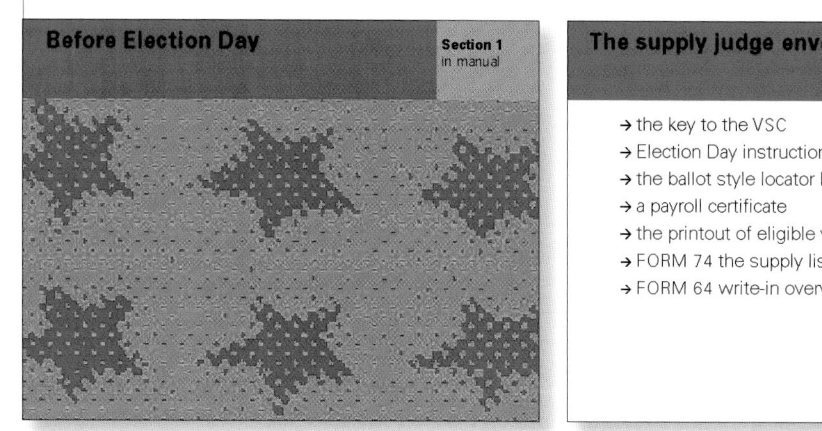

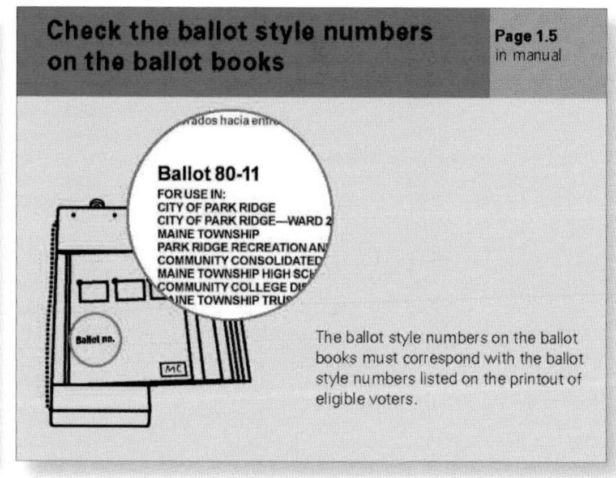

Right, the redesign of the Cook County election judge manual and, above, supporting electronic presentation. Shown at reduced size.

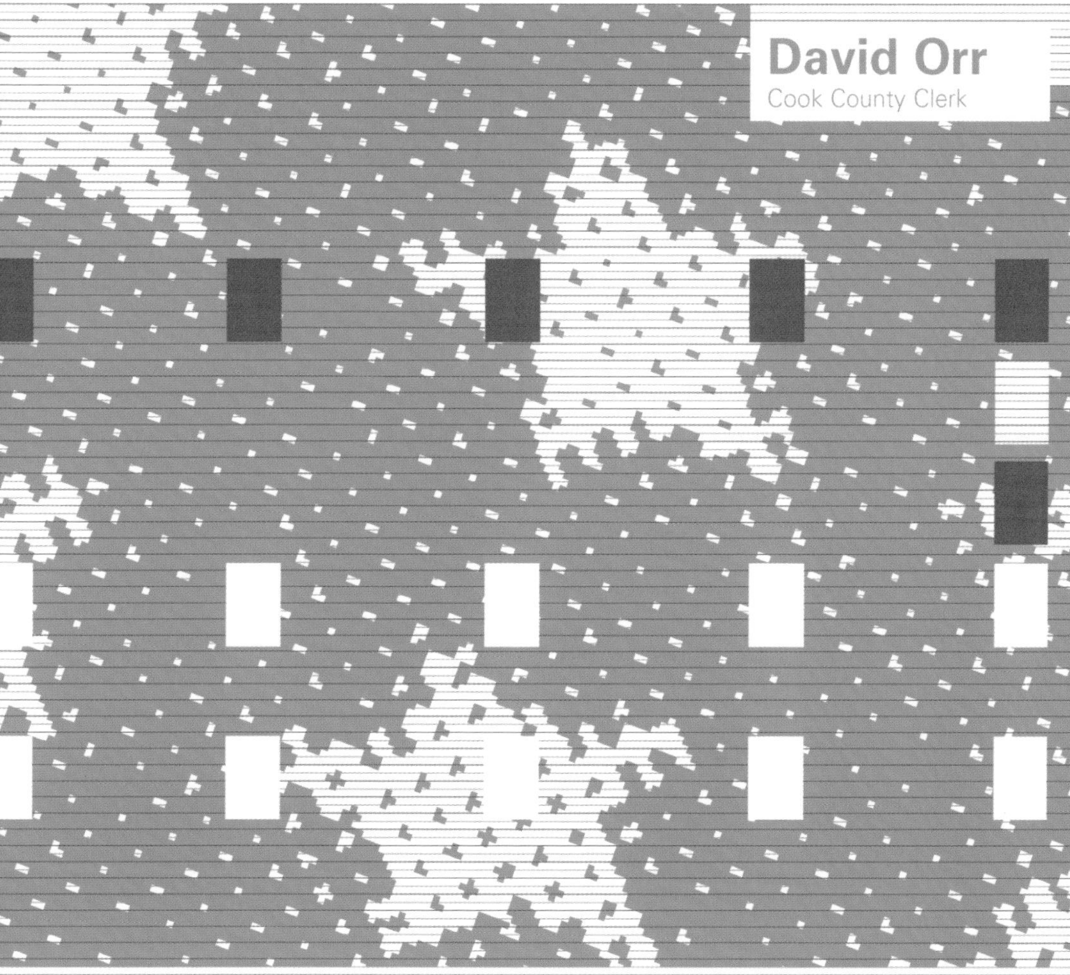

Graphics for the cover of a pollworker manual should be professionally designed. While amateur artwork may be solicited with the best of intentions, the results can be incompatible with the need to promote a culture of professional service.

Red and blue and stars and stripes are certainly appropriate election-related graphics. However, new interpretations of these well-known colors and forms, shown at left, provide a fresh look while supporting civic pride and responsibility.

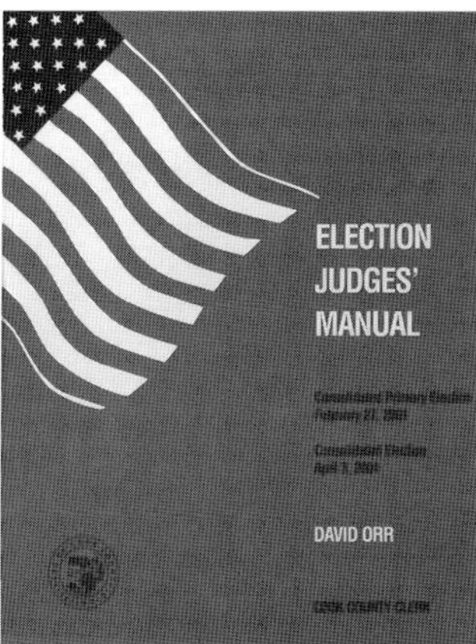

The artwork on the cover of an old Cook County election judge manual, above right, was likely selected in a student contest. While design contests are intended to involve members of the community, the results can look unprofessional.

The Cook County election judge manual, shown at right, is organized according to time-based activities, with an area in the front for general information. Sections are indicated with numbered tab dividers, allowing for easy access.

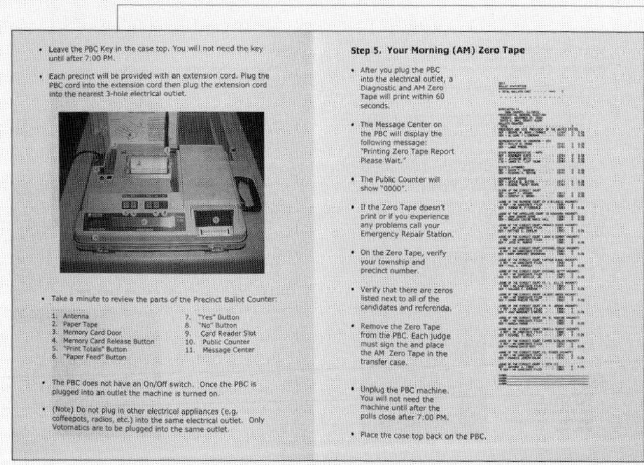

- Leave the PBC Key in the case top. You will not need the key until after 7:00 PM.
- Each precinct will be provided with an extension cord. Plug the PBC cord into the extension cord then plug the extension cord into the nearest 3-hole electrical outlet.
- Take a minute to review the parts of the Precinct Ballot Counter:

1. Antenna
2. Paper Tape
3. Memory Card Door
4. Memory Card Release Button
5. "Print Totals" Button
6. "Paper Feed" Button
7. "Yes" Button
8. "No" Button
9. Card Reader Slot
10. Public Counter
11. Message Center

- The PBC does not have an On/Off switch. Once the PBC is plugged into an outlet the machine is turned on.
- (Note) Do not plug in other electrical appliances (e.g. coffeepots, radios, etc.) into the same electrical outlet. Only Votomatics are to be plugged into the same outlet.

Step 5. Your Morning (AM) Zero Tape

- After you plug the PBC into the electrical outlet, a Diagnostic and AM Zero Tape will print within 60 seconds.
- The Message Center on the PBC will display the following message: "Printing Zero Tape Report Please Wait."
- The Public Counter will show "0000".
- If the Zero Tape doesn't print or if you experience any problems call your Emergency Repair Station.
- On the Zero Tape, verify your township and precinct number.
- Verify that there are zeros listed next to all of the candidates and referenda.
- Remove the Zero Tape from the PBC. Each judge must sign the and place the AM Zero Tape in the transfer case.
- Unplug the PBC machine. You will not need the machine until after the polls close after 7:00 PM.
- Place the case top back on the PBC.

Above, before the redesign, many years of minor edits had resulted in inconsistencies in layout, hierarchy, type size, column width, etc. Photographs are not as effective as simple diagrams that can place emphasis on the points of activity.

General Information 0

Before Election Day 1

Election Day 5:15 am to 6 am 2

2.2 Ballot counting table

Assemble the ballot counting table

1. Place the tabletop upside down on a flat surface with the leg holes facing upward. Push the four legs into the holes in the tabletop, using a twisting motion for a snug fit.
2. Stand the table upright and place the plastic ballot box, located on the top shelf of the VSC, into the ballot counting table.
3. Put the ballot box lid, found in the gray table case, on the ballot box. Use one of the nylon ties, found in the blue office supply box, to secure the lid to the ballot counting table. Place the table near an electrical outlet before continuing.

The ballot counting table is stored in a gray case outside the VSC. The ballot counting table serves as a base to hold the ballot box and the precinct ballot counter (PBC).

Ballot counting table assembly

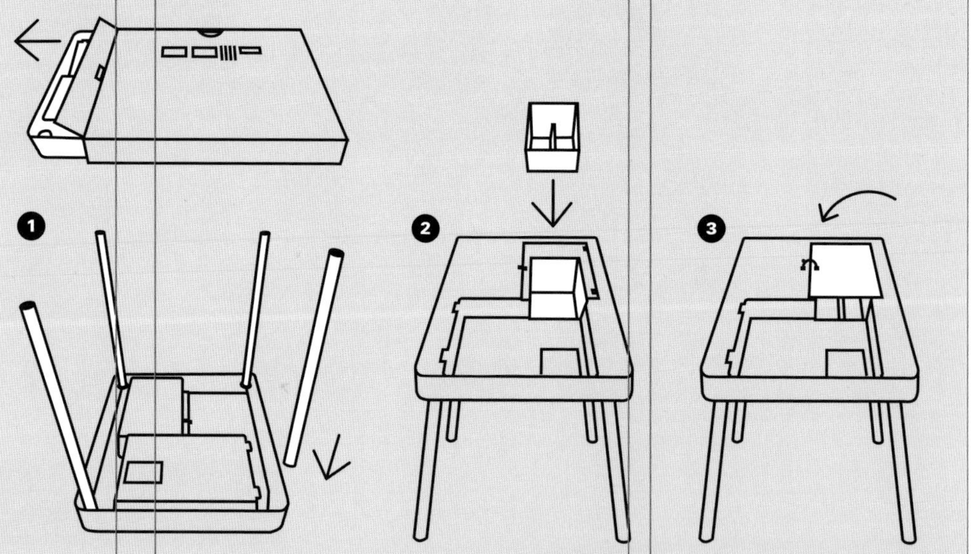

1 2 3

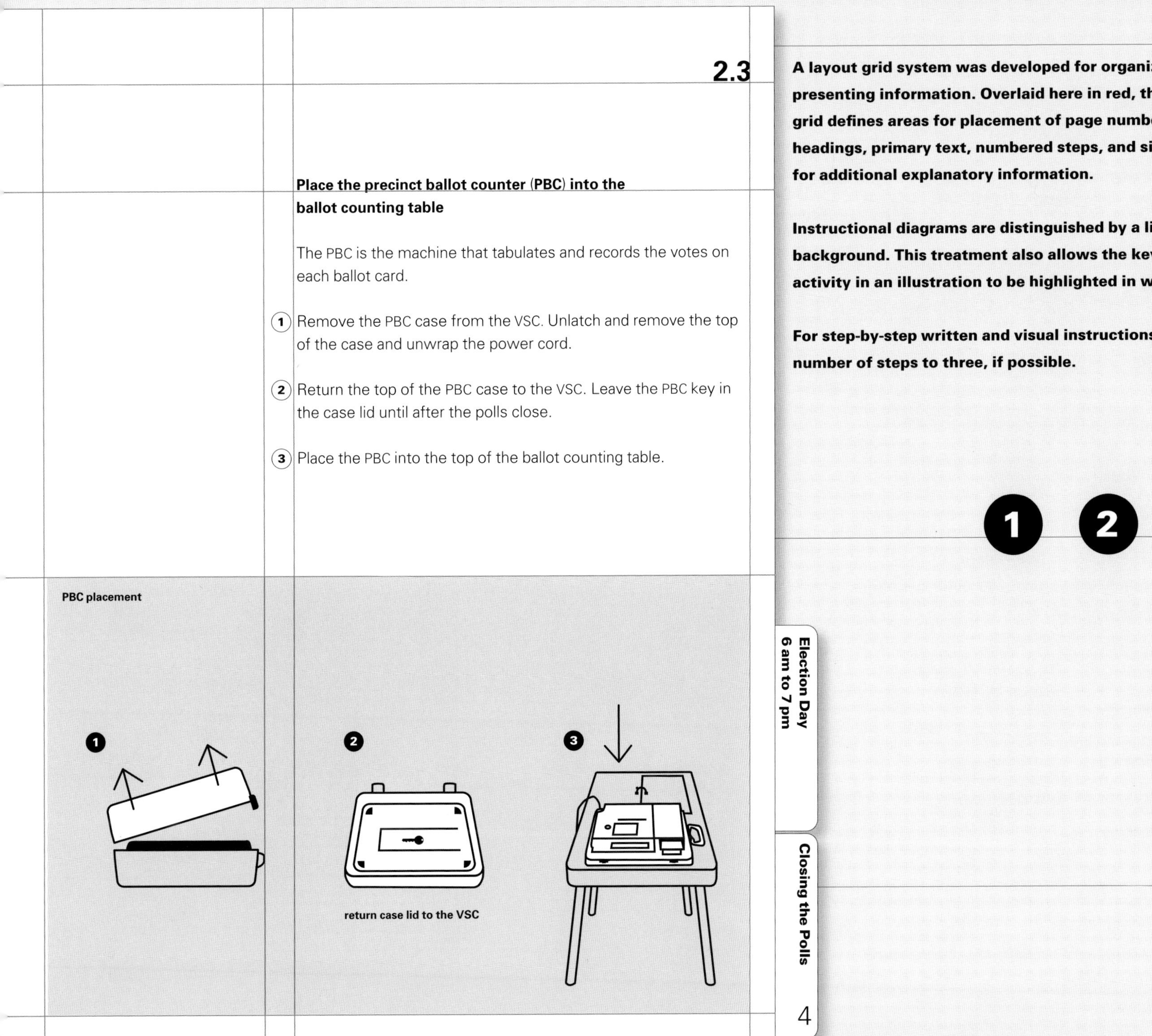

2.3

Place the precinct ballot counter (PBC) into the ballot counting table

The PBC is the machine that tabulates and records the votes on each ballot card.

1. Remove the PBC case from the VSC. Unlatch and remove the top of the case and unwrap the power cord.
2. Return the top of the PBC case to the VSC. Leave the PBC key in the case lid until after the polls close.
3. Place the PBC into the top of the ballot counting table.

PBC placement

A layout grid system was developed for organizing and presenting information. Overlaid here in red, the layout grid defines areas for placement of page numbers, headings, primary text, numbered steps, and sidebars for additional explanatory information.

Instructional diagrams are distinguished by a light gray background. This treatment also allows the key areas of activity in an illustration to be highlighted in white.

For step-by-step written and visual instructions, limit the number of steps to three, if possible.

The election judge manual employs a clearly defined typographic hierarchy, based on the same information design principles described in the previous chapter.

Because this is a reference manual, page numbers are very large, bold, and prominently placed at the top outer edge of the page. The modular numbering system always begins with the section number. Equally large page headings are placed visibly in white space near the page number. Primary instructional text is set in a large type size, with ancillary information made smaller and bolder in sidebar columns.

The entire document uses two weights of the Univers font family (45 light and 65 bold), keeping size variations to a minimum.

Main heading:
Univers 45: 22/36

Subheading/highlighted text:
Univers 65: 11.5/17

Page number:
Univers 65: 12.5/36

Primary text:
Univers 45: 12/17

Phone numbers:
Univers 65: 12.5/17

Sidebars/labels:
Univers 65: 8.5/13.5

Type specifications, above, are given in points, with type size listed first, followed by line spacing. For example, the primary text is set in Univers 45, 12 point type, on 17 points of line spacing.

General Information 0

Before Election Day 1

1.2 Supply judge duties

Visit the polling place

The supply judge will make arrangements to enter the polling place before Election Day with at least one other judge of the opposite political party from the precinct to inspect the contents of the voting supply carrier.

If you cannot gain access to your polling place prior to Election Day, call the Polling Place Department:
312 603 0973

Check the VSC's code number

The code number listed on the supply judge envelope should match the code number on the outside of the VSC and on the supplies inside the VSC.

If the code numbers do not match, call the Election Warehouse:
312 491 4000

The VSC

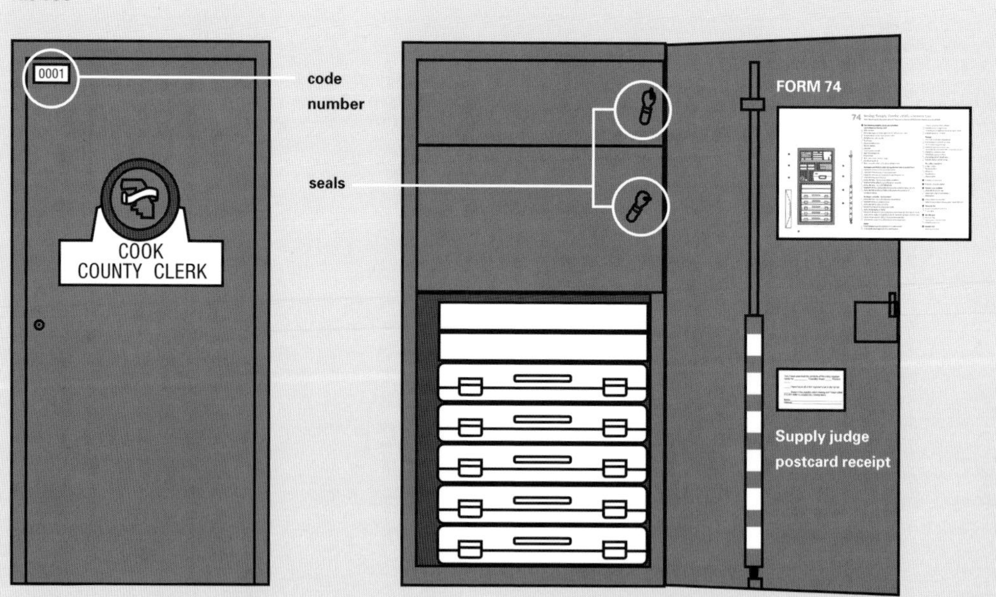

1.3

Check the VSC's contents

FORM 74

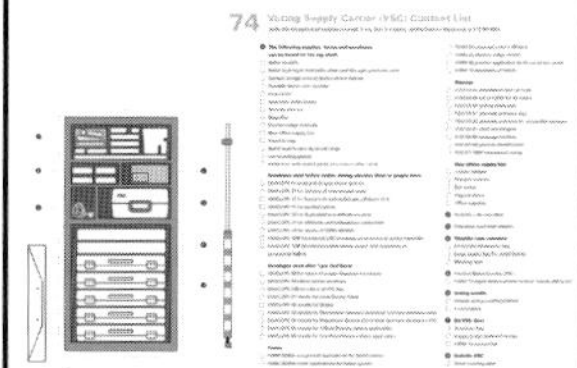

The supply judge must:
Unlock the exterior door of the VSC using the key from the supply judge envelope.

Open the interior doors of the VSC. To do this, break the two green seals by bending them back and forth. Place the broken seals on the top shelf of the VSC.

Locate a copy of the VSC content list FORM 74 inside the door of the VSC or in the supply judge envelope.

Check all of the contents of the VSC against the items on the VSC content list FORM 74.

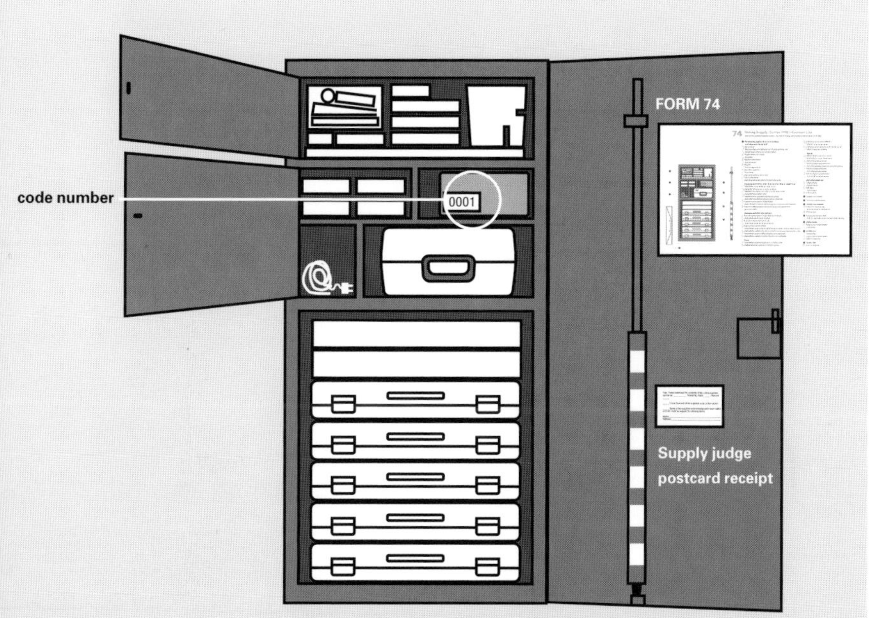

If any supplies are missing from the VSC, call the Election Warehouse:

312 491 4000

A telephone icon is used throughout the manual to indicate contact information for answering questions or responding to an emergency.

Close-up "bubbles" can be used to enlarge important areas of administrative forms and instructional diagrams. In some cases, as shown in the punchcard ballot diagram below, the enlarged area might be more effectively detailed as a photographic image.

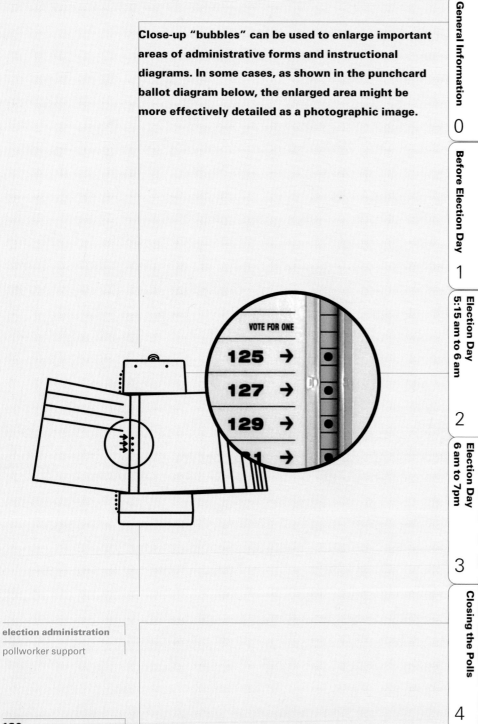

4.18 Recording provisional ballots (continued)

7. Place all Provisional Ballot ENVELOPEs 102P (with voted ballot cards inside) back into the Provisional Ballot Carrier Pouch 103P. All unused ballot cards must be returned to the VSC along with all unused Provisional Ballot ENVELOPEs 102P.

8. All election judges must sign Statement of Provisional Ballots.

9. Remove the seal from inside the purple pouch. Record the seal number and insert the Statement of Provisional Ballots back into the plastic pocket in front of the pouch.

10. Insert the seal in the lock with the number facing up. Lock the pouch with the seal number facing up so you can read it. (For complete instructions on locking the pouch, see Section 4.20)

! Return locked pouch to the receiving station.

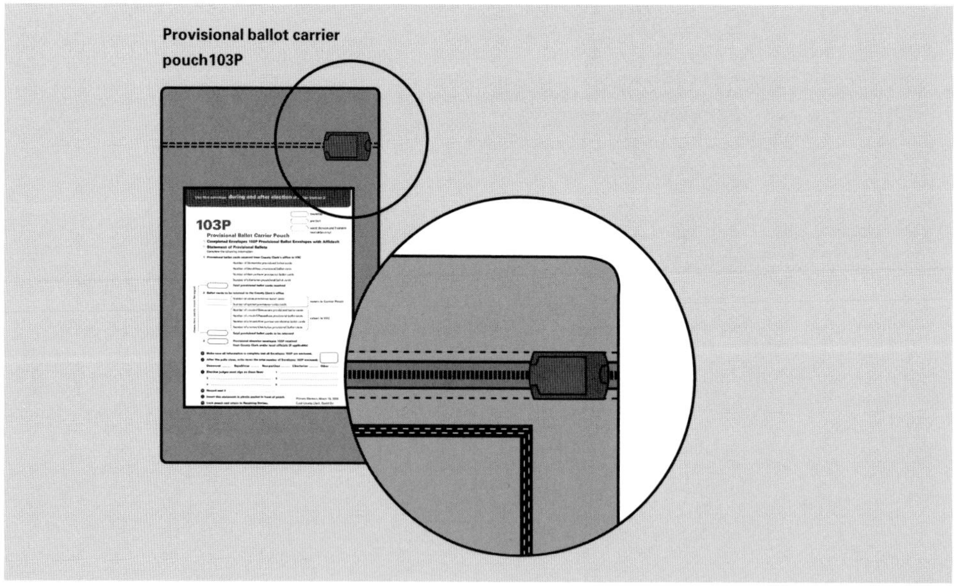

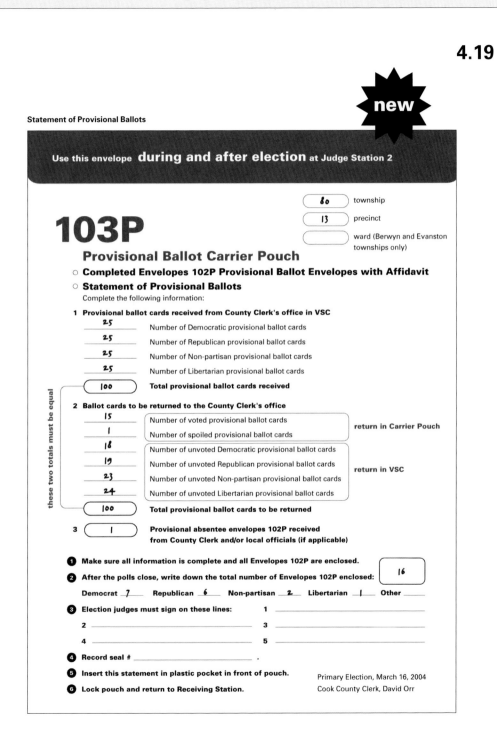

4.19

Statement of Provisional Ballots

Use this envelope **during and after election** at Judge Station 2

80 township

13 precinct

ward (Berwyn and Evanston townships only)

103P

Provisional Ballot Carrier Pouch

- **Completed Envelopes 102P Provisional Ballot Envelopes with Affidavit**
- **Statement of Provisional Ballots**

Complete the following information:

1 Provisional ballot cards received from County Clerk's office in VSC

25	Number of Democratic provisional ballot cards
25	Number of Republican provisional ballot cards
25	Number of Non-partisan provisional ballot cards
25	Number of Libertarian provisional ballot cards
100	**Total provisional ballot cards received**

2 Ballot cards to be returned to the County Clerk's office

15	Number of voted provisional ballot cards	**return in Carrier Pouch**
1	Number of spoiled provisional ballot cards	
18	Number of unvoted Democratic provisional ballot cards	**return in VSC**
19	Number of unvoted Republican provisional ballot cards	
23	Number of unvoted Non-partisan provisional ballot cards	
24	Number of unvoted Libertarian provisional ballot cards	
100	**Total provisional ballot cards to be returned**	

these two totals must be equal

3 1 **Provisional absentee envelopes 102P received from County Clerk and/or local officials (if applicable)**

1. **Make sure all information is complete and all Envelopes 102P are enclosed.**
2. **After the polls close, write down the total number of Envelopes 102P enclosed:** 16

   Democrat 7 **Republican** 6 **Non-partisan** 2 **Libertarian** 1 **Other** ____
3. **Election judges must sign on these lines:** 1 ____ 2 ____ 3 ____ 4 ____ 5 ____
4. **Record seal #** ____ .
5. **Insert this statement in plastic pocket in front of pouch.**
6. **Lock pouch and return to Receiving Station.**

Primary Election, March 16, 2004
Cook County Clerk, David Orr

Full-page examples of the administrative forms that will be encountered in the polling place help pollworkers to become familiar with detailed procedures in advance of election day.

In addition to the telephone icon used for indicating contact information, the redesigned election judge manual introduced the use of icons for indicating new policies and procedures and for special warnings.

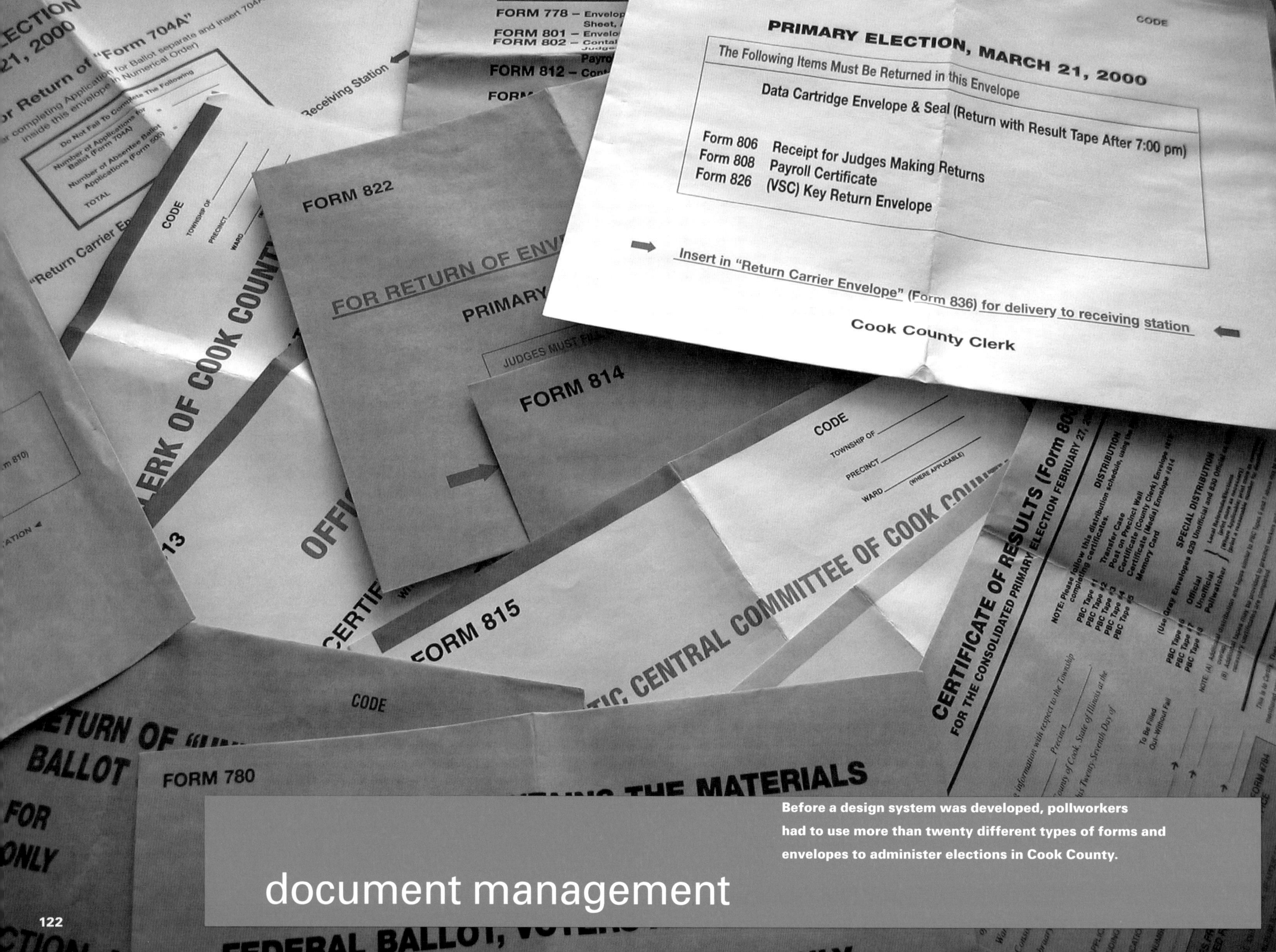

Before a design system was developed, pollworkers had to use more than twenty different types of forms and envelopes to administer elections in Cook County.

document management

Behind the scenes an election can seem frighteningly chaotic, and sometimes the chaos is real. There are dozens of forms—often with revised procedures for each new election—to be designed, printed, and completed. It is remarkable that election officials and pollworkers are able to keep up with the extraordinary quantity of election-related paperwork.

Further complications are caused by government requirements for obtaining competitive bids from printers and by the desire of elected officials to spread print work throughout a regional voting constituency. The efficiencies and quality control that can be achieved with a single trusted supplier are not generally available. Additionally, in elections it is all too common to treat printers as designers. Without an established design system and with a variety of printers involved, inconsistent quality of administrative materials is inevitable.

The design of administrative forms and envelopes can be improved by introducing

→ A design system that is visually consistent and intuitive
→ Modular sizing that establishes a direct relationship between an envelope and its contents
→ Color coding based on time-of-day usage and final delivery destination
→ A consistent information hierarchy through controlled placement, size, and weight of typography
→ Quality control guidelines that can be distributed to print suppliers

Developing a comprehensive design system for forms and envelopes requires close collaboration with election officials. Design for Democracy worked with the Office of the Cook County Clerk to evaluate its existing (and initially confusing) array of administrative materials. By determining specific functions and usage issues for all form types, more than twenty indeterminate variations in size, color, and paper stock were narrowed down to three distinct formats to be printed on three paper stocks.

Envelope sizes now relate to their contents. Custom ballot-shaped manila envelopes were designed to contain unused or spoiled punchcard ballots. Small envelopes contain results tapes, keys, seals, or other small items. Large envelopes are designed to contain sets of smaller forms and envelopes for transport or storage .

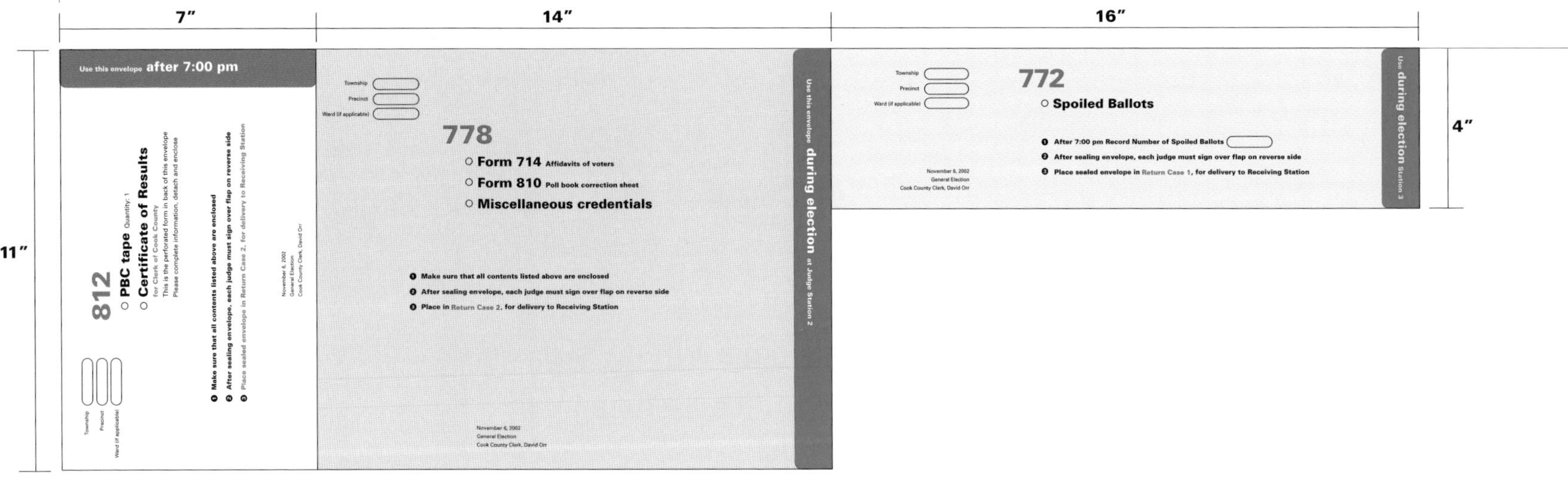

Above, the sizes of the document management system are modular. Large envelopes are twice the size of small envelopes, and custom-size envelopes hold unused or spoiled ballots. Prior to the redesign, the many different sizes of envelopes did not always relate to their contents.

Every design element in the document management system has informational meaning. The color of paper indicates the final destination of each envelope. White envelopes are to be delivered back to the clerk's office, gray envelopes are to be returned to the voting supply carrier, and manila envelopes are for ballot storage. Envelopes with a blue band are used before and during the election, and those with a red band are for use after the polls close. Form numbers are printed very large, in color, with consistent placement, and areas of the forms that require handwritten information are clearly indicated. The same set of icons used in the training and reference manual is used to indicate alerts and warnings. Contents lists are similar in design to the voting supply carrier checklist (see page 113).

812

Code #

Township

Precinct

Ward
(Berwyn and Evanston Townships only)

use this envelope **during election**

use this envelope **after 7pm**

Design elements of the document management system include alert icons, fill-in blanks, large form numbers, and color coding for timed usage.

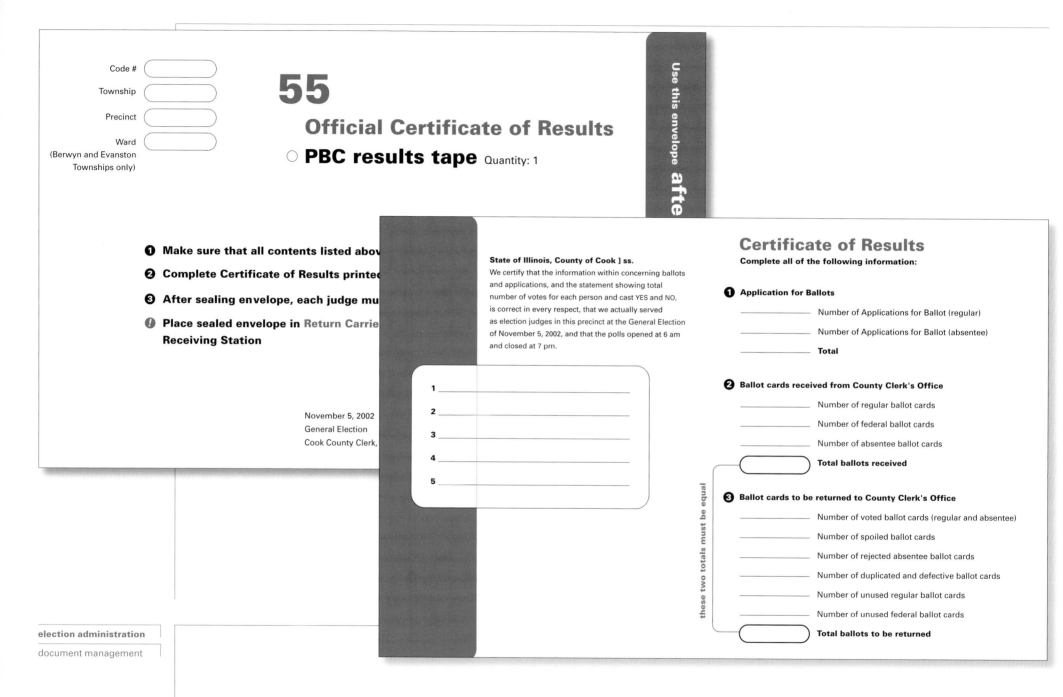

Code #

Township

Precinct

Ward
(Berwyn and Evanston
Townships only)

55

Official Certificate of Results

○ **PBC results tape** Quantity: 1

Use this envelope afte

1. **Make sure that all contents listed abov**
2. **Complete Certificate of Results printe**
3. **After sealing envelope, each judge mu**
4. **Place sealed envelope in Return Carrie**
Receiving Station

November 5, 2002
General Election
Cook County Clerk,

State of Illinois, County of Cook] ss.
We certify that the information within concerning ballots and applications, and the statement showing total number of votes for each person and cast YES and NO, is correct in every respect, that we actually served as election judges in this precinct at the General Election of November 5, 2002, and that the polls opened at 6 am and closed at 7 pm.

1 ____________
2 ____________
3 ____________
4 ____________
5 ____________

Certificate of Results

Complete all of the following information:

1. **Application for Ballots**
   - ______ Number of Applications for Ballot (regular)
   - ______ Number of Applications for Ballot (absentee)
   - ______ **Total**

2. **Ballot cards received from County Clerk's Office**
   - ______ Number of regular ballot cards
   - ______ Number of federal ballot cards
   - ______ Number of absentee ballot cards
   - ______ **Total ballots received**

3. **Ballot cards to be returned to County Clerk's Office**
   - ______ Number of voted ballot cards (regular and absentee)
   - ______ Number of spoiled ballot cards
   - ______ Number of rejected absentee ballot cards
   - ______ Number of duplicated and defective ballot cards
   - ______ Number of unused regular ballot cards
   - ______ Number of unused federal ballot cards
   - ______ **Total ballots to be returned**

these two totals must be equal

store ballots

31
Spoiled Ballots

32
Duplicated and Defective Ballots

return to voting supply carrier

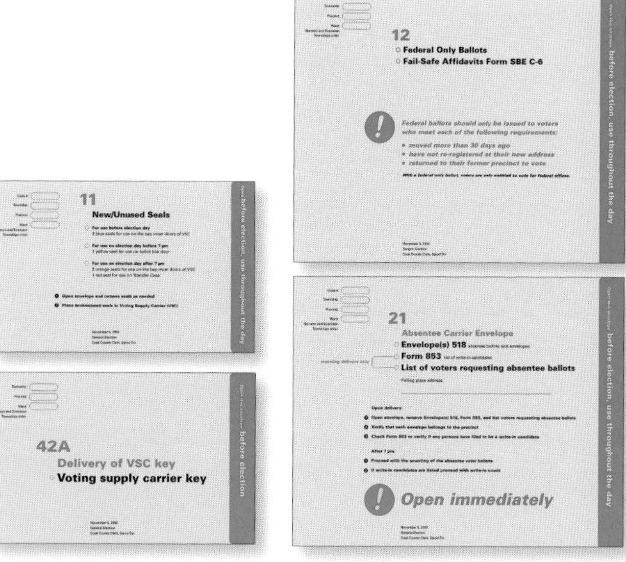

return to clerk's office

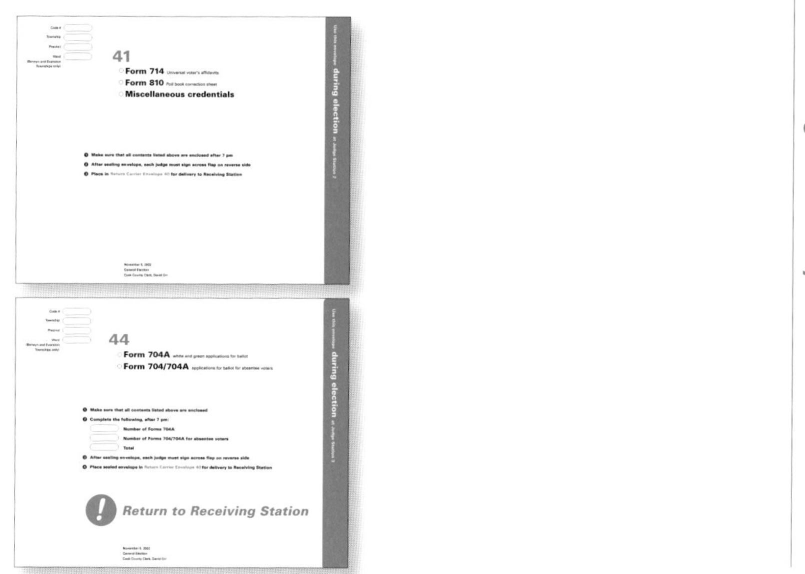

use during election day

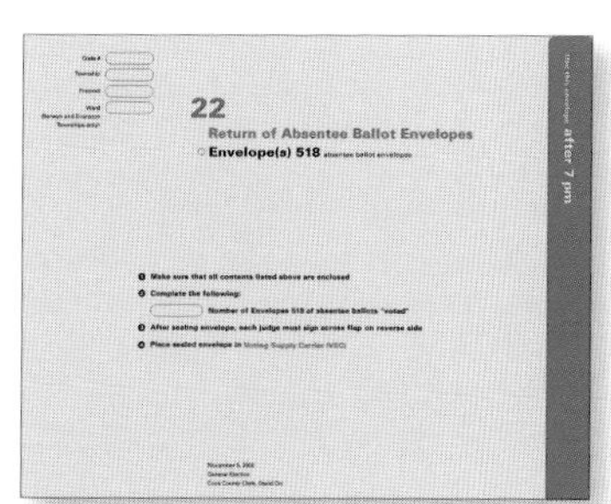

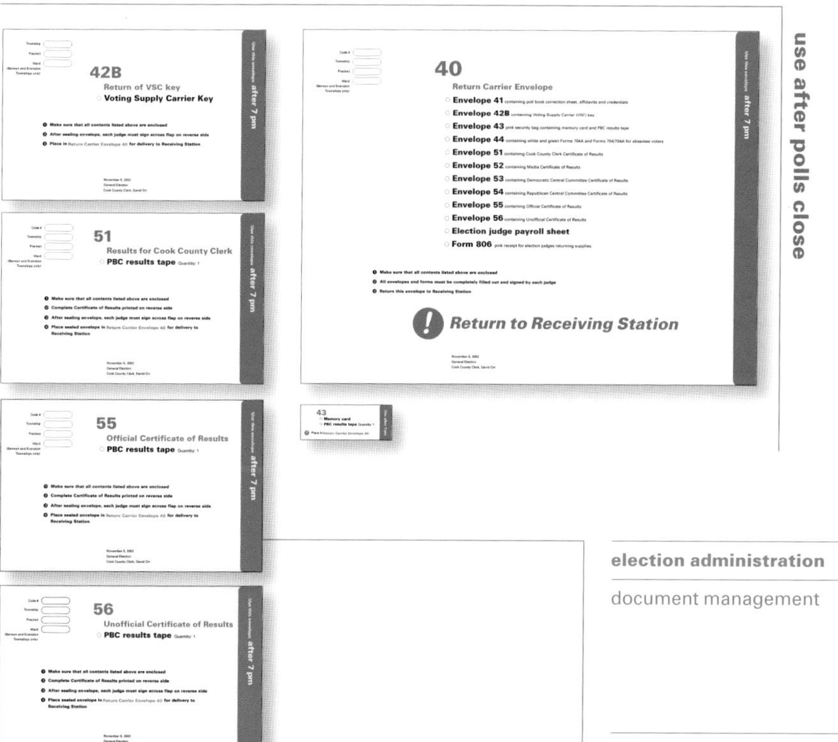

use after polls close

Above, a map of the document management system illustrates the variations in sizing and in paper and print colors. Shown at left are the front and back of a form that requires a special security feature: the signature of all pollworkers in the precinct across the seal of the envelope.

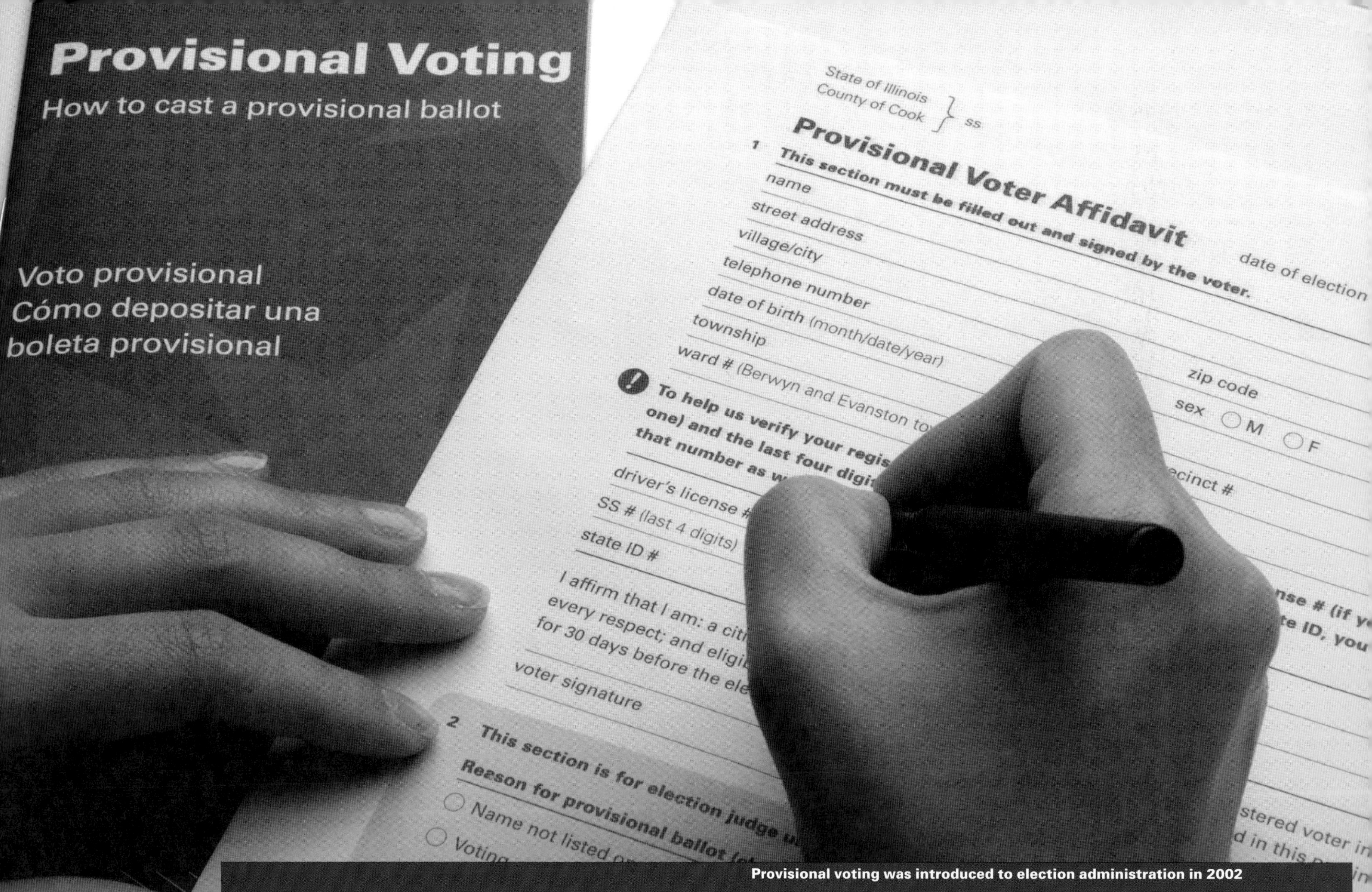

Provisional voting was introduced to election administration in 2002 by the Help America Vote Act.

provisional voting

A successful information design system can be adapted and expanded to solve new problems. For the Design for Democracy document management system, the first major expansion came with the introduction of provisional voting, mandated by the Help America Vote Act of 2002.

Provisional voting permits a voter whose record of registration cannot be found on election day to cast a ballot. A provisional ballot is held separately and is counted if and when the voter's registration is verified. For pollworkers already busy with their regular administrative duties, provisional voting further increases the amount of paperwork to be completed on election day.

To clearly identify all administrative and informational materials related to provisional voting, a new color, purple, was introduced to the design system. All other elements are identical.

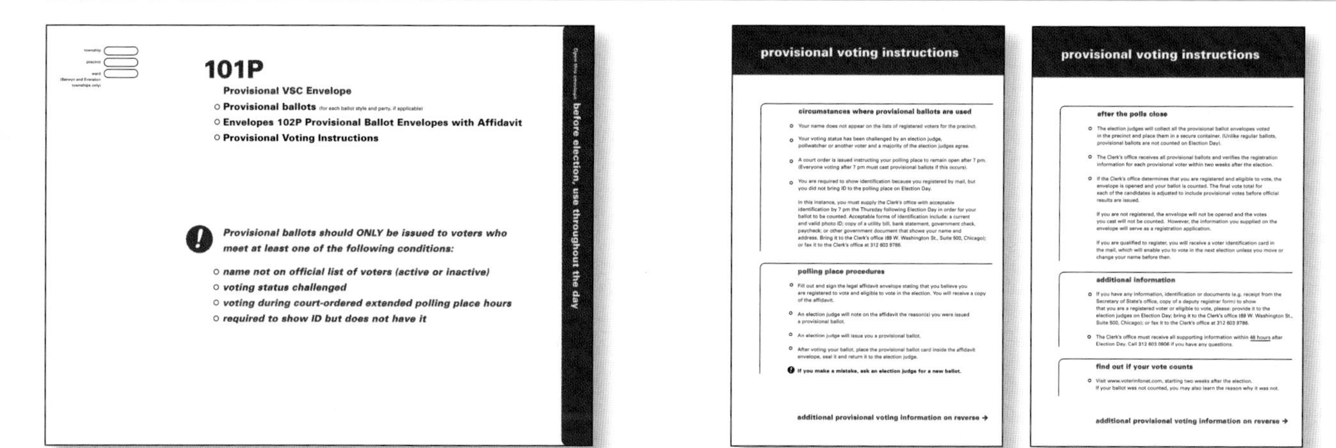

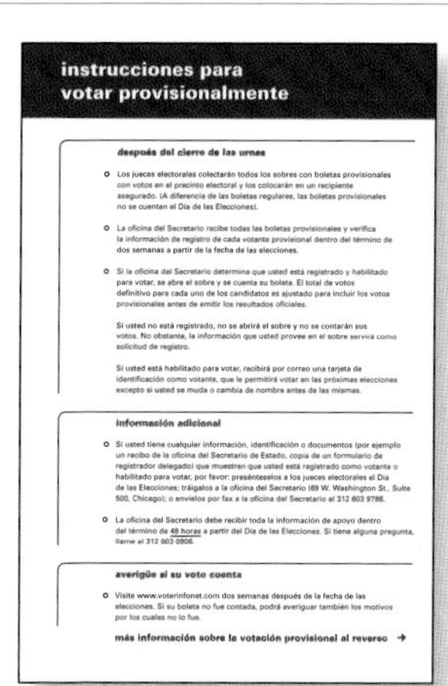

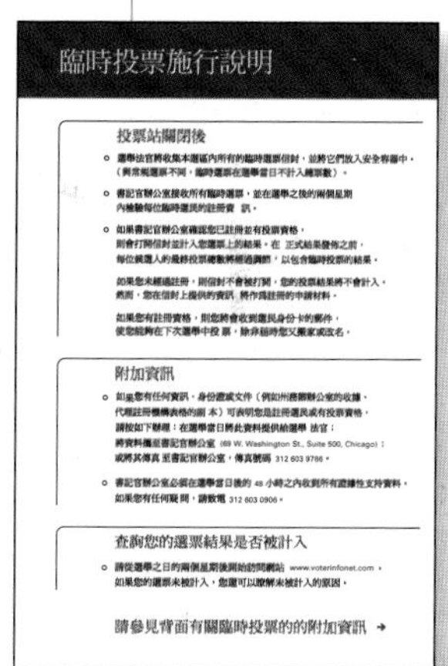

A purple color is used to identify all materials related to provisional voting.

Administrative forms and envelopes for provisional voting use the same design elements as the original system: Color-coded bars indicate when the materials should be used; very large form numbers help pollworkers to identify the needed documents; procedures are indicated by step-by-step instructions; and blanks to be filled in are clearly indicated.

The purple color differentiates provisional voting forms from other administrative materials.

Some provisional voting forms, such as the Provisional Voter Affidavit, shown on the facing page, are used not only by pollworkers but also by voters who cast provisional ballots.

Use this envelope **during and after election** at Judge Station 2

township

precinct

ward
(Berwyn and Evanston townships only)

103P

Provisional Ballot Carrier Pouch

○ **Completed Envelopes 102P Provisional Ballot Envelopes with Affidavit**

○ **Statement of Provisional Ballots**

these two totals must be equal

1 Provisional ballot cards received from County Clerk's office in VSC

______ Number of provisional ballot cards

Total provisional ballot cards received

2 Ballot cards to be returned to the County Clerk's office

______ Number of voted provisional ballot cards — **return in Carrier Pouch**

______ Number of spoiled provisional ballot cards — **return in Carrier Pouch**

______ Number of unvoted provisional ballot cards — **return in VSC**

Total provisional ballot cards to be returned

3 Provisional absentee envelopes 102P received from County Clerk and/or local officials (if applicable)

1. **Make sure all information is complete and all Envelopes 102P are enclosed.**
2. **After the polls close, write down the total number of Envelopes 102P enclosed:**
3. **Election judges must sign on these lines:** 1 ______ 2 ______ 3 ______ 4 ______ 5 ______
4. **Record seal #** ______
5. **Insert this statement in plastic pocket in front of pouch.**
6. **Lock pouch and return to Receiving Station.**

General Election, November 2, 2004

The provisional voting form that the voter must fill out may be needed in multiple languages. Consistent with multiple-language ballots, different versions of the form are printed, each with no more than one alternate language.

伊利諾州 } ss
庫克縣

臨時選民宣誓書

1 本節必須由選民來填寫和簽署。

姓名

街道地址

村/市

電話號碼

出生日期（月/日/年）

鎮區

城市選區編號（僅限伯溫市和埃文斯頓市）

駕駛執照號碼

社會安全號（最後四位數字）

本州身份證號碼

選民簽字

2 This section is for election judge use only.

Reason for provisional ballot (check all that

Name not listed on official list of eligible vo

Voting status challenged

Voting during court-ordered extended pollin

Required to show ID but does not have it

Party ballot given to voter (primary only)

Democratic / Republican

Non-partisan (if applicable) / Libertarian

election judge name

election judge signature

comments

State of Illinois } ss
County of Cook

Declaración Jurada pa

1 Esta sección debe ser llenada y firmada

nombre

domicilio

ciudad

número de teléfono

fecha de nacimiento (mes/fecha/año)

distrito municipal

\# de circunscripción (solo aplica para Berwyn

Para verificar su estatus como votante,
conducir (si tiene una) y los últimos cua
un documento de identidad estatal, pue

\# de licencia de conducir

\# de seguro social (últimos 4 dígitos)

\# de documento de identidad estatal

Declaro que soy ciudadano de los Estados
un votante debidamente registrado en tod
He residido en este estado y en este distrit
elecciones y no he votado en estas eleccio

firma del votante

2 This section is for election judge use on

Reason for provisional ballot (check all t

Name not listed on official list of eligibl

Voting status challenged

Voting during court-ordered extended p

Required to show ID but does not have

Party ballot given to voter (primary only

Democratic / Repub

Non-partisan (if applicable) / Liberta

election judge name

election judge signature

comments

State of Illinois } ss
County of Cook

Provisional Voter Affidavit date of election

1 **This section must be filled out and signed by the voter.**

name

street address

village/city zip code

telephone number sex ○ M ○ F

date of birth (month/date/year)

township precinct #

ward # (Berwyn and Evanston townships only)

To help us verify your registration status, please list your driver's license # (if you have one) and the last four digits of your Social Security #. If you have a state ID, you may list that number as well.

driver's license #

SS # (last 4 digits)

state ID #

I affirm that I am: a citizen of the United States; at least 18 years old; a duly registered voter in every respect; and eligible to vote in this election. I have resided in this state and in this precinct for 30 days before the election and have not voted in this election.

voter signature

2 **This section is for election judge use only.**

Reason for provisional ballot (check all that apply)

○ Name not listed on official list of eligible voters (active or inactive)

○ Voting status challenged

○ Voting during court-ordered extended polling place hours

○ Required to show ID but does not have it

Party ballot given to voter (primary only)

○ Democratic ○ Republican

○ Non-partisan (if applicable) ○ Libertarian (if applicable) ○ Other (if applicable)

election judge name

election judge signature

comments

Use this envelope **during election** at Judge Station 2

date of election

township

precinct

ward (Berwyn and Evanston townships only)

102P

Provisional Ballot Envelope with Affidavit

1. **Voter must fill out and sign the affidavit on the reverse side**
2. **An election judge must fill out and sign the bottom portion of the affidavit**
3. **Give one copy of the completed affidavit to the voter. The other two copies must remain attached to the envelope.**
4. **Voter must insert voted provisional ballot and seal the envelope.**
5. **Election judges must place this completed envelope in the carrier pouch.**

Place any documentation or materials provided by the voter that supports his/her registration in the attached plastic pocket.

To be completed by Cook County Clerk's Office:

Validated by ____________ ○ Valid ○ Invalid

Above, the provisional voting form to be completed by both the voter and the pollworker. Shown at reduced size, from left to right, are English/Chinese, English/Spanish, and English only versions.

in this section

the *vote!* logo

A simple visual mark that encapsulates the voting experience

color palette + typography

Basic building blocks of the election design system

symbols + icons

Simplify communication with universal visual language

illustration + photography

Images that provide information and add visual interest

The Design for Democracy election design system is a comprehensive program for improving the quality, legibility, and effectiveness of ballots and other election materials. All of the examples in this book—even the design of the book itself—were developed from this carefully conceived system of colors, typefaces, symbols, images, principles of organization, and methods of execution.

Examples on the previous pages demonstrate how the individual elements of the design system look and function as a whole. Some of these examples can be easily implemented by election officials working with print or electronic media suppliers. Other design problems require the attention of professionals versed in the principles of information design and the workings of a graphic design system. For guidance beyond simple adaptations of the examples provided, it is best to seek the services of a professional designer who has the specific skills and knowledge needed to extend the basic system into more complex or customized applications.

4 election design system

The Cross of Lorraine was chosen in 1902 as the symbol of the global fight against tuberculosis. Its designer is unknown.

One of the most enduring symbols in television is the CBS eye, designed in 1951 by William Golden.

The logo for IBM (International Business Machines) was created by design master Paul Rand in 1960.

Among the most pervasive symbols of popular culture are the McDonald's golden arches, designed by Jim Schindler and team in 1962.

A mark of certification for the International Wool Secretariat is symbolized by a ball of wool, designed by Francesco Seraglio in 1964.

One of the most widely recognized consumer logos, the Nike Swoosh was designed by a student, Carolyn Davidson, in 1971.

Symbolizing the election experience, the vote! logo was designed for AIGA Design for Democracy by a UIC student team in 2001.

the *vote!* logo

The foundation of a design system is often a logo. At its best a logo is simple, powerful, and timeless: a symbol used to establish recognition and to build identity. A logo can represent a company, a place, a product, a service, an idea, or, in the case of voting, a participatory civic experience. A symbol representing the voting experience ideally resonates with all involved: voters, politicians, election officials, pollworkers, and citizens of all ages.

A number of possible symbolic sources were considered by the team who worked to develop a logo for the U.S. voting experience. Stars and stripes, the graphic elements of the U.S. flag, have come to serve as symbols of national ideals like freedom, liberty, and democracy. These flag elements support national identity but they hold meanings beyond elections and do not specifically represent the voting experience. A check mark (✔) is a symbol more closely associated with voting, but it does not necessarily align with modern election technology. Punchcard chads and dimples, optical scan ovals and arrows, and computer screens, all more recent equivalents of the check mark, are fraught with potentially negative associations. These technology-based symbols were also ruled out. They draw attention to possible problems and to voting technologies that are likely to change with time.

The word ***vote*** is powerful, symbolic, and timeless. Developed into a logo, the word ***vote*** can come to represent the act of casting a single vote, the power of democracy, and the total voting experience.

Vote Vote
Vote
Vote
Vote
Vote
Vote
Vote
vote!
vote!
vote!
vote!
vote!
vote!
vote!
¡vota!

The Design for Democracy ***vote!*** logo was created to embody and communicate positive qualities inherent in the U.S. voting experience:

voice	*participation*	*activity*
confidence	*dedication*	*duty*
pride	*enthusiasm*	*community*

The word ***vote*** makes an ideal logo. It is simple and clear; immediate and expressive. It also functions as both a noun and a verb. The verb form is created by adding an exclamation point; this expresses the qualities of *voice, enthusiasm*, *activity*, and *duty*. The qualities of *participation* and *community* are expressed by using friendly, accessible lowercase letters—each letter a slightly different style, distinct but connected. The qualities of *confidence*, *dedication*, and *pride* are expressed through the strong bold weight of the type.

The ***vote!*** logo is freely available for use by any election authority. English and Spanish versions can be downloaded from the Design for Democracy website (www.designfordemocracy.org).

At left, development sketches for the *vote!* logo. University of Illinois at Chicago, School of Art and Design, spring 2001.

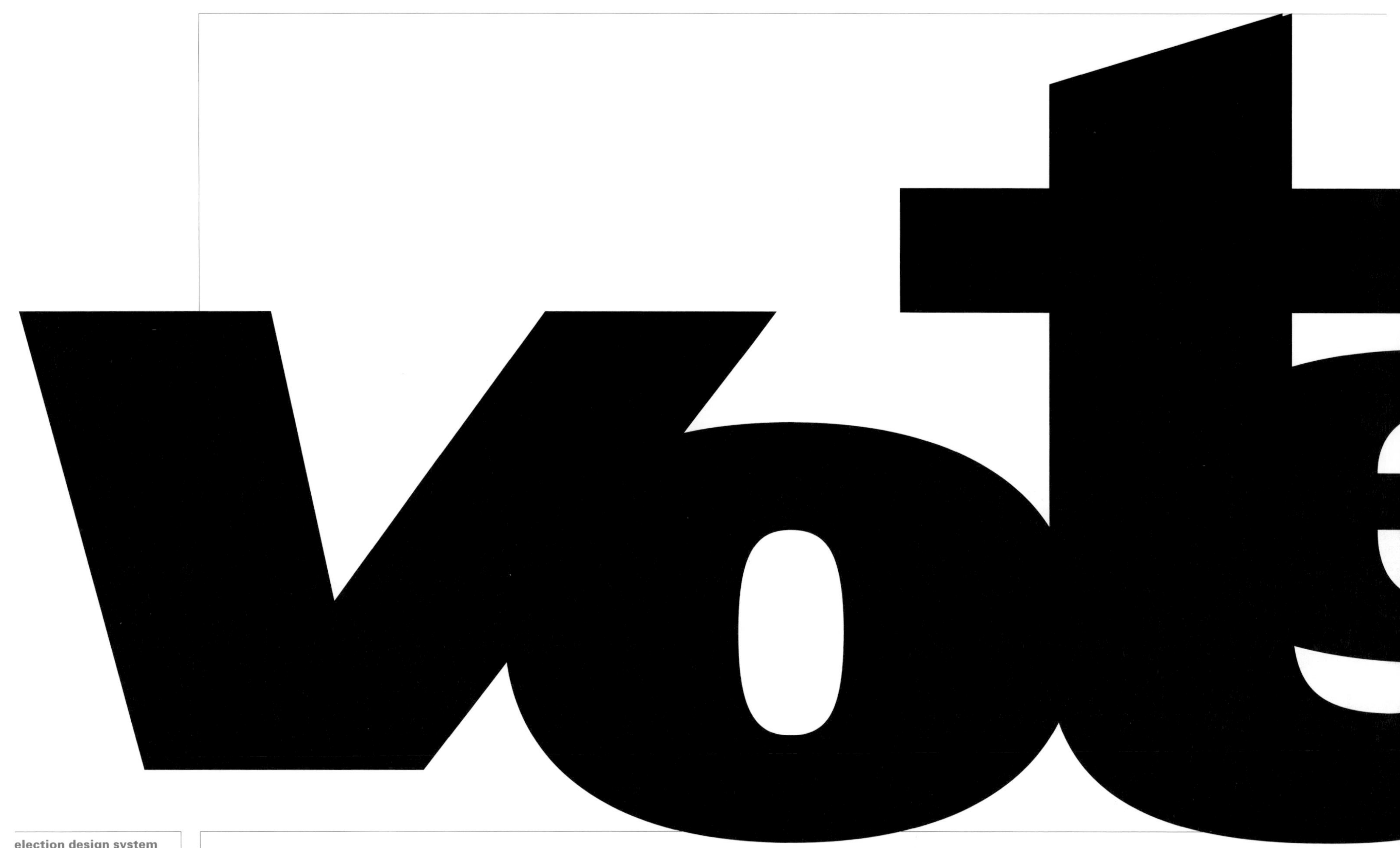

the *vote!* logo: size limits

The *vote!* logo is shown at right in various uses, including outdoor advertising in Oregon, with Secretary of State Bill Bradbury.

Maximum size:

Enlarge the *vote!* logo to any size. There are no maximum size restrictions.

Minimum size:

Do not reproduce the *vote!* logo smaller than .75 inches. (4.5 picas, 2cm, 54 pixels)

Cap height of type

register and

November 2, 2004

State General Election

To add custom messages to the *vote!* logo, place type above or below the logo, as shown above and on the facing page.

the *vote!* logo: type usage

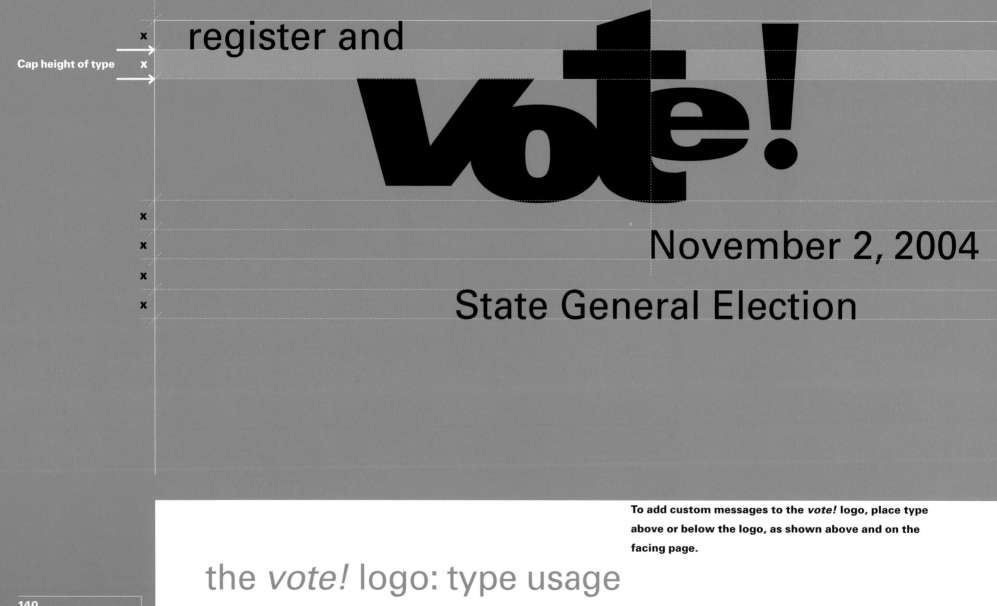

register and vote!

registrate y ¡vota!

November 2, 2004 vote!

It counts.

vote!

Let your voice be heard.

2 de noviembre del 2004 ¡vota!

Tu voto cuenta.

Oregon

vote!

March 16, 2004

Font:

Use Univers 55 as the typeface to add messages to the *vote!* logo.

Size:

Cap height of the type should match the height of the crossbar of the "t" in the logo, as shown in measurement "x" on the facing page.

hava graphics

As discussed in chapters 1 and 3, the Help America Vote Act (HAVA) of 2002 mandates a series of improvements that affect all areas of election administration. Changes in voter registration, voting equipment, and the administration of provisional voting are examples of HAVA initiatives that have a direct effect on the voters' experience.

To help share HAVA initiatives and their resulting improvements with constituents, some states have created special graphics to use in printed materials and on websites. Unfortunately, these HAVA graphics are often executed in an amateurish style, plagued by visual clichés and confusing use of type and color. Design for Democracy enthusiastically supports the use of graphics in HAVA-related communications to voters and has developed several versions of a HAVA logo—an extension of the ***vote!*** logo—that embody the same characteristics of confidence, pride, participation, and dedication that underlie the entire election design system. HAVA graphics are available along with the ***vote!*** logo on the Design for Democracy website.

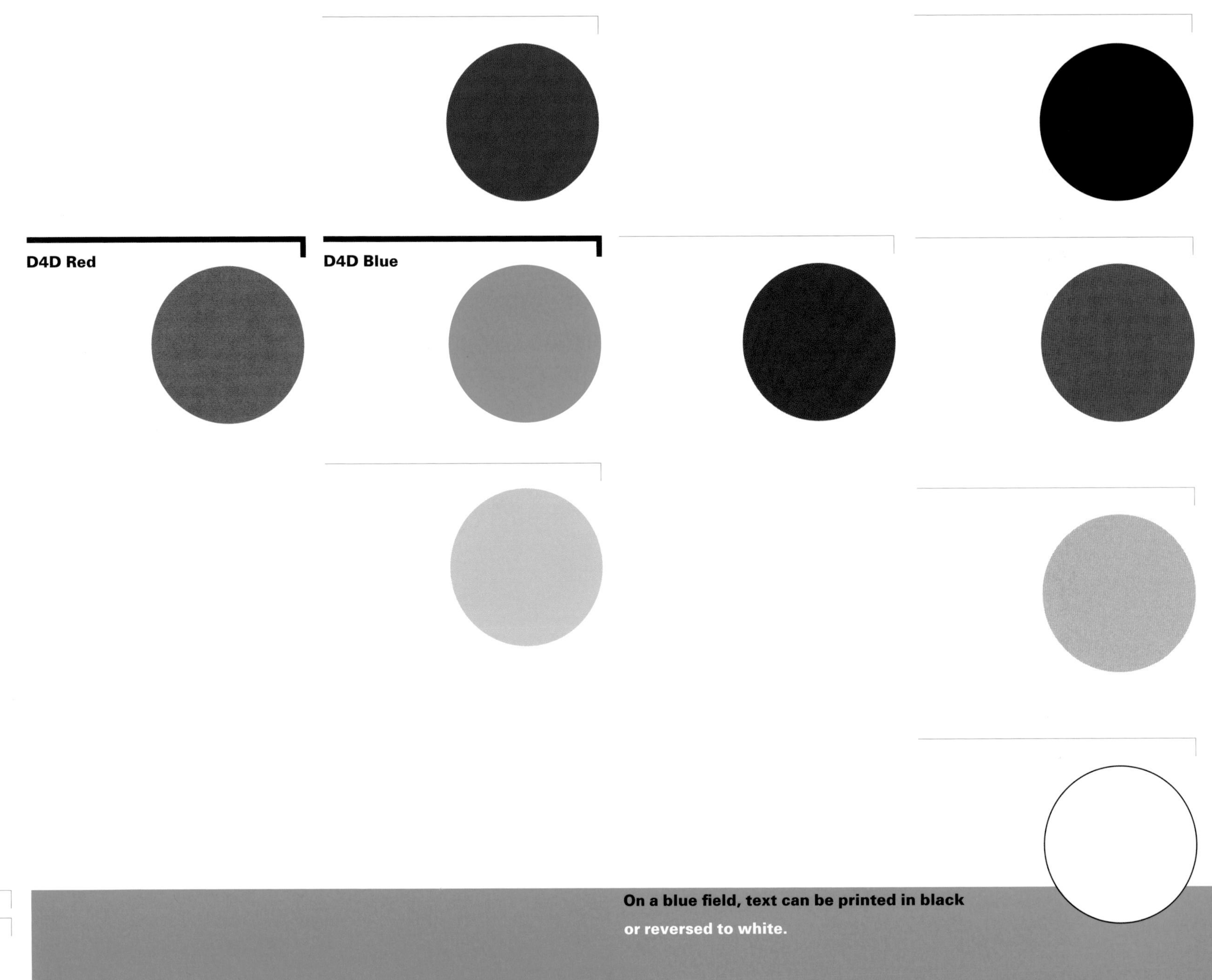

On a blue field, text can be printed in black or reversed to white.

color palette

Color plays an important role in the Design for Democracy election design system. A specific palette of colors has been selected to achieve the best possible communication results.

Red and blue are the core colors of the palette. Both were derived from the U.S. flag and adjusted for use in print and electronic media. The palette's red was selected for warmth, vibrancy, and impact, while its blue was chosen for its calm, approachable, friendly qualities. Type and graphics are legible in either black or white when printed on background fields of the palette's red or blue—a useful flexibility that cannot be achieved with the actual colors of the U.S. flag. Darker and lighter versions of blue can be used in the system. Purple, which combines red and blue, is a logical addition. Black, gray, and white are useful neutral colors.

Green and yellow are useful in many jurisdictions where party affiliations need to be distinguished in primary elections. Green is also useful in the palette for its association with environmental awareness. Finally, lighter shades of gray and yellow can be used to distinguish areas of special use on forms and other administrative materials.

Color can add cost to printed materials. Many of the examples in this book use only one or two colors.

Red

D4D Red

PANTONE® 1788

CMYK: 80M 85Y

RGB: 200R 100G 75B

Blue

D4D Blue

PANTONE® 279

CMYK: 70C 60M 35K

RGB: 120R 150G 200B

Purple

D4D Purple

PANTONE® 668

CMYK: 70C 60M 35K

RGB: 90R 95G 140B

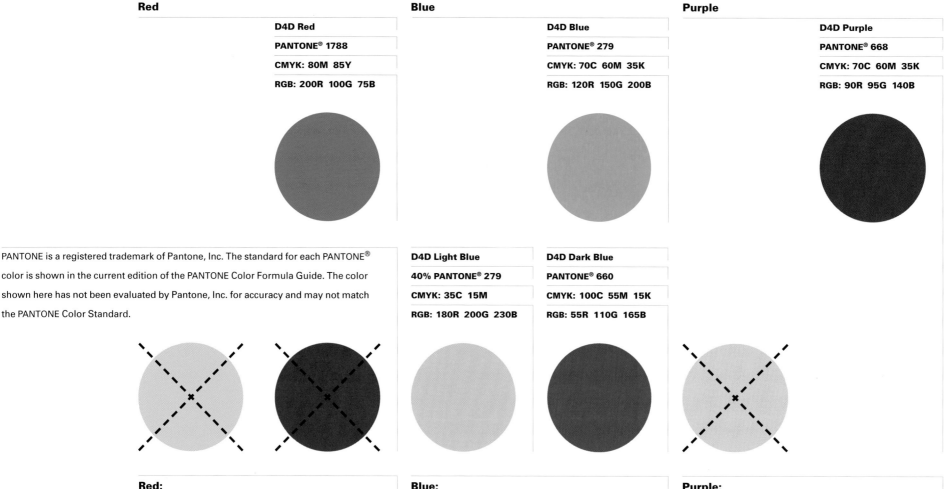

PANTONE is a registered trademark of Pantone, Inc. The standard for each PANTONE® color is shown in the current edition of the PANTONE Color Formula Guide. The color shown here has not been evaluated by Pantone, Inc. for accuracy and may not match the PANTONE Color Standard.

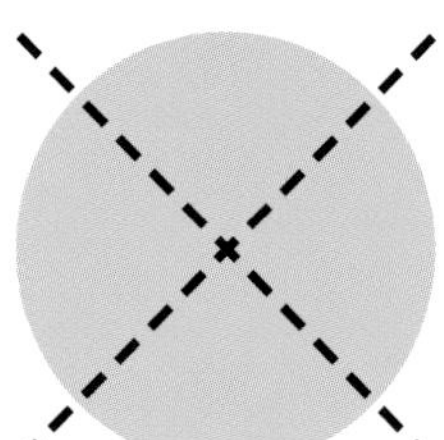

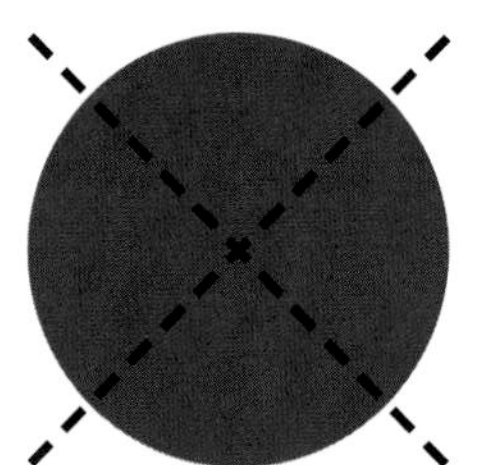

D4D Light Blue

40% PANTONE® 279

CMYK: 35C 15M

RGB: 180R 200G 230B

D4D Dark Blue

PANTONE® 660

CMYK: 100C 55M 15K

RGB: 55R 110G 165B

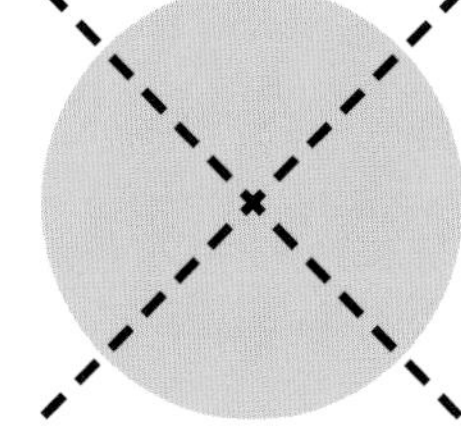

Red:

The design system's red is more vibrant and energetic than the red of the American flag. Use red for impact when communicating instruction and warning.

Blue:

The blue of the design system is more friendly and flexible than that of the U.S. flag. Blue is the system's most versatile color. It can be used successfully in many applications.

Purple:

The combination of red and blue, purple is a logical addition to the design system palette. One use of purple is to distinguish the administrative materials for provisional voting.

Caution:

Lighter versions of red appear pink or salmon and should be used sparingly. Darker versions have less energy and can appear harsh.

Do:

Use darker and lighter values of blue, if necessary, to achieve the desired message.

Caution:

Lighter versions of purple can appear pastel. Soft or subdued colors are not in alignment with the system's communication goals: confidence, pride, enthusiasm, activity, etc.

Green

D4D Green
PANTONE® 577
CMYK: 20C 45Y 10K
RGB: 195R 210G 160B

D4D Light Green
50% PANTONE® 577
CMYK: 10C 20Y
RGB: 225R 240G 210B

Yellow

D4D Yellow
PANTONE® 1215
CMYK: 35Y
RGB: 250R 245G 180B

D4D Light Yellow
50% PANTONE® 1215
CMYK: 15Y
RGB: 250R 250G 220B

Neutrals

Black
PANTONE® Process Black
CMYK: 100K
RGB: 0R 0G 0B

Dark Gray
50% Process Black
CMYK: 50K
RGB: 145R 145G 145B

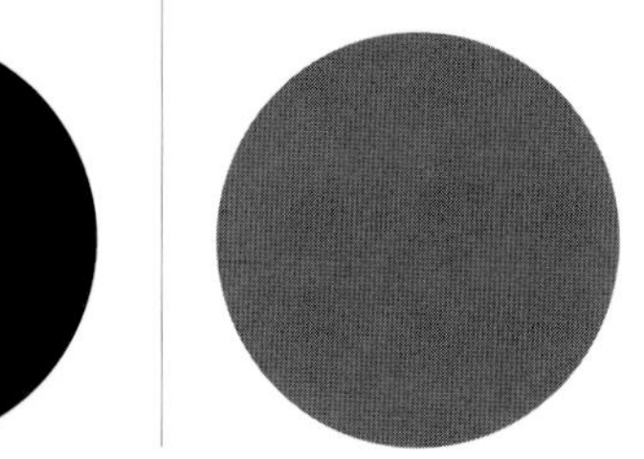

Light Gray
20% Process Black
CMYK: 20K
RGB: 210R 210G 210B

White

CMYK: 0C 0M 0Y 0K
RGB: 255R 255G 255B

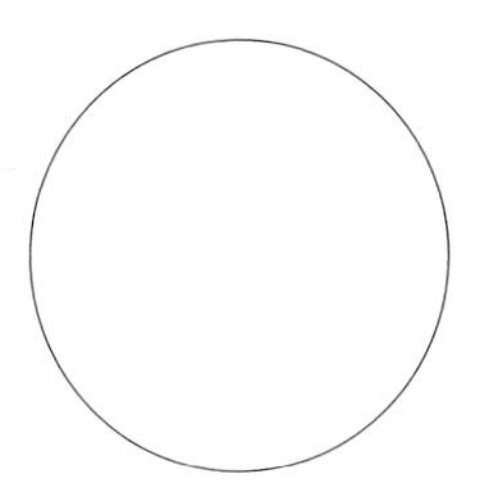

Green:
Often used in primary elections to indicate the Democratic Party.

Yellow:
Often used in primary elections to indicate the Republican Party.

Black, Gray, White:
Some of the most crucial election materials, including paper ballots, are printed only in black ink. Black plus one additional color can be used for most election design applications.

Do:
Use green within the system. Green can work effectively to communicate environmental awareness. Lighter tints of green can be used to distinguish areas of background color.

Do:
Use yellow within the system. Lighter tints of yellow have a cream/manila look that can be used to distinguish background fields in administrative forms.

Do:
Use black text on a white background for the bulk of any text to be read by voters. Use tints of gray for reduced contrast or to organize areas of information.

4 thin
4 light
5 roman
6 bold
7 black
8 extra black
55
56
65
66
75
76
extended
3
standard
5
oblique
6
condensed
7
condensed oblique
8
ultracondensed
9

typography

Good typography is critical to enabling written language. Headings, text, instructions, labels, and lists are used on ballots, forms, signs, brochures, and websites to educate and inform voters. Every U.S. citizen who is eligible to vote is a potential consumer of election information. Consequently, it is critical that written content be as accessible as possible. This means paying special attention to the selection of a typeface, its size, weight, width, spacing, and placement on a page or a screen.

The Univers font family was selected for the Design for Democracy election design system. Any and all materials for elections can be developed using this one font family. Created by the Swiss designer Adrian Frutiger in 1957, Univers is a sans serif font based on simple geometry and sound typographic principles. Revolutionary when developed, for its planned variations in weight and width, Univers has gone through periods of great popularity and is now considered a utilitarian modern classic.

Univers was selected because of its clarity, simplicity, and high degree of legibility. There are 21 font variations as shown on the facing page, with Univers 55 (roman) the standard height and width. All of these variations are designed to work together and can be successfully assigned and combined to achieve clear information hierarchy. This book has been typeset in Univers, using the guidelines of the Design for Democracy system. Only four fonts are needed for the entire text: Univers 55 (roman), 56 (oblique), 75 (black), and 76 (black oblique).

Univers is available in a range of compatible weights and widths. Most useful for the system are Univers 55 (roman), 65 (bold), and 75 (black), along with their italic (oblique) counterparts: Univers 56, 66, and 76. Univers can be purchased from the Adobe Type Library at adobe.com/type.

Univers 55 Roman

ABCDEFGHIJKLMNOPQRSTUVWXYZ

abcdefghijklmonpqrstuvwxyz 0123456789.,!?

Univers 65 Bold

ABCDEFGHIJKLMNOPQRSTUVWXYZ

abcdefghijklmonpqrstuvwxyz 0123456789.,!?

Univers 75 Black

ABCDEFGHIJKLMNOPQRSTUVWXYZ

abcdefghijklmonpqrstuvwxyz 0123456789.,!?

Univers 55 Roman (above top):
Use for paragraph text and for a second language in bilingual instructions.

Univers 65 Bold (above center):
Use for candidate names on ballots.

Univers 75 Black (above bottom):
Use for headlines and subheads and for English text in bilingual instructions.

Within the election design system, the most useful weights of the Univers font family are 55 and 75. Univers 55 is a standard text weight, useful for documents with large amounts of copy, like voter education brochures or pollworker training manuals. The bold weight of Univers 75 provides impact and emphasis, making it useful for headings or subheadings. At small sizes, Univers 75 is more legible than the lighter weights, especially when printed in color.

This is Univers 55	This is Univers 55
This is Univers 75	**This is Univers 75**

It is important to note the difference between one-step and two-step jumps in weight (for instance, 55 to 65 versus 55 to 75). The difference in weight in a one-step jump is minimal, and the result may look more like a typesetting error than a deliberate change in emphasis. A two-step jump provides clear contrast and deliberate emphasis.

This is Univers 55	This is Univers 55	This is Univers 45
This is Univers 65	**This is Univers 75**	**This is Univers 65**

Univers 65 has been used successfully for the names of candidates on a ballot. In ballot design, where space is at a minimum, Univers 75 is often too bold and takes up too much space.

Headings/subheadings:

Univers 75: 9.5/16

Text:

Univers 55: 10/16

Headings:

Univers 45: 23/36

Text:

Univers 45: 12/18

Text highlight:

Univers 65: 11/18

Sidebar text:

Univers 65: 8/14

Sidebar phone number:

Univers 65: 12/21

On Election Day

What if I'm not listed as being registered?
You can vote a provisional ballot if there is a question regarding your registration or eligibility to vote. A provisional ballot is just like a regular ballot, but it doesn't get counted unless election officials verify your registration and eligibility after the election.

What if I make a mistake?
If you make a mistake while voting your ballot, ask an election official for a new ballot.

Can I receive help voting my ballot?
If you have difficulty punching your ballot, you may request assistance from a friend, family member, or election judge in your precinct. Both the voter and the individual(s) providing assistance must sign a legal affidavit.

People allowed in the polling place

Aside from election judges and voters, specific individuals are allowed to observe and monitor operations inside the polling place during the day and after the polls close. Each observer must present proper identification or credentials and must never interfere with the election procedures or disturb voters.

A **pollwatcher** is an individual who represents a candidate, political party, independent organization, or a proponent or opponent of a referendum who is legally inside the polling place to observe the conduct of the election.

If you cannot gain entry to the polling place, call the Polling Place Department:

312 555 0123

If the supply judge does not arrive call the Election Judge Department:

312 555 3210

Voter education brochure text (above left): Headings are distinguished from text by the use of bold type. Subheadings, which direct the voter to areas of specific content, are printed in red.

Pollworker manual text (above center): Univers 45 can be used as a text font at larger sizes. Headings are distinguished from text by size. Terms included in a glossary are highlighted in bold throughout the text.

Pollworker manual sidebar (above, in red): Bold text in a narrow column creates areas for special information.

Introductory text

Univers 57: 16/24

Sign heading

Univers 75: 120pt

Sign heading

in second language

Univers 55: 60pt

Bilingual voting instructions

Univers 75: 10.5/16

Univers 55: 11/16

Absentee voting is a convenient way of casting a ballot if you're unable to make it to your polling place on Election Day.

In most cases, voters choose to vote absentee when they will be out of town on Election Day or are physically disabled.

The most common method of voting absentee is by mail, but you may also cast ballots in-person at your local village or township hall.

polling pla

lugar de vota

Hold the stylus straight up and down next to your selections. Press down firmly.

Sostenga el estilo perforador recto hacia arriba y hacia abajo sobre sus selecciones. Oprima con firmeza.

Voter education brochure introduction (directly above):
Highlight introductory text by reversing a large type size out of a color field. The condensed width of Univers 57 is useful for narrow formats.

Polling place sign heading (top):
Univers 75 is recommended for headings in polling place signs. Type size will vary based on the specific application.

Bilingual voting instructions (directly above):
For bilingual communications, distinguish English from a second language by weight.

Use symbols to simplify communication.

Symbols and icons provide immediate visual impact. They can be used effectively to clarify instructions and to place emphasis on important or new information.

symbols + icons

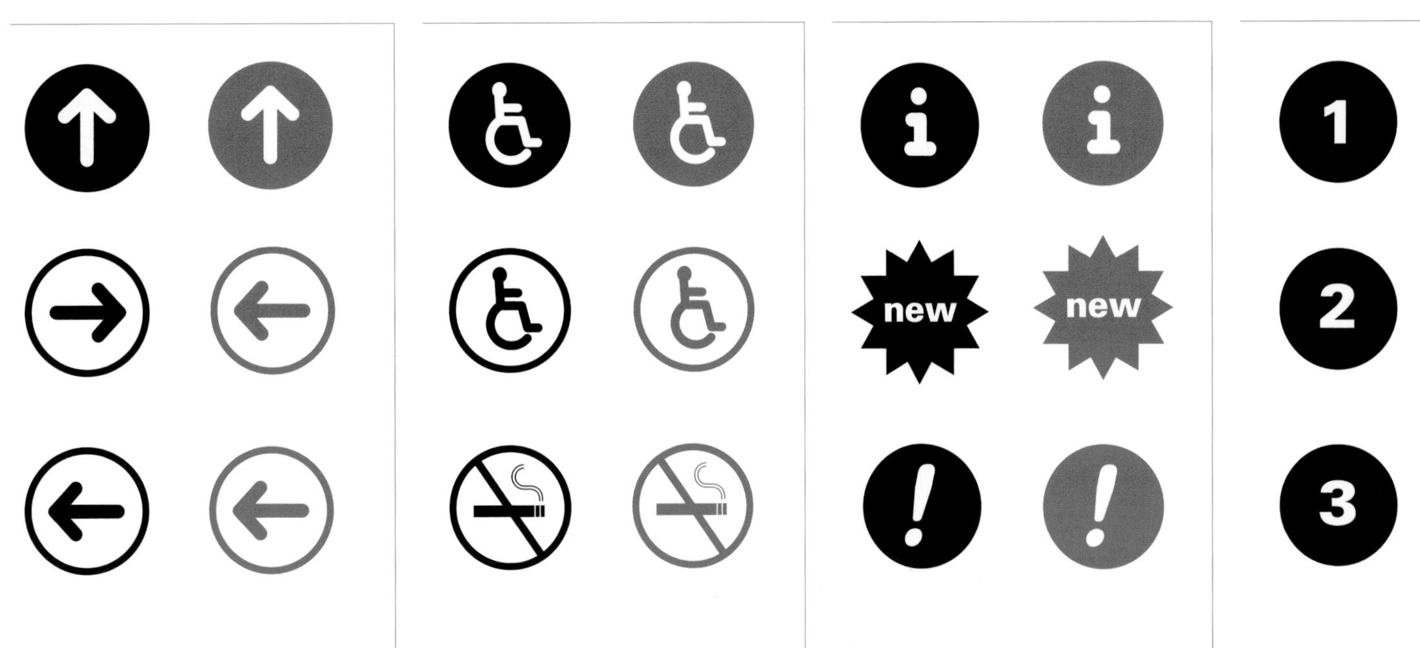

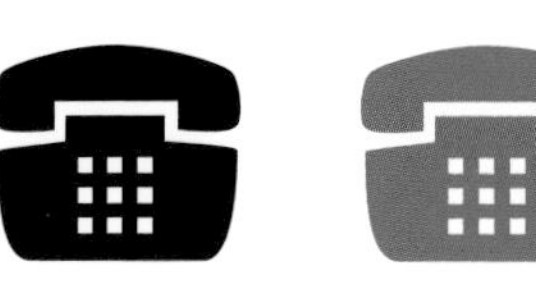

Use symbols to help people find their way. The polling place is often difficult to navigate. Accessibility icons and arrows from this system can easily be used to provide guidance to voters.

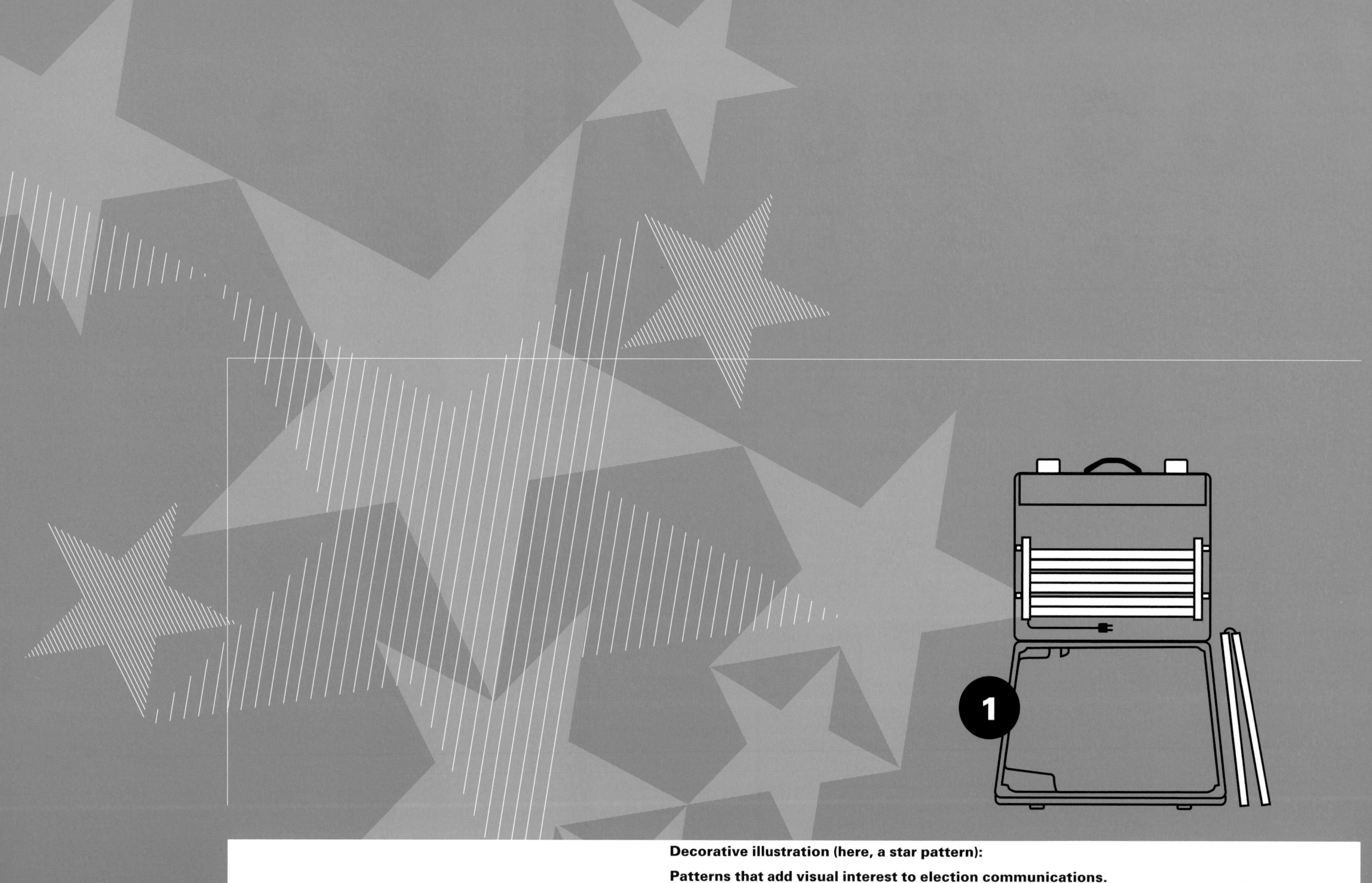

Decorative illustration (here, a star pattern):
Patterns that add visual interest to election communications.

illustration

Within the design system there are two types of illustrations that can be used to communicate election information. Decorative illustrations are graphic patterns of stars and stripes that add visual interest to election communications. Instructional illustrations are graphic diagrams that provide visual explanations of procedures for voters and pollworkers.

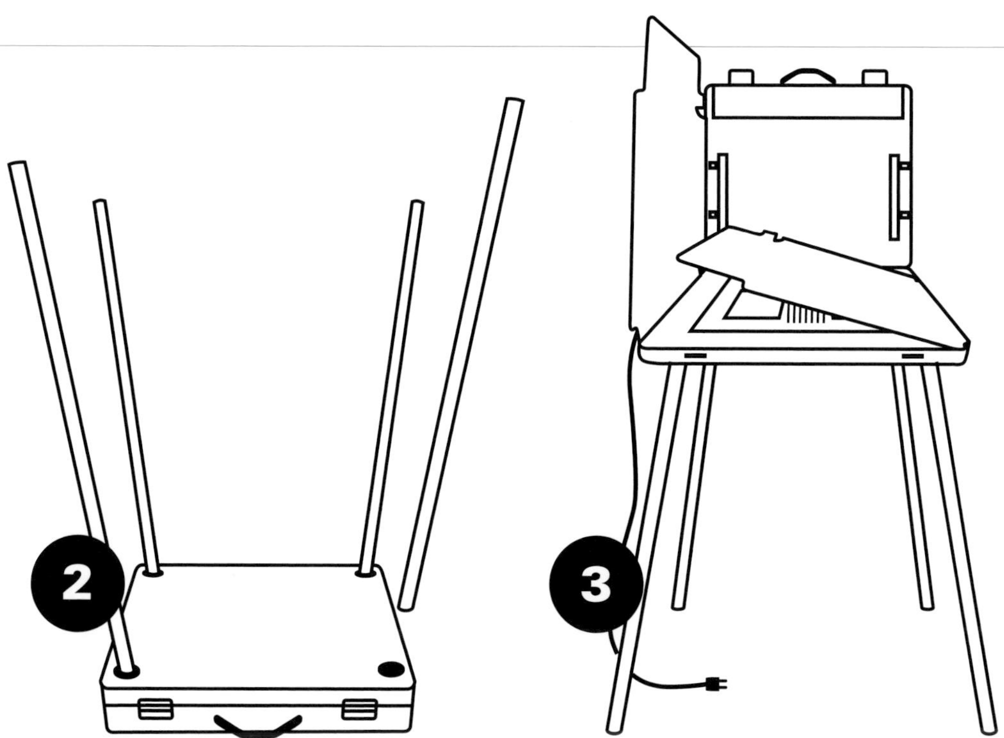

The instructional illustration style is defined by a heavy black outline in a single line weight.

This simple diagrammatic style works successfully using only black. However, areas of flat color can be added for interest and emphasis.

It is best to commission a professional artist to create instructional illustrations, but this style also can be created by tracing photographs (see page 163).

Instructional illustration (numbered diagrams, facing page and above): Diagrams that clearly describe procedures for voters and pollworkers.

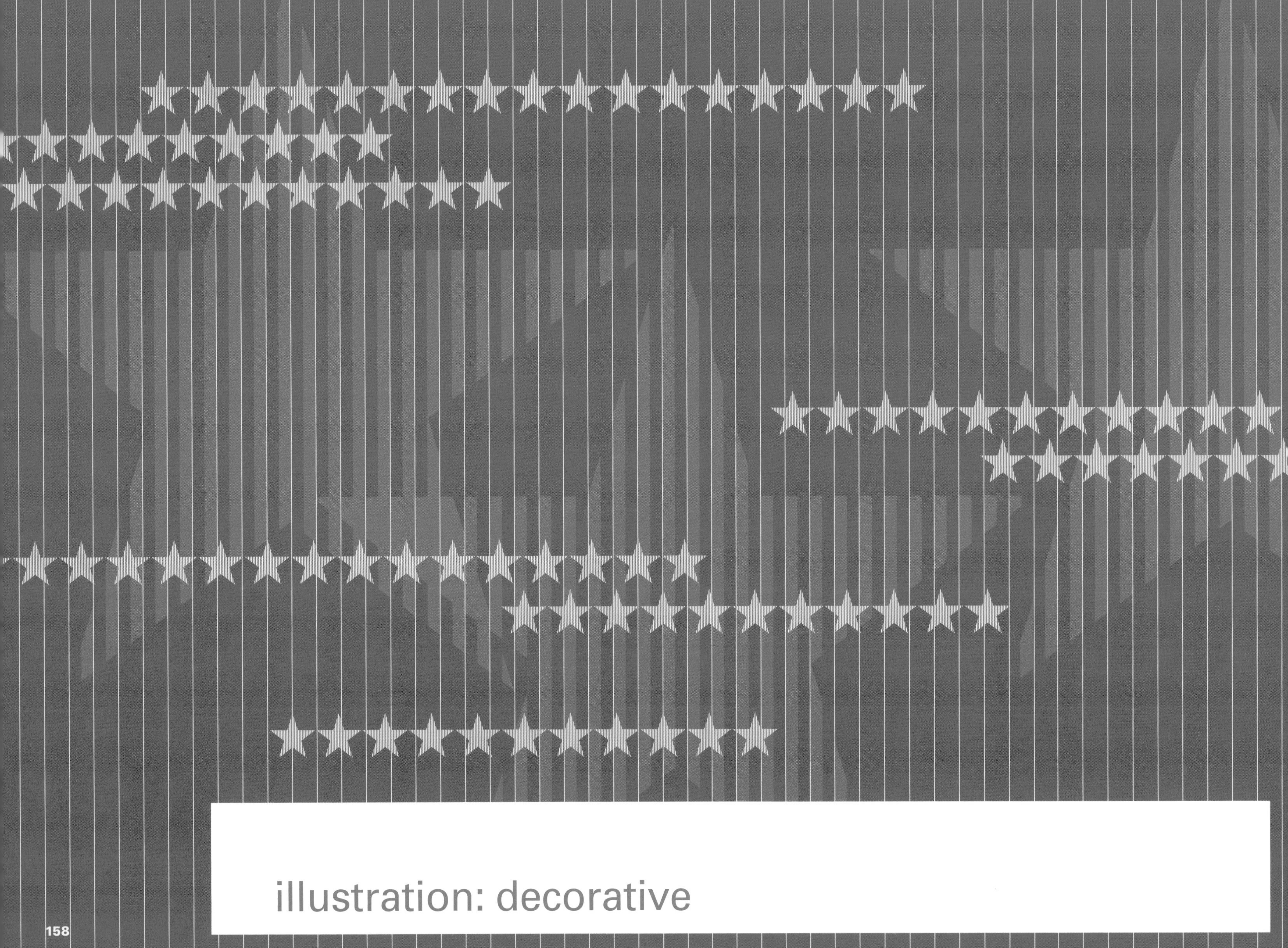

illustration: decorative

Decorative illustrations can be used to make voter education materials interesting and accessible. In addition, color variations can be used to indicate different categories of information, as shown below in the Cook County voter education brochure covers.

Graphic patterns of stars and stripes should be designed to express the most desirable characteristics of the voting experience: confidence, enthusiasm, participation, activity, and community. They need not, and should not, be literal interpretations of the stars and stripes of the U.S. flag. For example, the graphic pattern used for the cover of this book, and on the Cook County young-voter brochures shown on pages 48–49, is designed to suggest the high energy and ordered chaos of election activities.

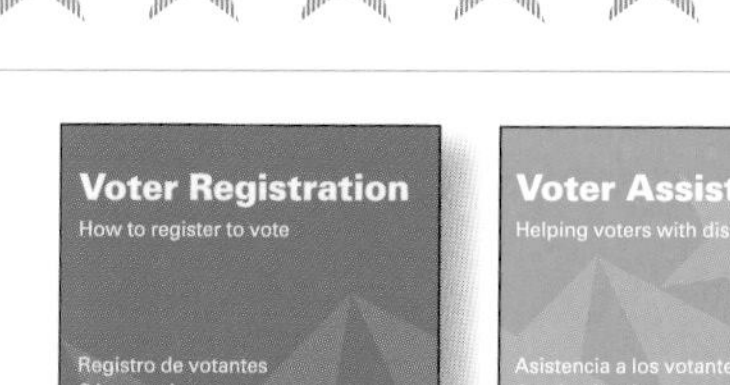

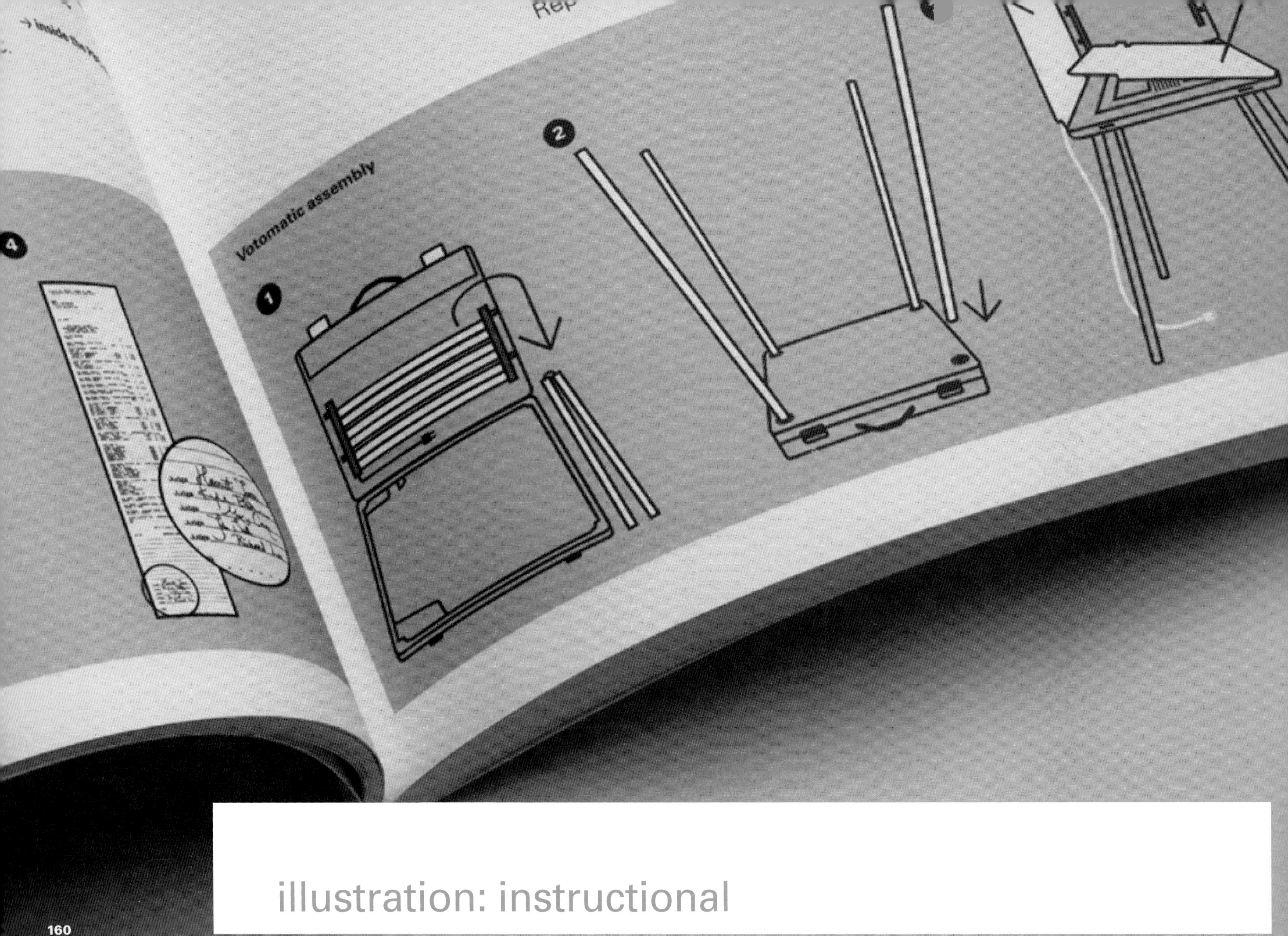

illustration: instructional

Photographs of the voting process can be difficult to decipher, whereas illustrated diagrams can be used to convey instruction with simplicity and clarity. In the examples below, the diagrams are more effective than photographs in depicting the activity critical to each step. Shades of gray, or areas of color, create emphasis that allows the ballot to come forward as the only area of bright white. The use of illustration also allows for focused exaggeration, as in the arrows directing the voter to place the ballot on the red pins. In comparison to the photographs, the diagrams better present the voting process as straightforward and unintimidating.

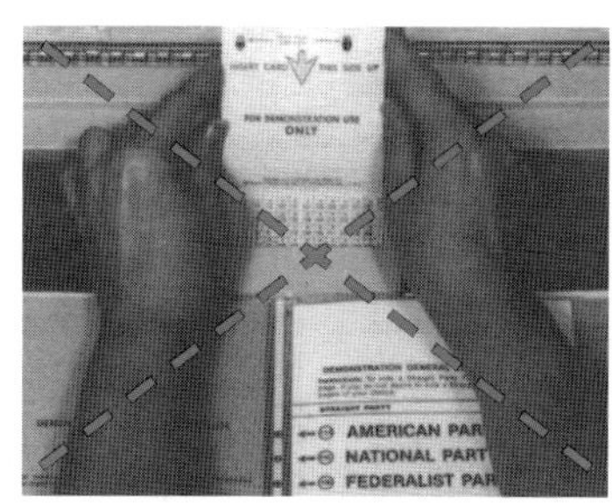

Use contrast to place emphasis on the most important information. The ballot card being inserted into the vote recorder stands out because it is the only area of white in the illustration.

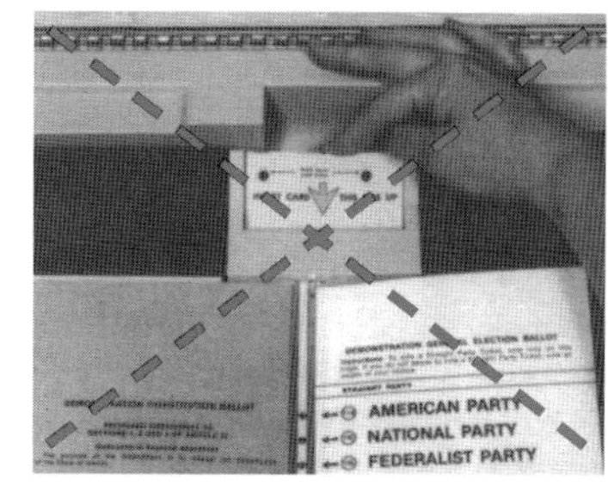

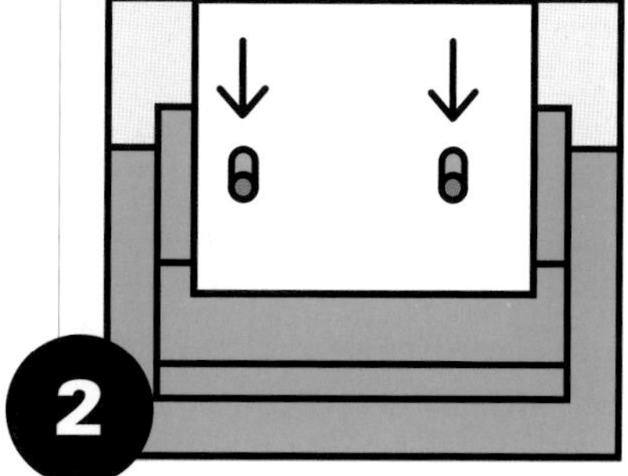

Use color and bold graphics to focus on areas of activity. The pins that hold the ballot in position are shown in red. Arrows shown at an exaggerated scale provide directional guidance.

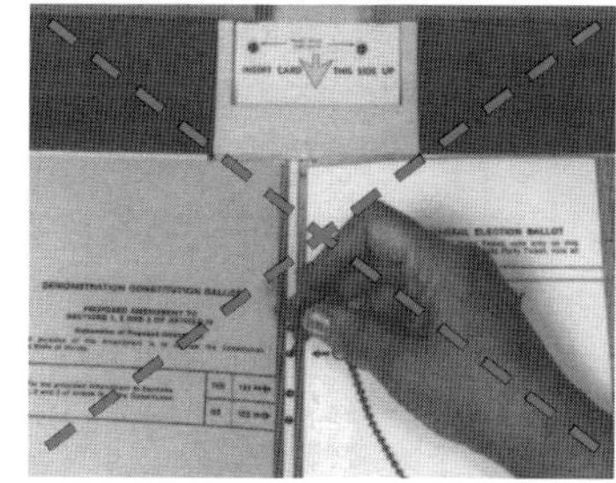

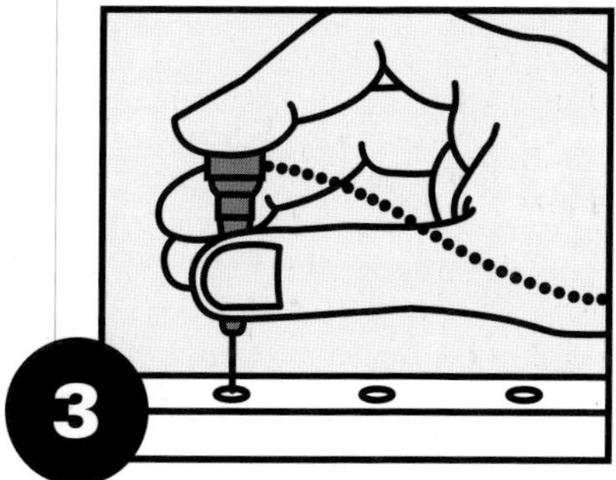

Illustrations allow for angles of view that are difficult to achieve in a photograph. Here, the voter is instructed to hold the stylus perpendicular to the ballot.

When illustrating step-by-step procedures it is important to be mindful of the actual number of steps required. In 2000, voters in the City of Chicago were mailed voting instructions that described the voting process in four steps. They then arrived at the polling place to discover that the instructions in the voting booth had increased to ten. Ideally, the number of steps presented in instructions of this kind should be limited to three. In redesigning the voting instructions, a necessary fourth step was converted to a special warning and was isolated with an alert icon. This preserved the three-step limit.

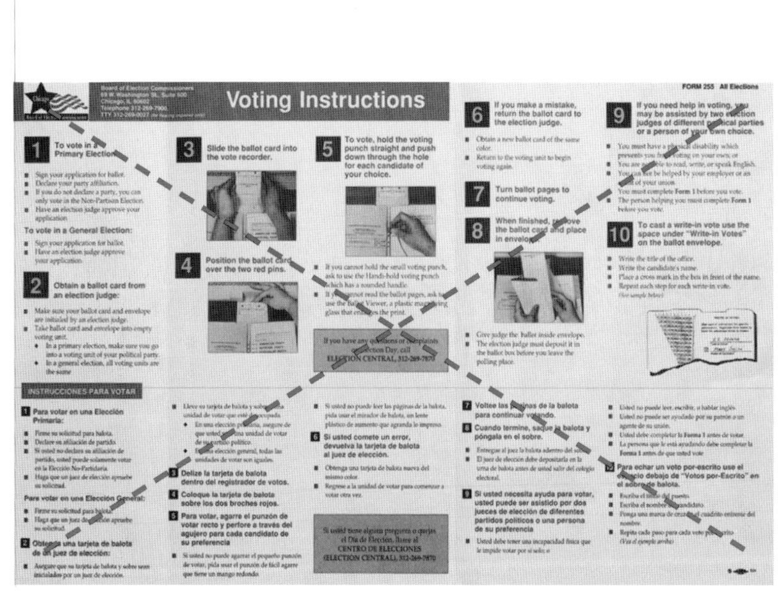

Voting Instructions

FORM 255 All Elections

1 To vote in a Primary Election:

To vote in a General Election:

2 Obtain a ballot card from an election judge:

3 Slide the ballot card into the vote recorder.

4 Position the ballot card over the two red pins.

5 To vote, hold the voting punch straight and push down through the hole for each candidate of your choice.

6 If you make a mistake, return the ballot card to the election judge.

7 Turn ballot pages to continue voting.

8 When finished, remove the ballot card and place in envelope.

9 If you need help in voting, you may be assisted by two election judges of different political parties or a person of your own choice.

10 To cast a write-in vote use the space under "Write-in Votes" on the ballot envelope.

If you have any questions or complaints on Election Day, call ELECTION CENTRAL, 312-269-7870

INSTRUCCIONES PARA VOTAR

Para votar en una Elección Primaria:

Para votar en una Elección General:

Obtenga una tarjeta de balota de un juez de elección:

Deslice la tarjeta de balota dentro del registrador de votos.

Coloque la tarjeta de balota sobre los dos broches rojos.

Para votar, agarre el punzón de votar recto y perfore a través del agujero para cada candidato de su preferencia

Si usted comete un error, devuelva la tarjeta de balota al juez de elección.

Voltee las páginas de la balota para continuar votando.

Cuando termine, saque la balota y póngala en el sobre.

Si usted necesita ayuda para votar, usted puede ser asistido por dos jueces de elección de diferentes partidos políticos o una persona de su preferencia

Para echar un voto por-escrito use el espacio debajo de "Votos por-Escrito" en el sobre de la balota.

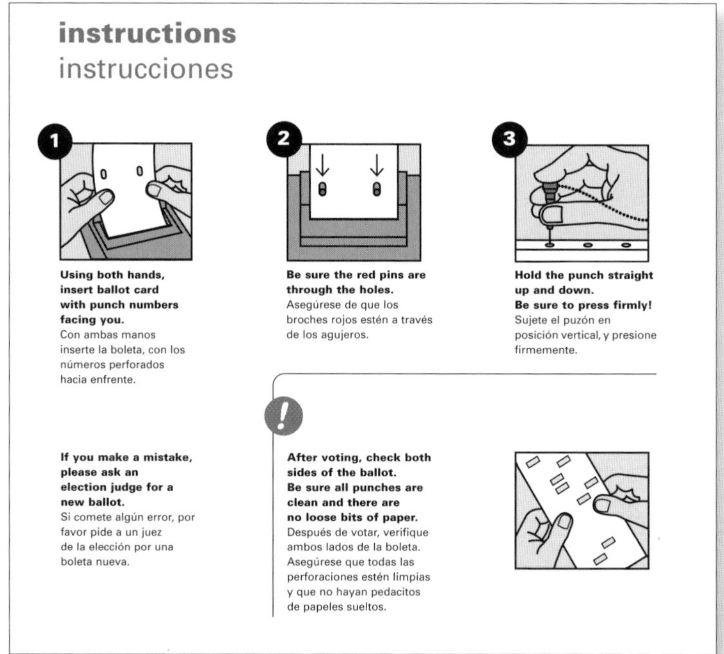

instructions
instrucciones

1 **Using both hands, insert ballot card with punch numbers facing you.**
Con ambas manos inserte la boleta, con los números perforados hacia enfrente.

2 **Be sure the red pins are through the holes.**
Asegúrese de que los broches rojos estén a través de los agujeros.

3 **Hold the punch straight up and down. Be sure to press firmly!**
Sujete el puzón en posición vertical, y presione firmemente.

If you make a mistake, please ask an election judge for a new ballot.
Si comete algún error, por favor pide a un juez de la elección por una boleta nueva.

! **After voting, check both sides of the ballot. Be sure all punches are clean and there are no loose bits of paper.**
Después de votar, verifique ambos lados de la boleta. Asegúrese que todas las perforaciones estén limpias y que no hayan pedacitos de papeles sueltos.

Before the redesign, instructions in the voting booth included procedures that had already taken place at other stations in the polling place. Items of general information had also been listed as steps—making voting a cumbersome ten-step process.

The redesign provides only the information needed in the voting booth. Voting is now a manageable three-step process, with a warning to check for loose chads.

Instructional illustrations in the style developed for the design system can be created without difficulty using a digital camera and graphics software (see below). 1] The object or activity to be illustrated is photographed, and 2] the photograph is used as a template for tracing an outline. 3] The most important information is presented in white, emphasis is created using different shades of gray, and irrelevant or unimportant details are omitted. Strong black outlines provide additional clarity and a friendly look and feel.

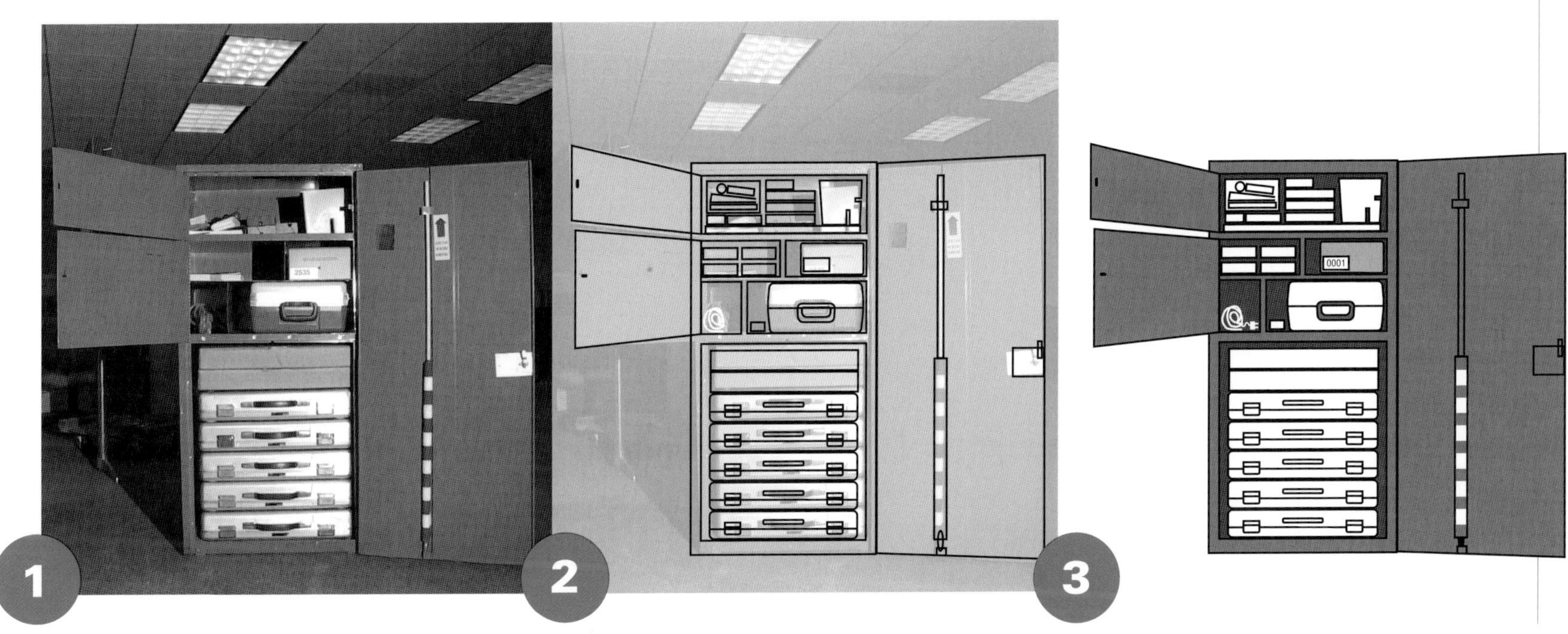

A photograph is taken of the object to be illustrated. A brightly lit direct front view is best, as shown here in this image of an open voting supply carrier.

The photograph is used as a template to trace the outline of the object. The outline includes only those details important for providing instruction to the voter or pollworker.

Shades of gray are used to distinguish objects, leaving the most important information in white. This diagram serves as a quick visual inventory of the supply carrier's contents.

photography

Photographs can provide visual interest and add meaning to election communications. Voting is all about people and community. Images of people voting and serving in elections provide emotional and environmental context for election information. As described in the previous section, there are drawbacks to using photographs as instructional images. However, photography can be used to add warmth and impact and convey a spirit of civic pride.

An effective combination of illustration and photography can improve both the emotional and the educational aspects of election communications. As distinguished below, photographs and decorative illustrations are better suited to communicate emotion and feeling. In contrast, instructional illustrations are better used to provide functional understanding of the materials and procedures that the voter will encounter in the polling place.

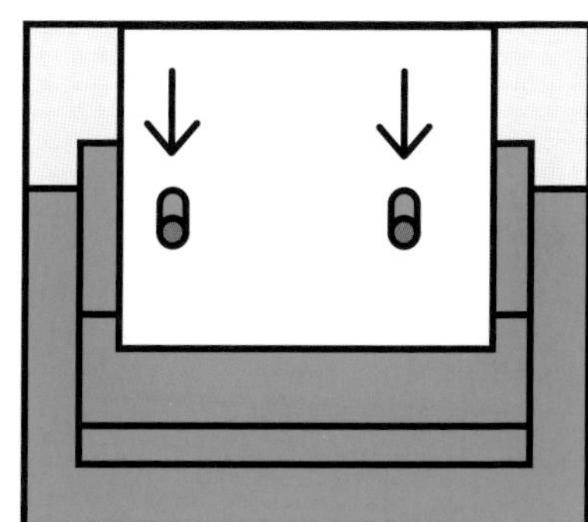

Photographic images and decorative illustrations help voters to *feel* what it is like to participate in the voting experience.

Instructional diagrams help voters to *understand* how things work.

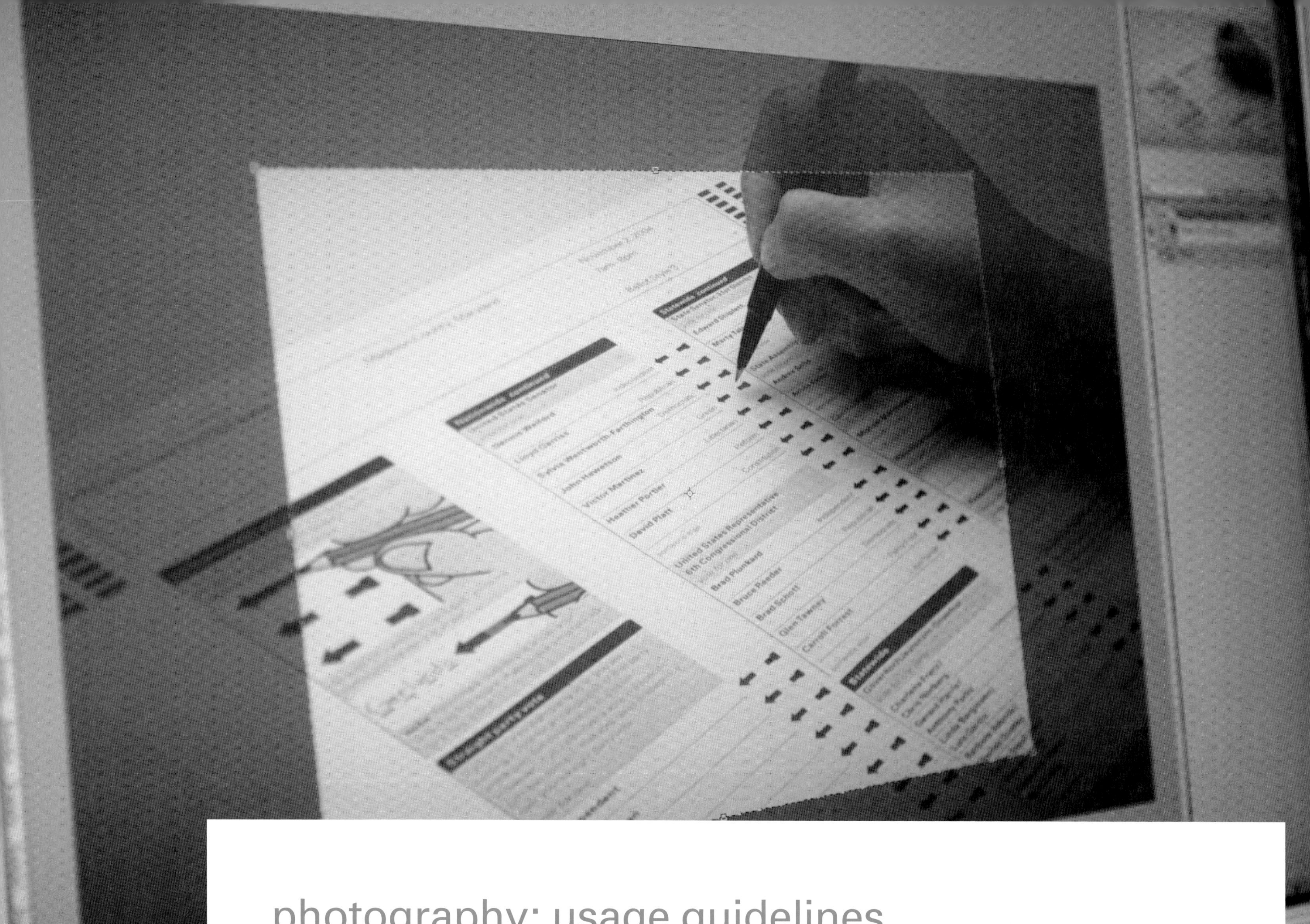

photography: usage guidelines

A few simple guidelines can maximize the effectiveness of photographic images in election materials. For instance, to create a strong visual statement, use the full width of a page or spread to display a photograph. Also, whenever possible, use large photographs with dramatic cropping.

Black and white photography (rather than color) is recommended for images of polling place environments. These settings are often visually complicated by materials and objects that have little or nothing to do with the voting experience. Black and white photography simplifies the environment and directs focus toward individuals and activities. Black and white photography is also less expensive to reproduce in printed materials.

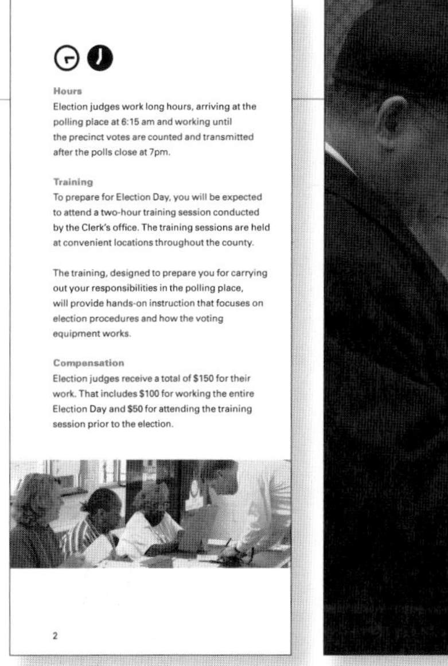

Hours
Election judges work long hours, arriving at the polling place at 6:15 am and working until the precinct votes are counted and transmitted after the polls close at 7pm.

Training
To prepare for Election Day, you will be expected to attend a two-hour training session conducted by the Clerk's office. The training sessions are held at convenient locations throughout the county.

The training, designed to prepare you for carrying out your responsibilities in the polling place, will provide hands-on instruction that focuses on election procedures and how the voting equipment works.

Compensation
Election judges receive a total of $150 for their work. That includes $100 for working the entire Election Day and $50 for attending the training session prior to the election.

2

Do:

Extend photographs to the full width of the page. For large images, extend to all four sides and use dramatic cropping to focus on activity or expression.

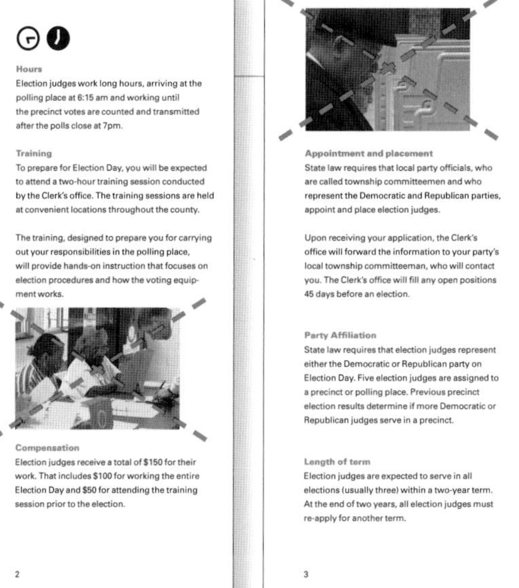

Hours
Election judges work long hours, arriving at the polling place at 6:15 am and working until the precinct votes are counted and transmitted after the polls close at 7pm.

Training
To prepare for Election Day, you will be expected to attend a two-hour training session conducted by the Clerk's office. The training sessions are held at convenient locations throughout the county.

The training, designed to prepare you for carrying out your responsibilities in the polling place, will provide hands-on instruction that focuses on election procedures and how the voting equipment works.

Compensation
Election judges receive a total of $150 for their work. That includes $100 for working the entire Election Day and $50 for attending the training session prior to the election.

2

Appointment and placement
State law requires that local party officials, who are called township committeemen and who represent the Democratic and Republican parties, appoint and place election judges.

Upon receiving your application, the Clerk's office will forward the information to your party's local township committeeman, who will contact you. The Clerk's office will fill any open positions 45 days before an election.

Party Affiliation
State law requires that election judges represent either the Democratic or Republican party on Election Day. Five election judges are assigned to a precinct or polling place. Previous precinct election results determine if more Democratic or Republican judges serve in a precinct.

Length of term
Election judges are expected to serve in all elections (usually three) within a two-year term. At the end of two years, all election judges must re-apply for another term.

3

Do Not:

Place a photograph in a box in the center of a page or above body text. This use of photography is too closely tied to text and appears as instructional illustration rather than environmental context.

Election Judge
Working in the polling place
Juez Electoral
Trabajando en el precinto electoral
David Orr
Cook County Clerk
Serve!

Every election, 12,500 election judges in 2,500 suburban Cook County precincts make sure that polling place operations run smoothly and that elections are carried out fairly, honestly and accurately.

Serving as a gatekeeper of democracy, you are responsible for supervising the conduct inside the polling places and helping voters.

You also get paid for it. Election judges can receive up to $150 every election.

Responsibilities
Election judges have many responsibilities and perform several tasks on Election Day, including:

→ Opening the polling place in the morning and closing it at night
→ Setting up election equipment
→ Providing assistance to voters
→ Signing in voters
→ Verifying voter qualifications
→ Distributing ballots
→ Operating voting equipment
→ Filling out forms
→ Processing and transmitting votes at the end of the day
→ Certifying vote totals

Eligibility
To be eligible to serve as an election judge, you must be:

→ A U.S. citizen
→ A resident of Cook County
→ A registered voter
→ Able to speak, read and write English
→ Of good understanding and capable of performing duties

! Candidates running for office and elected political party committeemen are prohibited from serving as election judges.

1

This is one of a series of brochures developed by Design for Democracy and the Office of the Cook County Clerk. It demonstrates the successful use of photography in election materials.

Formulario de solicitud para servir como Juez Electoral

Marque todas las casillas aplicables:

- ☐ Deseo servir como juez demócrata.
- ☐ Deseo servir como juez republicano.
- ☐ Deseo servir como juez para cualquiera de los partidos.
- ☐ Deseo obtener más información, por favor, llámenme.

También hablo con soltura: Español Chino
(marque si es aplicable)

Nombre

Dirección domiciliar

Pueblo/Ciudad Código postal

No. de teléfono durante el día

No. de teléfono durante la noche

Firma

Si tiene alguna pregunta, sírvase llame al Departamento de Jueces Electorales de la oficina del Secretario del Condado al 312 603 0964 o envíe un correo electrónico a electjudge@cookcountygov.com

Envíe por correo o fax esta solicitud a:
Cook County Clerk's Office
Attn: Election Judge Department
69 W. Washington St., Suite 500
Chicago, IL 60602

12

The dotted red lines, directly above, show how cropping can be used to simplify the complicated environment of a polling place and to focus in on a specific election activity.

Designación y colocación

La ley estatal exige que funcionarios de partidos locales, que se denominan miembros de comités de distritos municipales y representan a los partidos Demócrata y Republicano, designen y coloquen a los jueces elecorales.

Al recibir su solicitud, la oficina del Secretario enviará la información al miembro del comité del distrito municipal local de su partido, el cual se pondrá en contacto con usted. La oficina del Secretario llenará todas las posiciones vacantes 45 días antes de una elección.

Afiliación partidaria

La ley estatal exige que los jueces electorales representen al partido Demócrata o al partido Republicano el Día de las Elecciones. Cinco jueces elecorales son asignados a un distrito electoral o precinto electoral. Los resultados de las elecciones previas en el distrito electoral (precinto) determinan si un número mayor de jueces demócratas o republicanos servirán en un precinto electoral.

Término

Se espera que los jueces electorales sirvan en todas las elecciones (usualmente tres) en un término de dos años. Al final del período de dos años, todos los jueces electorales deben volver a solicitar para servir otro término.

8

Jueces estudiantes

La ley estatal, patrocinada por la oficina del Secretario, permite a estudiantes del último año de secundaria que llenen los requisitos establecidos, servir como jueces electorales. Los jueces estudiantes comparten las mismas responsabilidades, la misma autoridad y reciben la misma page que los jueces adultos.

Cualquier persona interesada en servir como juez estudiantil debe contactarse con la Oficina del Secretario:

llame al
312 603 0964

correo electrónico
electjudge@cookcountygove.com

Jueces bilingües

Aunque la ley estatal sostiene que todos los jueces electorales deben leer y escribir inglés, la oficina del Secretario siempre está buscando jueces electorales bilingües. Las leyes electroales federales exigen que la oficina del Secretario detecte distritos electorales (precintos) en el área suburbana del Condado de Cook con atlas concentraciones de votantes que hablen español y chino y no hablen soltura inglés y puedan necesitar asistencia especial en las urnas.

9

Photographs of materials to be used and activities to be performed in the polling place provide context and add meaning to a brochure that explains to potential pollworkers the responsibilities of election administration.

Votar le da el poder de influir en asuntos en su comunidad y en todo el mundo seleccionando candidatos para cargos públicos que toman decisiones cruciales sobre una variedad de asuntos.

Registrarse para votar, aprender las técnicas de votación adecuadas y obtener información sobre los candidatos y sus posiciones son los primeros pasos para convertirse en una persona políticamente activa.

Las elecciones son la piedra angular de la Democracia, por lo que debe ejercer su derecho a registrarse y votar.

David Orr
Cook County Clerk
69 W. Washington St.
5th floor
Chicago, IL 60602

312 603 0906
www.voterinfonet.com

¿Qué opciones tienen los votantes incapacitados?

La oficina del Secretario tiene el compromiso de ampliar el acceso a las urnas para que les resulte más fácil a los votantes incapacitados depositar sus boletas de forma independiente.

Están disponibles varios programas y servicios de asistencia, incluyendo votación en la acera, votación en ausencia, equipo de votación accesible en silla de ruedas y materiales de ayuda para votantes. Para más información, llame al Coordinador de servicios a incapacitados de la oficina del Secretario del Condado al 312 603 0929 o comuníquese por correo electrónico a accessibility@cookcountygov.com.

¿Qué sucede en el precinto electoral?

Los jueces electorales son personas que residen en su vecindario y presiden las votaciones en su precinto electoral. Si usted necesita ayuda para comprender un procedimiento o necesita otro tipo de asistencia, pídasela a un juez electoral. En la página siguiente se describe en detalle a los jueces electorales y sus deberes.

20

Photographs can also be used to provide detailed information in support of instructional diagrams. Shown below in these examples from the Cook County election judge manual, close-up "bubbles" contain photographic enlargements of a punchcard vote recorder. The enlargement at left indicates the location of the ballot style number, and the enlargement at right provides a clear look at punch numbers, arrows, and holes.

This combination of image styles provides the best possible visual instruction. The diagram simplifies and focuses attention, while the photographic enlargement provides realistic detail.

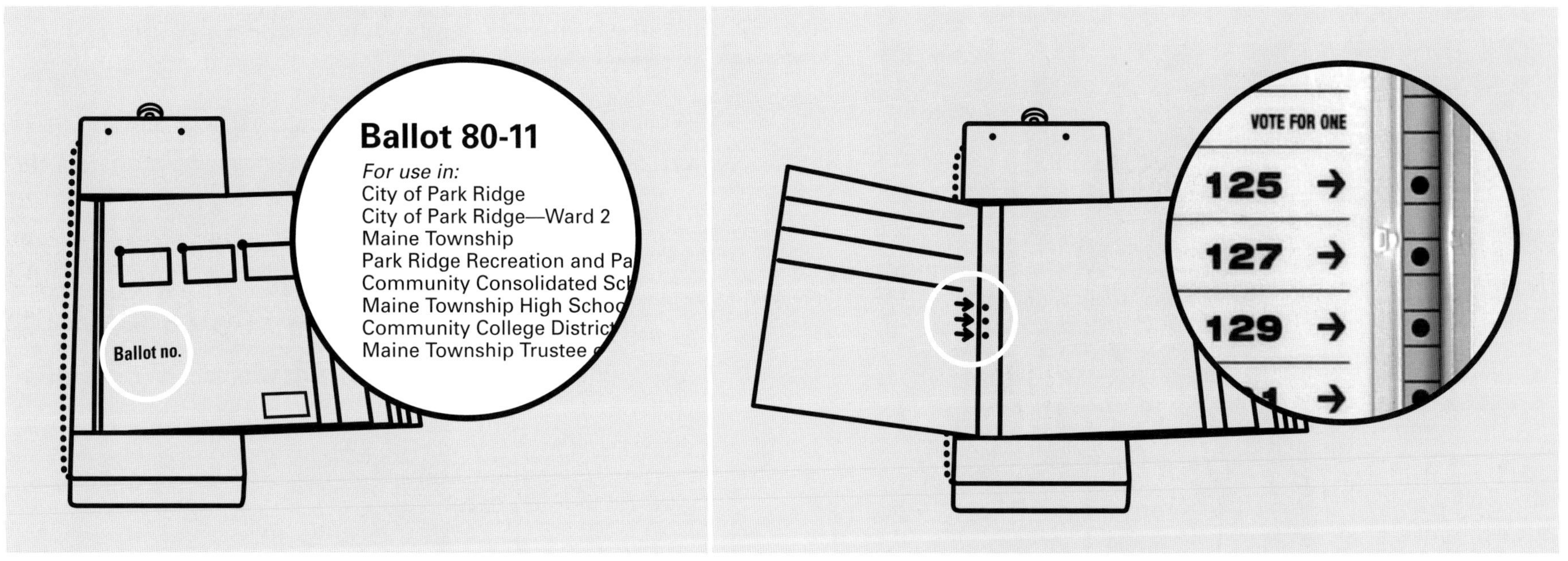

These diagrams, which combine instructional illustrations with photographic enlargements, instruct pollworkers to check for the correct ballot style number and to be sure that ballot numbers and directional arrows are in proper alignment with punch holes.

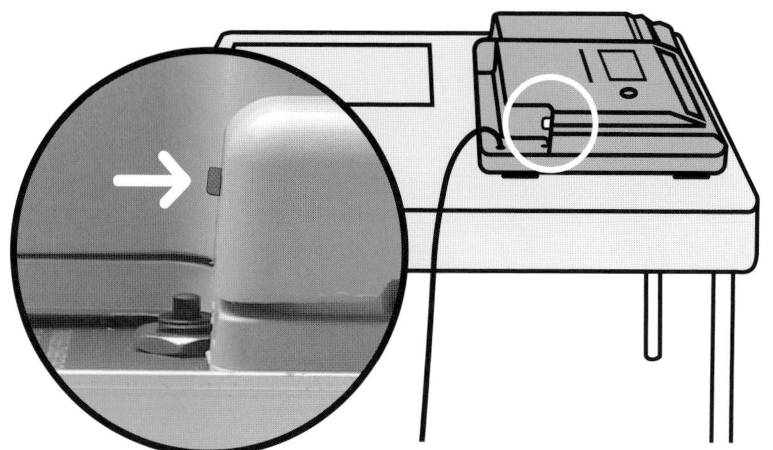

Photographic enlargements of ballot counter features are particularly helpful in pollworker training and reference.

In order to process an undervoted ballot, the pollworker must press a red override button on the left rear of the ballot counter. This combination of diagram and close-up photograph, shown at right, provides the needed visual instruction to locate a frequently used but difficult-to-find machine part.

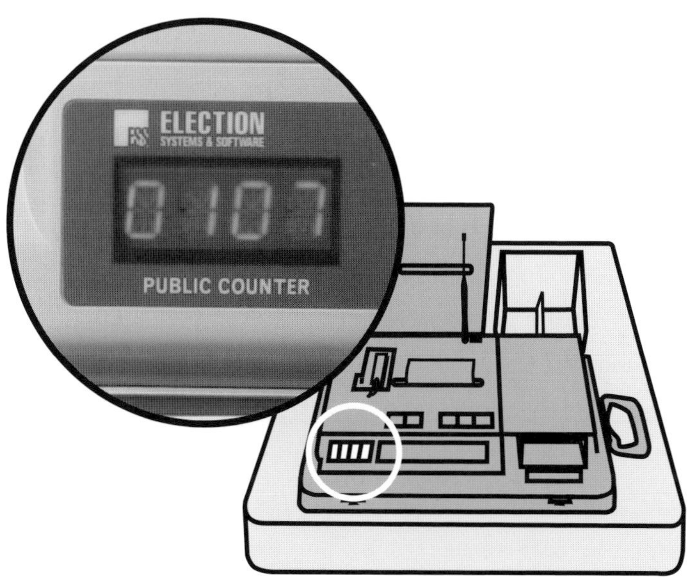

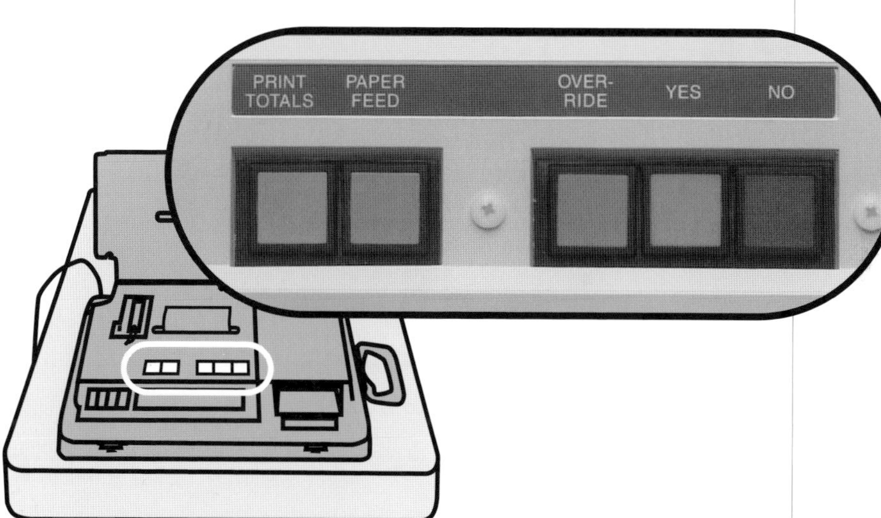

Above left, a photographic enlargement is combined with an instructional diagram to show a pollworker where to find a ballot counting display, and above right, to provide a detailed picture of the ballot counter's primary control panel.

Good design is good leadership

This book seeks to demonstrate the tremendous impact that good design can have on the functional, experiential, and emotional aspects of complex systems of communication—like those that need to occur between a government and its citizens.

Design can improve the functional aspects of a communication system. It can streamline processes and present information in the clearest possible light. It can make things easier to access, learn, and use.

Design can address the experiential aspects of a complex procedure or an unfamiliar environment. It can improve the way groups and individuals encounter information, undergo processes, and navigate space. It can help people to successfully interact with tools, equipment, and one another.

Beyond the functional and the experiential, good design can have positive emotional outcomes. It can influence how a system is perceived, recorded, remembered, and shared. It can inspire confidence, change negative perceptions, and build trust.

The material presented here has successfully addressed all three aspects of communication design for elections. Important functional improvements have been introduced in the design of ballots, registration applications, administrative forms, polling place signs, and voter information. Improving the presentation of information and planning how information is delivered and accessed has made the voting experience better for all involved. Such improvements result in a positive emotional experience, supported and sustained through a design system founded on ideas of pride, participation, activity, community, and duty. Examples and guidelines for the effective use of type, color, and image provide the tools necessary for long-term success.

It took an unusual set of circumstances to bring this work about. Ideally, election design reform would have been identified as an area of national concern. In an analysis of government design needs, it would likely be one of many initiatives to be defined, prioritized, and approached strategically. Instead, this work was initiated in response to a glaring mistake that called into question the outcome of a presidential election. The Design for Democracy election design initiative grew from a single regional case study into a comprehensive national design system because the right people were in the right place at the right time to make it happen. It was not the result of a unified demand for good design from our local, state, and national leadership.

Today good design seems to be low on the list of government priorities. However, this was not always the case. In the early 1970s a federal initiative led to the Federal Design Improvement Program of the National Endowment for the Arts. Among other things, this program produced four federal design assemblies that fostered relationships between government officials and designers of all disciplines and the 1972–1981 Federal Graphics Improvement Program, under which more than 45 government agencies worked to transform haphazard graphics into rational systems of communication.

There is an obvious need for government leadership to return to this level of commitment. Enlightened leaders who advocate for improvement and who engage the design disciplines to apply proven ideas and imagine new possibilities can have an immensely positive impact on future democracies.

All prototypes and guidelines for the design of ballots, voter education and outreach, pollworker support, absentee and provisional voting, and election administration materials were developed by AIGA professional and student members.

Student work was completed as partial fulfillment of BFA coursework at the University of Illinois at Chicago under the direction of Marcia Lausen, professor of graphic design; Stephen Melamed, clinical associate professor of industrial design; and Cheyenne Medina, teaching assistant in graphic design.

Through the U.S. Election Assistance Commission, Design for Democracy continues work to establish federally recommended guidelines and best practices documentation for polling place signage and for optical scan and touch-screen ballots.

UIC students for Cook County

Graphic design:
Veronica Belsuzarri
Katie Boston
Thomas Brandenburg
Carrie Butera
Lydia Cervantes
Sandra Champion
Claudio Fucarino
Matt Granstrom
Sabine Krauss
Alice Leaf
Vedran Residbegovic
Jennifer Stratton
Matthew Terdich
Arlene Torman
Sofia Vaitsas
Joanna Wilkiewicz

Industrial design:
Susan Bullis
Olivier Currat
Jay DeMerit
Randy Estiller
Justin Geagan
Tim Jones
Brian Mak
David Sagan
Ronaldo Santiago
Joe Schifano
Brian Urbanik
Marcus Wolff

UIC students for the State of Oregon

Graphic design:
Manyi Au
Nolan Chan
Citlali Diaz
Lizelle Din
Abrahem Hasan
Tamara Hastings
Jacqueline Howard
Luis Ibarra
Dawn Joseph
Stefani Klayman
Laura Martinez
Gretchen Schulfer
Jennifer Snyder
Kristin Tobin
Ya-Yu Tseng
Noah Weinstein

UIC students for community outreach

Graphic design:
Kelly Bullard
Lenka Cechova
Vincent Cerasani
Tricia Fleischer
Luz Hernandez Nieto
Christy Claire Katien
Benjamin Kim
Karen Liwanpo
Brian Mak
Sasa Matijevic
Martha Maxwell
Jennifer Murfay
Kimberly Murfay
Jose Ruiz
Lesa Sewick
Charles Sherman
Michelle Tan

Participating professionals

Design:
Veronica Belsuzarri
Thomas Brandenberg
Hillary Geller
Gus Granger
Michael Konetzka
Mattie Langenberg
Marcia Lausen
Cheyenne Medina
Meeyoung Melamed
Lance Rutter
Gretchen Schulfer
Hanna Smotrich
Jennifer Snyder
Matthew Terdich
Jody Work
Bob Zeni

Retention election research:
Albert Klumpp

Design research:
Joan Afton
Todd Cherkasky
Anna Choi
Martha Cotton
Tamara Hamlish
Jean Maiorella
Elizabeth Tunstall
Rob Vellinga
Frank Romagosa
Brianna Sylver

Sachnoff & Weaver, Ltd. attorneys:
Neil Petty
Marshall Seeder

Consultants:
Roberta Feldman
Cathy Kokontis
Charles Kouri

About AIGA

AIGA, the professional association for design, is the oldest and largest membership association for design professionals engaged in the discipline, practice, and culture of designing. Its mission is to advance design as a professional craft, strategic tool, and global cultural force.

Founded in 1914, AIGA now represents more than 18,000 designers of all disciplines through national activities and local programs developed by more than 50 chapters and 200 student groups. AIGA supports the interests of professionals, educators, and students who are engaged in the process of designing.

Design for Democracy is a strategic initiative of AIGA. The mission of Design for Democracy is to engage design and social research professionals to enable compelling, efficient, trust-building experiences between government and the governed.

AIGA Design for Democracy leadership

President:
Richard Grefé

Advisory Board:
Susan King Roth
Marcia Lausen
John Lindback
Stephen Melamed
Whitney Quesenbery
Elizabeth Tunstall

I certainly was not the only graphic designer who understood the need to act after the 2000 presidential election. As a college professor involved in AIGA leadership, I was simply in a position to do so.

Bob Zeni ignited the spark, immediately following the 2000 election, by suggesting that AIGA Chicago submit a redesign of the Cook County butterfly ballot to the *Chicago Tribune*. Lance Rutter, who was president of AIGA Chicago, had the insight to establish a multidisciplinary team of professional experts, many of whom are still active today.

That core team included Stephen Melamed, my friend and colleague at the University of Illinois at Chicago. In 2001, Stephen and I combined our advanced undergraduate industrial and graphic design classes to undertake the research and development work that formed the basis of the design system presented here. Although this book focuses on graphic design, I want to acknowledge the importance of the contributions of the industrial designers and the enriched experience that resulted from the collaboration. I have no doubt that the ideas for equipment improvements developed by the industrial design team will gain attention as the nation continues to grapple with changes in voting technology.

Also at UIC, my high expectations were often exceeded by the graphic design students who worked on this project over the course of two years. Our efforts were ardently supported by Judith Russi Kirshner, dean of the College of Architecture and the Arts, and Philip Burton, chair of our graphic design program.

Our work was informed by user research conducted by the experience modeling group of Sapient, Chicago. The research team included Joan Afton, Todd Cherkasky, Anna Choi, Martha Cotton, Jean Maiorella, Elizabeth (Dori) Tunstall, PhD, and Rob Vellinga.

Dori Tunstall went on to serve as Design for Democracy's first managing director. She led us deeper into multidisciplinary territory and through the development of the research foundation that is now enabling broad implementation.

Albert Klumpp, PhD, made two remarkable contributions without which this work would not have been fully realized. His research in retention elections provided unexpected and unprecedented evidence that improved design can have a direct impact on voter participation. He also generously served as the book's editor. Clarity of design means very little without clarity of word. It was Albert who expertly finessed the latter.

Without cooperation and guidance from election officials willing to lead us through administrative and procedural realities, our efforts would be meaningless. David Orr, Cook County clerk, and Scott Burnham, director of communications, were committed partners from day one. Many of the materials presented here were developed for the Cook County Elections Division. Scott provided us with many opportunities to grow and test the system by presenting new design problems to solve and by providing a continuous flow of resources and information. I also know, and much appreciate, that Scott insulated us from challenges, big and small, that must be met in order to implement and promote design changes in a bureaucratic environment.

John Lindback, Oregon's director of elections, truly understands the power of design. By inviting us to address audiences of election officials, and by seeking our help to develop materials for Oregon's vote-by-mail program, he enabled us to move our work into a national arena. John's innovative division, under the leadership of Secretary of State Bill Bradbury, hired a graphic designer—the first ever to work full-time in a state elections office. That designer, Gretchen Schulfer, a former student and an admired colleague, has been an incredible resource and contributor.

Ric Grefé, AIGA executive director, is a respected leader, mentor, and friend. He founded Design for Democracy and aggressively inspired, supported, and advocated for the election design initiative. Ric's voice of leadership is behind every word and image in this book.

Cheyenne Medina is a truly inexhaustible source of design energy who has worn many hats in the service of election design: designer, project manager, and teaching and research assistant. Cheyenne knows this material inside out. She greatly contributed to this book's strategic vision while keeping track of design and production details.

Finally, a special thanks to everyone at Studio/lab, including fellow founders Greg Lynch and Susan Verba, and my husband, Tim Wilson, for putting up with the distractions, the absences, and the drain on resources this project has brought. All have supported the effort, either with direct contributions or with enthusiastic cheers from the sidelines.

This book is dedicated to my parents, who provided the rare experience of growing up in a loving bipartisan household. My father taught me that democracy is messy. I guess I just want to do what I can to clean it up a bit.

6: November 2000 Palm Beach County ballot

Veer

12: Nutrition Facts Label

Corbis

Label designed by Burky Belser, AIGA

U.S. Food and Drug Administration

Center for Food Safety and Applied Nutrition

www.cfsan.fda.gov

14–16: November 2000 Cook County retention ballot

Tim Wilson, Studio/lab

22: March 2006 Cook County demonstration ballot

Tim Wilson, Studio/lab

24: Illinois Election Code

Tim Wilson, Studio/lab

34: voting systems: lever

Cindy Koren

34: voting systems: optical scan, paper, electronic

Tim Wilson, Studio/lab

34: voting systems: punchcard

Nathan Mandell

46: registering

Nathan Mandell

48–49: recruiting registrants, *Vote!* buttons

Tim Wilson, Studio/lab

50–51: Cook County voter registration brochure

Nathan Mandell

54: voter registration form

Tim Wilson, Studio/lab

60: getting information

Tim Wilson, Studio/lab

62: Cook County voter education literature

Tim Wilson, Studio/lab

64, 66, 68: Oregon voter information

Tim Wilson, Studio/lab

80: voting

Nathan Mandell

82: election judge identification badge

UIC students

82: polling place, ballot counter

Nathan Mandell

83: optical scan, electronic voting

Tim Wilson, Studio/lab

83: punchcard voting

Nathan Mandell

84: election judge stations

Nathan Mandell

85, 88, 90–91: voting equipment setup

UIC students

86: election judges

Nathan Mandell

92: signage + wayfinding

Matthew Terdich

94: Cook County polling place setup

Nathan Mandell

99: security sleeve, ballot counter

Nathan Mandell

102: absentee voting

Tim Wilson, Studio/lab

108: behind the scenes

Tim Wilson, Studio/lab

110: pollworker training + support

Tim Wilson, Studio/lab

112: inside the voting supply carrier

UIC students

122: document management

Cheyenne Medina, Studio/lab

128: provisional voting

Tim Wilson, Studio/lab

136: Veronica + *vote!* logo studies

UIC students

139: registering voters

Nathan Mandell

139: recruitment van

Office of the Cook County Clerk

139: Bill Bradbury + *vote!* billboard

Oregon Elections Division

155: confusing corridor

UIC students

160: instructional illustration

Tim Wilson, Studio/lab

164: small images on contact sheet

Nathan Mandell

Tim Wilson, Studio/lab

165: voter close-up

Nathan Mandell

166: photography usage guidelines

Tim Wilson, Studio/lab

167–171: Cook County brochure series photos

Nathan Mandell

photography credits

Voting: What Is, What Could Be.
Caltech/MIT Voting Technology Project
California Institute of Technology and
the Massachusetts Institute of Technology Corporation
July 2001

To Assure Pride and Confidence
in the Electoral Process
The National Commission on Federal Election Reform
July 2001

Voting and Registration
in the Election of November 2000
Voting and Registration
in the Election of November 2002
Voting and Registration
in the Election of November 2004
U.S. Census Bureau
2002, 2004, 2006

Judicial Retention Elections in Cook County:
Exercise of Democracy, or Exercise in Futility?
Albert J. Klumpp
Ph.D. dissertation
University of Illinois at Chicago
2005

Choosing Among 133 Candidates
John E. Mueller
Public Opinion Quarterly
Volume 34, No. 3, Fall 1970

Beyond the Butterfly: The Complexity of U.S. Ballots
Richard G. Niemi and Paul S. Herrnson
Perspectives on Politics
Volume 1, No. 2, 2003

bibliography

A

B

C

D

T

U

V

W

Y

colophon

This book was designed at Studio/lab using the information design principles and the graphic design system set forth herein.
It is typeset in the Univers font family, designed in 1957 by Adrian Frutiger.